Praise for *Brand Immortality*

"This unique book rightly shifts attention from myopia, so often the scourge of advertising, to the long-term. Brand equity drives the bottom line, is the message, so prolong its active life. Supported by the brilliant IPA Effectiveness Database, Pringle and Field provide grounds for debate but, more importantly, a feast for thought."
Tim Ambler, Senior Fellow, London Business School and co-editor of The SAGE Handbook of Advertising

"Hamish Pringle and Peter Field deserve our thanks for this challenging and convincing book. It makes a uniquely valuable contribution, combining both practical brand-building advice based on hundreds of case histories together with revealing analyses of the main theoretical branding frameworks. I am sure it will be widely read and closely studied in Asia: today's manufacturing power, tomorrow's brand power. If Western brand owners don't learn from it too – look out!"
Tim Broadbent, Regional Planning Director, Ogilvy & Mather Asia Pacific

"For many companies, their brands have greater value than their people. This is an uncomfortable truth for people to accept. But people have to die and brands don't. *Brand Immortality* uses solid case evidence to show how we mere mortals can achieve a sort of proxy immortality by investing our brands with the gift of eternal life."
Jeremy Bullmore, WPP

"Extending a brand's profitable life is of critical importance to marketers and *Brand Immortality* should serve as an antidote to those who think that infinite profitability is an impossibility."
Hugh Burkitt, Chief Executive, The Marketing Society

"New complexities and subtleties constantly surround that iconically simple entity: the brand. Field and Pringle have disentangled the complexities, using hard data to identify those strategies which can make brands thrive forever – and those which can kill them off."
Winston Fletcher, Chairman, Advertising Standards Board of Finance and author of Powers of Persuasion: The Inside Story of British Advertising

"Truly understanding and managing brands towards immortal status is a poorly understood art and science. In *Brand Immortality*, the wise insights provided by Hamish and Peter help to unlock some of the key secrets to long-term success."
Gillian Graham, CEO, Institute of Communication Agencies (ICA)

BRAND
Immortality

How brands can live long and prosper

Hamish Pringle **IPA** Peter Field

**KOGAN
PAGE**

London and Philadelphia

First published in Great Britain and the United States in 2008 by Kogan Page Limited

120 Pentonville Road
London N1 9JN
United Kingdom
www.koganpage.com

525 South 4th Street, #241
Philadelphia PA 19147
USA

© Institute of Practitioners in Advertising (IPA), 2008

ISBN 978 0 7494 4928 5

Cover design concept by Hamish Pringle and Peter Field.

British Library Cataloguing-in-Publication Data

A CIP record for this book is available from the British Library.

Library of Congress Cataloging-in-Publication Data

Pringle, Hamish.
   Brand immortality : how brands can live long and prosper / Hamish Pringle and Peter Field.
        p. cm.
   Includes bibliographical references and index.
   ISBN 978–0–7494–4928–5
   1. Brand name products. 2. Branding (Marketing) I. Field, Peter. II. Title.
   HD69.B7.P749 2008
   658.8′27--dc22
                                            2008022897

Typeset by Saxon Graphics Ltd, Derby
Printed and bound in Great Britain by MPG Books Ltd, Bodmin, Cornwall

To all the authors of IPA Effectiveness Awards cases, whose intellect, diligence and accountability have created such a great source of learning about brands, their successful advertising and communication strategies, and their proven return on marketing investment for clients.

Hamish Pringle

To the late Simon Broadbent, father of the IPA Effectiveness Awards, without whose foresight this book would not have been possible.

Peter Field

'I don't want to achieve immortality through my work. I want to achieve it through not dying.'

Woody Allen (1935–)

'Immortality lies not in the things you leave behind, but in the people your life has touched.'

Anon

Contents

About the authors

Hamish Pringle

Hamish graduated from Trinity College, Oxford with a BA in PPE and joined Ogilvy, Benson & Mather as a graduate trainee in 1973. After spells at McCormick Richards, Boase Massimi Pollitt, McCormick Intermarco-Farner/Publicis, Abbott Mead Vickers, his own agency Madell Wilmot Pringle, and Leagas Delaney, Hamish joined KHBB in 1992 and became Chairman and CEO in 1995. Following the re-launch as K Advertising and the subsequent merger in 1997, he became Vice-Chairman, and Director of Marketing of Saatchi & Saatchi.

During this 26-year period in the advertising industry, Hamish had a variety of involvements with the IPA, including being Chairman of the IPA Effectiveness Awards Committee. He was also Chairman of NABS, the industry charity (1996–98), and a recipient of its Ron Miller Award. After two years running his own branding and marketing communications consultancy, Brand Beliefs, he became Director General of the IPA in 2001.

He has co-authored two books, *Brand Spirit: How cause related marketing builds brands* with Marjorie Thompson, and *Brand Manners: How to create the self-confident organisation to live the brand* with William Gordon. His third book, *Celebrity Sells*, was published in April 2004.

Hamish is a Fellow of the IPA, a Fellow of the Marketing Society, a member of the Marketing Group of Great Britain, and a member of the Editorial Board of *Market Leader*.

Peter Field

Peter graduated from St John's College, Cambridge with an MA in Engineering and spent 15 years as a strategic planner in advertising, starting his career in 1982 at Boase Massimi Pollitt (now DDB London). He spent nine years working for Abbott Mead Vickers BBDO Ltd, leaving to join the management team of Bates London (now absorbed into WPP) and, subsequently, Grey London.

In 1997, Peter left advertising to pursue a consultancy role supporting both clients and their agencies as well as founding Express Train, a training partnership for the advertising and marketing industries. In 1999, he helped start Eatbigfish, the challenger brand consultancy, and supported it in its early years.

Peter was a member of the IPA Effectiveness Awards Committee for five years and helped set up and run the IPA dataBANK. He has been a judge of the prestigious IPA Effectiveness Awards and has contributed over many years to IPA education and training programmes, most recently as a module editor for the Excellence Diploma – a role that has involved selecting and reviewing a wide range of marketing and advertising literature. Peter contributed a chapter to *Advertising Works 10* on learning from the IPA dataBANK and to the *Handbook of Advertising*, which attempts to bring together an extensive body of collective learning from the dataBANK. Most recently he co-authored the second IPA dataMINE monograph, *Marketing in the Era of Accountability*, with Les Binet – based on the most complete meta-analysis of the 880 case studies of the dataBANK yet conducted. In this book, he extends that analysis further.

Peter has written widely for the various journals of the marketing and communications sectors and has undertaken many public speaking engagements for the IPA and others. In 2006, he was elected an honorary Fellow of the IPA.

Institute of Practitioners in Advertising (IPA)

The Institute of Practitioners in Advertising is one of the world's leading trade bodies for advertising, media and marketing communications agencies. Since 1917 the IPA has represented only agencies – not clients, advertisers or media owners – so its focus is single-minded when it comes to promoting their best interests. Currently, the IPA has over 270 of the UK's brightest and best agencies in membership, drawn from a broad range of disciplines, who between them handle an estimated 85 per cent of all UK advertising spend for clients, and employ over 19,000 people. The IPA's mission is straightforward: to promote the value of the agencies in its membership. It does this in two main ways: first, by acting as a spokesperson and representing members on issues of common concern; and second, by contributing to their professional operation via a range of advisory, information and training services. On a day-to-day basis the IPA operates in a similar way to its agency members. Each of its departments manages a key aspect of the business, from Research to Creative, Production to Media, and through dedicated groups of agency people is able to develop thinking and appropriate policy, publications, events and a range of support services for all aspects of the business. These different groups report into the IPA Council, which, through its elected President, is responsible for overall strategy and direction. One of the most important areas of activity is the development, organization and promotion of the IPA Effectiveness Awards. Established in 1980, this competition generates the outstanding case histories that form the IPA dataBANK, and that are the basis for the analyses on which the core of this book depends.

Institute of Practitioners in Advertising (IPA)
44 Belgrave Square, London SW1X 8QS
Tel: (020) 7235 7020 Fax: (020) 7245 8804
www.ipa.co.uk

Foreword

Since Procter & Gamble started in 1837, our brands have been crucial to our success. Today our brands are serving over 3 billion consumers around the world and among them are 23 brands each worth over a billion dollars, and that number continues to grow. Clearly, our success is driven by putting our consumers at the heart of everything we do, and as our consumers change, our brands and our marketing need to change too. The pace of this evolution accelerates daily and the new digital media are just one set of factors bringing not only new opportunities, but also new challenges. Our aim is to improve our consumers' lives through our brands, but our consumer is better informed and more demanding than ever before. Thus we need constant and relevant innovation in our products and marketing to win and keep winning their trust. So when the concept of 'brand immortality' came along, naturally I was interested. The case studies and analysis in this book presented me with some important new insights. Given the marketing challenges we face, I'm pleased to have been among the first to read it!

Roisin Donnelly
Corporate Marketing Director, UK & Ireland
Procter & Gamble

Preface

Originally this was going to be a book about the life cycle of brands and how marketing can be most effective at different stages. Our going-in position was: 'Brands are born, grow, mature and then die, right?' But of course we were wrong.

On reflection, it became obvious that some outstanding brands have lived for a very long time despite many decades of significant social, technological and economic change. We realized that there are many brands among the IPA Effectiveness Awards case histories in the IPA dataBANK that for one reason or another ought to be dead or dying, but are in fact in rude good health. Our detailed analysis of the case histories also showed that although there were common rules for keeping brands healthy, whether *they* were young or old, the same was not true of their *category's* life stage. It was clear that successful brand strategies differed considerably in young, growing, mature and declining categories. So it is important for a brand to modify its strategy over time to achieve optimum performance, and to live long and prosper. And while some brands may become victims of their category life cycle, the implication is that brands can live for ever if they're managed professionally.

This book illustrates the value and resilience of the brand as a promise that exists in an individual's mind. Carefully constructed and nurtured, that promise can not only support product innovations and line extensions within its original category, but also enable the brand to transfer to a completely new market sector. Indeed, a well-managed brand can live on in people's minds for successive generations. This book is about how to manage strategy so that the brand rides the product and market life-cycle waves, and outlives them. It shows how to ensure your brand is immortal.

Acknowledgements

A special thank you to all our interviewees, who offered such fascinating insights, giving colour and detail to the text: Les Binet, Richard Brasher, Elisa Edmonds, Laurence Green, Nick Hough, Lucy Jameson, Martin Lambie-Nairn, Sophie Maunder-Allan, Chris Moss, James Murphy, Ian Priest, Steven Sharp, Simon Thompson, Charles Vallance, Will Whitehorn, Robin Wight and Jerry Wright.

Many companies have generously allowed us to reproduce their data, analyses and research findings. In particular, we would like to thank David Haigh at Brand Finance, Dominic Twose at Millward Brown, Vanella Jackson at Hall & Partners, Heather Stern at Focalyst, Layla Forster, Paul Dunn and Josie Lamey at Nielsen Media, Jim Law at MRUK, James Lawson at Ledbury Research, Graeme Griffiths at TNS Media, Andrew Fenning at AcuPOLL, Mary Ellen Young at Information Resources Inc, James Mundell at IPSOS ASI, Ross Wightman and Justin Sampson at AGB Nielsen Media Research, Doug McConchie at Malik PIMS, Matthew Coombs and Catherine Gardner at WARC and Roger Ingham at Data Alive.

There are many other senior industry people that we must thank for providing us with ideas, data and insights: Tim Ambler, Reg Bryson, Leslie Butterfield, David Cowan, Charlie Dawson, Jan Hofmeyr, Janet Hull, Andrew Marsden, Angela Pirrie, Jagdish Seth and Karl-Erik Sveiby. Special thanks go to Judie Lannon, Editor of *Market Leader*, who kindly agreed to critique the manuscript for us. Her comments were invaluable and we are most grateful for her contribution to the final book.

We very much appreciate all those at the IPA who have helped. Particular thanks must go to Caroline Roberts for her key role in delivering this book through exemplary project management, diligent research and intelligent contributions to the text. Victoria Murray has been a truly worthy successor, and Sian Bateman, Maureen Gonsalves, Ralph Lock, Steve Mill, Pamela Perl and Lena Roland have all provided valuable support, while Martin Coomber and Claire Post did an excellent job in sourcing the images.

Finally, we must thank Jon Finch for his patience and commitment to this project, as well as the rest of the team at Kogan Page for producing a book we are all proud of.

Introduction

This book is a practical health manual for brands that seek immortality – brands of all types and of all ages. Our premise is that, properly managed, no brand need die: that immortality is within the reach of any brand. Although there will always be brand 'disappearances', these should be regarded as avoidable deaths, not some inevitable consequence of an ineluctable process of decay. If the right decisions, the right resources and the right imagination are brought to bear, brands can renew continuously and outlive their creators. There are, after all, many brands around us that have transcended multiple generations of human beings. If brands of all types and sizes can survive from one human generation to the next, why should they not continue to do so thereafter? Many in business make the mistake of judging the prospects of brands by the state of the category in which they operate. Worse still, many assume that the brand is inextricably tied to the market (ie product) life cycle associated with its current product or service range. Why should this be so, when the halls of brand fame are filled with examples of brand transformations from Apple to Zanussi?

The book examines how many of the best-known and most widely accepted theories and tools of marketing work *against* brand immortality, not *for* it. It distinguishes the *useful* from the *dangerous* and the *valid* from the altogether *wrong*. And it pulls together a wide range of experience of how marketing thinking can benefit brands at different stages of the market life cycle, distilling it into some key lessons for marketing, procurement and agencies. It also examines how the nature of brands has changed over time and continues to evolve, and the implications this has for marketing: once again, in an area well served with hype and pet theories, the book sets out to distinguish the reliable from the fanciful.

Our assertion that brands could be immortal is based on observations of how many brands (of widely differing types and ages) have defied the challenges they faced at different stages of their evolution and prospered. In particular, we draw heavily on the findings of the IPA dataBANK and on the core 880 case studies of effectiveness that constitute it. We have discerned the factors that are essential to a brand's long-term survival, and especially those that defend and strengthen a brand's place in the hearts and minds of consumers.

Andrew Marsden, when Marketing Director at Britvic Soft Drinks and President of the UK's Marketing Society, often recounted what his first boss at Unilever said when he began his career there as a trainee: 'Always remember that the brand was here before you arrived and it had better be there long after you are gone. Your job is to ensure you leave it in at least as good a shape as you found it.' These are watchwords for us all, and by providing actionable learning from the IPA Effectiveness Awards case studies and elsewhere, this book aims to help brand teams live up to this challenge.

In addition to the IPA effectiveness case study database – the IPA dataBANK – the book draws on the findings of leading market research companies to help identify winning brand strategies. In addition, many examples of success and failure from around the world are used to bring the chapters alive, enriched by interviews with key people who were directly involved with the brands, to probe for their insights. Hopefully these will help more marketers and their agencies beat the odds in winning, retaining and satisfying customers, and thus achieving brand immortality.

PART 1

Brands as shareholder assets to be managed

1 Why immortality should matter to investors

These are the key points in this chapter:

- Intangible assets, particularly brands, account for a growing proportion of companies' stock market value.
- Successful brand development requires a full understanding within the whole company of the value of the brand, and how it is created.
- CEOs, CFOs and boards of directors need to take a closer interest in marketing and communications in the development and maintenance of brands, and the 12 per cent of shareholder value they create.
- The value of brands as assets needs to be preserved; companies need to appreciate that successful brand management is essential to their survival.
- With careful management, brands have the potential to be immortal, preserving value and customer relationships.

Brand immortality is fundamentally important to businesses in the 21st century because in Westernized economies the balance of shareholder value has shifted irrevocably from *tangible* assets to *intangible* assets. Intangible assets account for a growing proportion of companies' market value, as corporate performance and profitability are driven more and more by the exchange and exploitation of ideas, information, expertise and service, and less and less by control over physical resources. Intangibles include patents, strategic alliances, customer lists, employee know-how and other forms of non-physical assets, but in many companies the most important intangible assets are *brands*. Intangible assets have therefore always existed, but only recently have they begun to be valued properly. Brands, in some sectors, comprise up to 70 per cent of companies' market capitalization. These non-material assets have never been more important. Raoul Pinnell, when chairman of Shell Brands International, went so far as to say, 'Intangible value is the issue of the decade. Shareholders will place increasing emphasis on a management's ability to manage intangible assets, rather than tangible assets, in the understanding that a growing proportion of companies' value will derive from intangibles.' In this context it's worth remembering that intangible brand assets have some very tangible aspects. Angela Pirrie of Chartered Brands has a good way of picturing these benefits of a brand to both its owner and its consumers (Figure 1.1).

What's important to note is that the proportion of tangible to intangible assets has changed dramatically over the past 50 years. A study by the US Federal Reserve Board shows that in 1955 tangible assets accounted for nearly 80 per cent of the value of non-financial businesses; by 2005 that proportion had fallen to just over 50 per cent. A study of the market capitalization of the Standard & Poor's 500 by Millward Brown Optimor concludes that the value of intangibles has trebled over the past 30 years (Figure 1.2).

According to Brand Finance's 'Invisible Business' report of 2005, 78 per cent of the market value of the Fortune 500, 72 per cent of the value of the FTSE 350 and 35 per cent of the market value of all listed companies world-wide is now intangible.

Although intangibles are now the key drivers of our modern economy, they are still rather poorly understood by management and investors alike.

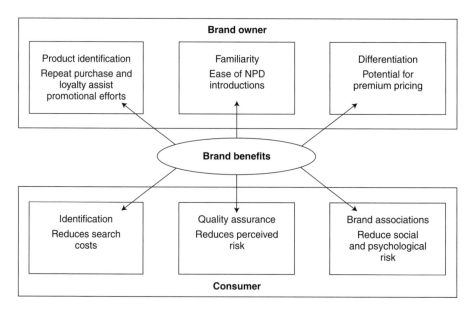

Figure 1.1 Brand equity
Source: 'What value brands?' *Admap*, October 2006, Issue 476, p 40. Reproduced by kind permission of Angela Pirrie/Admap

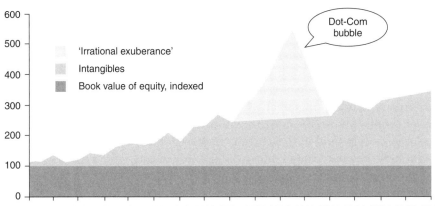

Figure 1.2 The growth of intangibles
Source: The Intangible Revolution, IPA 2006. Reproduced by kind permission of the IPA

Qualitative research among 50 financial analysts by Populus on behalf of the IPA in 2005 revealed that nearly half the respondents were uninterested in brands when evaluating companies. They saw no objective or scientific way of measuring marketing or brands except when 'hard numbers show up on the balance sheet'. The other half did use, or would consider using, non-financial data in their appraisals and see marketing strategy and sales performance as most important. But these analysts tended to rely on their own subjective experience of brands as a consumer, rather than on any more objective data. The Populus research showed they would be interested in more information, but didn't understand marketing or know what to ask for. This leads potentially to poor decision-making by companies and the risk of mis-pricing of stock by investors.

Traditional accounting, which remains largely focused on tangible assets, has not encouraged better practice, because business tends to manage what it measures, and to measure only what it appreciates. Developments such as the new Business Review or Narrative Report are now putting real pressure on companies to appreciate, then measure, and manage far better the contribution of intangible assets to their current and future performance. The Narrative Report requires directors to look at the risks their businesses face and review non-financial information about factors like environmental concerns and employees. This is an opportunity for those, like agencies, who are experienced in demonstrating the effectiveness of what they do for brands, and can help boards improve the way they identify, explain and monitor their intangible assets.

We hold the view that the concept of the brand life cycle is an old-fashioned and outmoded one. While there are product or category life cycles, which go through the phases of birth, growth, maturity and decline, we believe that brands have the potential to be immortal. This is because the company's relationship with the customer is based upon much more than the functional performance of the product or service that the company provides. It explains why brands may be immortal while mere products and services can die. Therefore, brands can liberate companies from the limitations of category (or product) life cycle and its destruction of shareholder value. This idea is now increasingly widely accepted, but sadly not universally, which is worrying for the shareholders in companies whose CEOs, CFOs and directors have yet to grasp the full importance of intangibles.

Given the intense interest in brands and how to preserve their asset value, they must appreciate with much greater clarity the financial implications of brand management. In this context the concept of 'customer capital' is a valuable tool. It was originated by Karl-Erik Sveiby, now professor in Knowledge Management at Hanken Business School, Helsinki, Finland. He created his theory of 'knowledge capital' in 1988, dividing it into three categories: customer capital, structural capital and human capital. In 1989 it was published in Swedish as *The Invisible Balance Sheet*. Skandia, the Swedish insurance company, adopted the approach around 1993. Subsequently, a key conversation took place between Thomas Stewart of *Fortune* magazine and Hubert Saint-Onge, then a vice-president of the Canadian Imperial Bank of Commerce, in which Saint-Onge also mooted the idea of 'customer capital'. Stewart then published an influential article, 'Brainpower', in *Fortune*. He concluded that intellectual capital was the product of three elements working together: individual skills needed to meet customers' needs (human capital), organizational capabilities demanded by the market (structural capital), and the strength of its franchise (customer capital). A book then followed, *Intellectual Capital: The new wealth of organizations*, which was published in 1997, and helped popularize the concept. But while the accounting standards and regulations have embraced this thinking, it has yet to be fully adopted within the marketing discipline.

The key role of marketing resides in expertise in managing a company's customers by identifying, influencing, acquiring, serving, satisfying and retaining them at a profit. The product of this marketing process – its 'customer capital' – is the company's customer base and, to a large degree, the present and future value of the business, as it is usually its prime revenue-generating asset. Stewart argued that the primary focus of boards of directors should be on how many customers of what value a company has and how many and which of those people are likely to remain customers in future, and for how long. Boards should be keenly aware of, and planning to mitigate, the risk factors for the company in terms of the rate at which it is winning or losing customers and the rising, or falling, future revenues that implies. The nature and strength of a brand's relationships with its customers can vary significantly over time and according to factors beyond the control of marketing that may affect either the company or the customer, or both. These factors might include the economic climate, social trends, technological advances, product or service performance, competitive activity, editorial coverage, and word of mouth as well as customer life stage, employment and personal experience, to name but a few. So the concept of 'customer capital' can be used to build a bridge between the inputs of business and marketing strategy and the outputs of revenue growth, profitability and shareholder value.

Although it is a powerful idea, Tim Ambler from the London Business School expressed some reservations in a 2005 *Market Leader* article. His main point is that it is dangerous to replace the *asset* of brand equity with the *capital item* (or resource) of customer capital, because this will shift the role of marketing towards the short term and take attention away from the longer-term building of shareholder value through brand equity. His worry therefore is that the good intentions of customer capital may backfire in practice. It is difficult to know without trying whether his concern is valid. He also points out that in the final analysis it is no less complex a concept than the asset measure – brand equity – that it is intended to simplify. Judging by the difficulty of explaining the concept, he may well be right, but that is not necessarily a reason to give up if the measure brings benefits. The key issue is whether it is possible to arrive at a universally acceptable means of calculating customer capital. This entails knowing the value of a brand's customers and the likelihood of recruiting or retaining them over a given time period, which is a function of the brand's competitive strength. This calculation is clearly easier for companies that have a direct relationship with their customers via catalogues, direct mail or the internet. However, for brands sold through wholesalers, retailers and other intermediaries the calculation is much less certain. A decision by Wal-Mart or Tesco to list or de-list a brand can be hard to build into a forecast of customer capital but has massive implications for it. The inability to reach a common definition of brand equity has hugely weakened its value, so there is both reason to try and reason to be sceptical when it comes to defining customer capital.

Capitalism creates a vested interest in keeping brands alive, and every year, as the cost and complexity of creating brands increase, this interest strengthens. So success for companies will increasingly depend on the longevity of their brands. But successful brand management requires a full understanding within the company of the value of a brand. Only if this value is known and fully appreciated will there be less of a tendency to allow it to wither away: a new direction will be found for the brand to preserve its value and hence safeguard the historical investment made in it. Or it will be sold to someone who can make better use of it, but at full value rather than a distress sale price. The problem is that most companies do not have an accurate understanding of the value of their brands, and therefore many allow them to decline, while retaining ownership. It seems unlikely that this is in the interests of their shareholders in more than a tiny minority of cases.

In some extreme situations the death of the brand through re-branding can become unavoidable if the product or service has been allowed to become too old-fashioned or uncompetitive to be sustainable. This rebirth is made a lot easier in retail by habitual shopping patterns and the fixed nature of outlets combining to ensure the new format starts with inherited customer footfall. Overnight, old-fashioned Hepworth Menswear became trendy, innovative and profitable Next, as did Chelsea Girl when it turned into River Island. It is rare outside retail, but killing off a neglected brand can sometimes be the only way to save the business. But well-managed brands should never get themselves into such a situation.

With hindsight, Andersen Consulting was fortunate to be forced to re-brand when it bought itself out of the parent accountancy firm because it could no longer legally use the name under the separation agreement. At the time, well before the collapse of Andersen due to its involvement with Enron, this was seen as a negative requirement and a difficult one – what should be the new brand's name? When the competition winner 'Accenture' was announced, there was a decidedly mixed reaction. The same thing happened when the UK's Royal Mail declared its international brand name as 'Consignia' and wags suggested it should be 'consigned to the wastepaper bin'. But there was one big difference between the two companies' approaches, which helped lead to huge success on the one hand and an embarrassing climb-down on the other. Whereas Royal Mail spent little behind Consignia, Andersen Consulting committed at least $75,000,000 in advertising and marketing communications support in the first year alone to establishing its new identity as Accenture. Nowadays not many people can recall what Accenture used to be, and that's a sure sign of a successful re-branding exercise.

Another recent example of a 'phoenix' brand rising from the funeral pyre of another is that of O_2. Struggling mobile phone company BT Cellnet was transformed into the O_2 brand in order to distance it from BT as a condition of its separate stock market flotation, and also to signal its rejuvenation. As Nick Hough, former managing director of O_2's branding consultants Lambie-Nairn, recounts, 'Peter Erskine was Chief Executive of the company and an extremely good marketer. He said, "if I'm going to run this business, we're going to change the name, we're going to change everything. We're going to give this brand a complete refresh…".'

Refreshment for O_2 entailed a two-pronged strategy of improving retention of the existing customer base with improved service and transparency, and winning new customers with better marketing and intelligible customer-friendly promotional packages. In 2006 O_2 was sold to Spain's Telefónica for £18 billion, a sum approaching the total market value of BT, its original parent, and triple the value of BT Cellnet at its initial public offering (IPO).

The brilliance of O_2 is rare. Brand owners and their agencies are operating in an environment where mediocrity is commonplace and major success relatively unusual. Even those with the most successful careers in marketing and advertising would find it difficult to point to their involvement in more than a handful of campaigns which have truly transformed the fortunes of a brand. But this is no reason to be downhearted: their efforts are usually valuable, even if it's only maintaining the brand's status quo in the face of fierce competition. It is also no reason to stop aspiring to achieve that once or twice in a lifetime campaign that goes off the scale and really changes the fortunes of the brand. Our focus on the IPA dataBANK will enable examination of these rare peak performances and unearth the secrets of their success.

The few beneficial brand deaths are very much the exception that proves the general rule of the value of brand immortality. More usually the demise of a brand signals the unnecessary destruction of shareholder value, through a reduction in the intangible asset base of the company. The CEOs and boards of companies, their investors, analysts, advisers and the journalists who write about them, all need to take a much closer interest in the role of marketing and communications in the creation and maintenance of brands and in the 12 per cent of all shareholder value they account for on average across the world's stock exchanges.

2 Is death inevitable?

These are the key points in this chapter:

- Paul Ormerod argues persuasively that almost all companies fail eventually, but we are unconvinced that this is true of brands.
- Using the Boston Matrix as a brand management tool can be dangerous as it can create a self-fulfilling prophecy.
- Brands do not have to die: they can be immortal if they are managed properly.
- Ailing brands can be resurrected or evolve into different markets and survive.

In his book *Why Most Things Fail*, Paul Ormerod puts a persuasive case for the inevitable mortality of corporations. He draws intriguing analogies with nature and the extinction of species (Figure 2.1). Indeed, he refers throughout to the 'extinction of companies' (Figures 2.2 and 2.3).

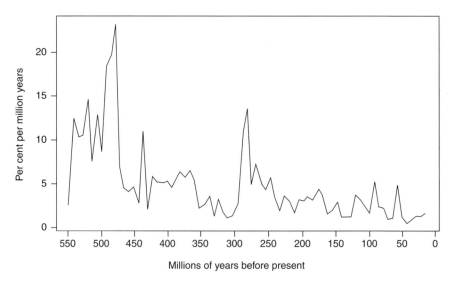

Figure 2.1 % species becoming extinct per million years
Source: Ormerod (2005). Reproduced by kind permission of Faber & Faber Ltd

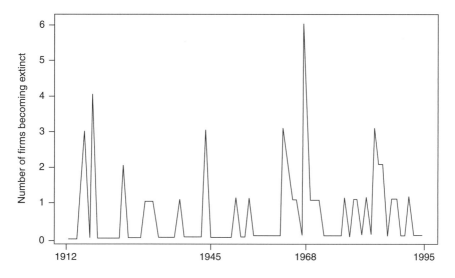

Figure 2.2 Number of extinctions of the world's largest 100 companies in 1912 (annual basis 1912–95)
Source: Ormerod (2005). Reproduced by kind permission of Faber & Faber Ltd

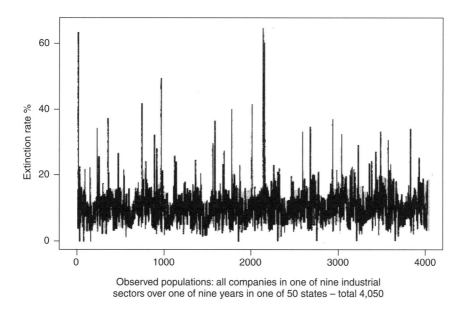

Observed populations: all companies in one of nine industrial sectors over one of nine years in one of 50 states – total 4,050

Figure 2.3 % of US firms that become extinct each year by industry and state
Source: Ormerod (2005). Reproduced by kind permission of Faber & Faber Ltd

His case is made with unarguable data that corporations are subject to an inexorable process of birth, life and death. As with human life, good care can stave off the inevitable for a while, but, eventually, time catches up with them all. His analysis suggests that there is a continuous extinction of companies at the rate of about 10 per cent per annum, but every so often there is a dramatic peak, during which short period very large numbers go out of business – as many as 60 per cent in a single year. To take a recent example, the invention of the World Wide Web in 1989 led to an explosion of innovative activity, the huge growth in the number of dot.com start-ups, an investment-banking-funded bubble and a massive spike in the number of failed companies when the crunch came in March 2000. Another spectacular incidence within living memory was the Wall Street Crash of 1929, with the South Sea Bubble of 1720 and the Dutch 'Tulip Bulb Mania' of 1637 as other historical precedents.

Companies also disappear as a result of mergers and acquisitions. Not such a long time ago there were 15 different UK regional commercial television stations. Now just one, ITV plc, owns all the licences in England and Wales (accounting for over 90 per cent of TV advertising revenues) – and within only a couple of years of its creation, it too has been the subject of a takeover bid. Perhaps this law is immutable, despite the growth of the global corporation?

But finally, on the last page of Ormerod's book, he asserts that 'almost all brands fail eventually'. We beg to differ with him: we refuse to lie down and accept death. Why should brands die? Time and time again we see brands outliving the corporations that gave birth to them, like KitKat, a confectionery bar first created by Rowntree and now made by Nestlé, or Airfix model kits, originally part of Humbrol, then Heller and now Hornby Railways, or the British ICI and Dulux brands recently acquired by Dutch company Akzo Nobel. Often it is the expectation that those brands may be better off in the hands of another corporation that is responsible for the extinction of the original owner.

Les Binet is the Chief Econometrician and European Director of DDB Matrix, a leading market analysis consultancy. He has spent a career analysing and modelling many categories from cars to carbonates and has witnessed the fallacy of the brand life cycle many times:

> People talk about brands having a life cycle, a sort of profile of birth, growth, death. But you've got to distinguish between three different things: the life stages of a brand, the life stages of products (which are not necessarily the same as the brand – they usually have different products within a brand) and then also the life stages of the market. If you start to distinguish between those you start to think about what you do at the different stages. For example, you can have new brands in declining markets and declining brands in mature markets and declining products within a mature brand. So it's essential to distinguish between the brand and the product. Brands can go on for ever, by attaching themselves to different products.

Meanwhile, brands are sometimes allowed to die, often justified by the spurious mantra of the 'brand life cycle'. While it may not be possible to rejuvenate every stricken brand, and within a multi-brand company it may not always make commercial sense, there's too much grievous bodily harm done to brands and sometimes outright 'brand slaughter'. We argue that in many cases brands have the potential to be immortal: their death is usually a result of the failure of imagination and/or investment by their owners. So this book is about how to cheat brand death – not just in old age, but in infancy and at all stages in between.

One of Damien Hirst's most celebrated works is a shark preserved in a vitrine full of formaldehyde and its title is *The Physical Impossibility of Death in the Mind of Someone Living* (Figure 2.4). We need to get into that mindset in the way we think about brand immortality. Brands are like sharks – they keep moving to stay alive and the role of brand managers is to ensure they move in the right direction, at the very least going with the flow of market evolution, riding the waves of competition and modulating communications in tune with ever-shifting customer sentiment.

One of the best-known strategic marketing tools has unintentionally done more than any other to perpetuate the myth of the mortality of brands. This is

Figure 2.4 Damien Hirst: *The physical impossibility of death in the mind of someone living* (1991). Glass, steel, silicone, shark and 5% formaldehyde solution. 2,170 × 5,420 × 1,800 mm (85.43 × 213.39 × 70.87 in). © Damien Hurst.
Source: Photo: Prudence Cuming. Courtesy Science Ltd (London)

the Boston Matrix with its widely known, but little understood, categories of 'Stars', 'Cash Cows', 'Dogs' and 'Question Marks'. The application of the Boston Matrix to brands carries with it the assumption that, at some point, when category growth falters, a brand will progress to 'Cash Cow' status, and thence fade. In fact, the Boston Matrix was never formulated as a brand management tool, but rather as a category management one, and the potential problem with applying it to a brand is that it can create a self-fulfilling prophecy: growth falters so marketing support is cut, so growth falters further and so on.

David Cowan of FORENSICS, formerly Planning Director of Boase Massimi Pollitt (now DDB London), has seen this problem played out first hand. His observations are a useful warning to us all:

You ask what are the main sins managers commit in murdering brands?

Quite a complex subject, but here are some initial observations. The first point is that although there are cases of sudden death by execution, I suspect that in most cases brands aren't murdered, but their veins are opened and they slowly bleed to death.

I suspect that one model is that, for some reason (perhaps share has started to slip or resources are needed in another part of the company), more profit is required from the brand so investment in it is cut. Sales don't collapse and the company gets used to the extra profit from not investing in advertising the core brand. These cuts go on for a few years and the company gets to a position where advertising is only, or predominantly, used when launching new products. What then happens is that the sector itself starts to decline and if there is own label, this gains an even greater share.

This is a very difficult position to recover from because starting to advertise the core brand again won't lead to commensurate short-term increases in sales and most managers won't move heaven and earth (because this is what it takes) to get out of this downward spiral, and therefore it doesn't happen. A few more years pass and the brand has become a shadow of its former self and it is very difficult to make the business case for more investment. If the brand 'is the company' then the company is now in trouble and is eventually taken over, but rarely does the brand get revived by its new owners. If the brand was already part of a larger group, it may be killed off and other brands in the portfolio given the task of serving the market. Or the brand may be sold and probably continues life in some very reduced form, being milked for profit. There are cases, for example McVitie's, where I've seen this sort of thing happen, although I wasn't in the room when the decisions were actually taken.

In 1986, the Imperial Group was acquired in a hostile takeover by Hanson plc for £2.5 billion. Hanson subsequently divested all the non-tobacco business, including Ross Foods, to United Biscuits in 1988, netting a total of £2.3 billion, and only retaining the hugely profitable tobacco business. As a part of a strategic review, UB got the management consultants in. The McVitie's biscuit division was designated a 'Cash Cow' and KP, the snacks business, a 'Star'. Advertising spend behind the McVitie's lines dropped steadily between 1985 and 1991, when I started to have some involvement. McVitie's share was in decline and own labels were growing. However, my analysis showed that, contrary to what management thought, McVitie's sales, and hence market share, were declining because its users were decreasing their consumption of biscuits per se, not because they were switching to own label. I was able to show that the major cause of this was lack of advertising: McVitie's users, who were highly loyal, were simply forgetting to have biscuits with their tea and coffee.

The then managing director of McVitie's, Brian Chadbourne, was aware of the danger of the downward spiral and was pushing through a programme of production cost efficiencies to release £12m of savings which were to be invested in advertising McVitie's core brands – Digestives, Rich Tea, Hob Nobs etc. This was a way of breaking out of the vicious circle. Unfortunately, a crisis arose within UB's American subsidiary Keebler and Brian was parachuted in as CEO. His McVitie's job was given to a production man who didn't believe in advertising, so the investment was never made. A few years later UB fell to private equity.

A powerful analogy to bring this point to life is that of an aircraft in flight (Figure 2.5). If the plane's fuel supply is cut and the engines stop, the plane does not fall out of the sky immediately. Indeed, it can glide for some time before inevitably hitting the ground. The same thing happens to brands whose investment in marketing and communications is cut off.

We suggest that the application of the term 'Cash Cow' to a brand is the first seductive contact in the long, slow, lingering kiss of death for the brand. It heralds the loss of sense of purpose and dynamism that is essential for immortality. The question for such brands is: would the continuation of marketing effort behind new strategies have rejuvenated the brand, or would it have been folly to have continued the effort?

Figure 2.5 Plane flying
Source: Photographed by Tom Collins

Perhaps Allied Domecq, now part of Pernod Ricard, and former owner of Plymouth Gin, might have cause for regret. They saw their languishing gin brand as surplus to their portfolio and in 1996 Plymouth Gin was sold off at a knockdown price. The buyer, John Murphy, had been a founder of Interbrand, one of the world's leading branding agencies, and so knew a valuable asset when he saw one. He and his team engineered a very successful renaissance, inspired by brand archaeology, which revealed that the original Martini cocktail had been created using Plymouth Gin. He capitalized upon it by improving packaging, restoring the original 'Navy strength' variant (while the market leader reduced its alcoholic strength) and reinvesting in marketing communications. In 1995, Allied Domecq sold just 7,500 cases of Plymouth Gin, but now, under the new brand management, it has become the UK's leading premium gin brand in a growing market, selling 130,000 cases worldwide in 2005/6.

Pernod Ricard has pulled off a similar brand resurrection in the United States with Seagram's Gin. To achieve this, they employed a three-pronged strategy: first, by appealing to younger African American consumers with a new campaign (Figure 2.6). Second, they updated the packaging for the first time in 40 years. Third, they introduced a premium line-extension called Distiller's Reserve. At the time of the purchase in 2001, Seagram's Gin had seen sales fall a million cases per annum over 10 years, to just 3 million cases per annum. The brand had been steadily deserted by its drinkers. The Pernod Ricard re-launch halted the decline in its tracks, stabilizing sales at 3m cases in 2006.

Of course we see corporate casualties, but set against this there are many companies with decades, if not centuries, of longevity. There are also lots of examples of companies that were established in one market and that over time have evolved to occupy positions in many others, and in some cases ended up not being represented in their original one at all. Perhaps the most famous contemporary example is the mobile phone handset company Nokia, which started out life in 1865 as a Swedish wood pulp company (Figure 2.7).

It may be impossible to rejuvenate a brand within its existing category, but what about extending to other categories or even creating new ones? The transformation of Lucozade from a quasi-medical bedside restorative to a dynamic out-of-home sports drink is a great example. Look how brands such as Dove and Lux have evolved to transcend the categories they were in. But set against that there's the failure from neglect of retailers such as C&A and Dickens & Jones in the UK, and car-maker Rover. Media brands too can become victims. The BBC's *Top of the Pops*, one of the original and best UK chart shows, was allowed to die in 2006 after 46 years. Perhaps if the show's format had been revamped to reflect the era of the download and use had been made of interactive technologies, it could have been saved. As Noel Edmonds, one of

Figure 2.6 Seagram's Gin 'Urban Elegance' campaign, TBWA/Chiat Day, New York
Source: Photo by Hashi Studio Inc. Illustration by Andrea D'Aquino. Reproduced by kind permission of Pernod Ricard USA

Figure 2.7 Nokia Wood Pulp Company
Reproduced by kind permission of the National Board of Antiquities, Sweden

the UK's leading TV presenters, said of the programme's demise, 'It's a tragedy when a broadcaster doesn't understand such a powerful brand.'

We are convinced that many of these casualties would have been avoidable if only imagination and investment had been applied earlier, rather than things being allowed to drift for too long.

3 How the changing nature of brands affects brand resilience

These are the key points in this chapter:

- Brands not only have physical attributes, they have emotional and psychological ones too.
- Brands are promises that exist in people's minds.
- Much of brand management is all about creating, communicating and keeping promises.
- Nowadays, customers are increasingly involved in a two-way communications process with brands.

Before delving into the myriad factors and tools that influence a brand's ability to keep itself alive and thriving, it's worth considering the nature of brands in terms of how they're created, how they live and are evolving. We have already begun to examine the impact of certain strategic thinking models on brand longevity, but what is the process of brand birth, life and survival in people's minds?

Writing in 1971, the late Stephen King, one of the architects of account planning in agencies and a leading light at JWT, outlined his view of what would make brands successful. His booklet *What is a Brand?*, is a formidably prescient thought-piece that resonates to this day. He identified that brands were entering a period of retailer power in which only strong brands ('brands that are more valuable to consumers than competitive brands, brands that have added values') would be able to sustain healthy margins. He predicted that these values would become increasingly non-functional, and that the creation of integrated brand 'personalities' that unite the non-functional and functional values would become essential. He observed that a brand personality must be unique and constantly developing to stay unique in order to remain salient and profitable. And he rolled his insights up into a three-point test for any piece of brand communication that many would do well to study now:

1. Does it enhance the brand's total personality?
2. Does it contribute to the blend of appeals to the senses, the reason and the emotions?
3. Does it bring the brand to the front of mind?

'And if it does not do any of these things, what *is* it for?' he concluded.

Helpfully, Jeremy Bullmore, another famous alumnus of JWT, has provided us with a wonderful image of what a brand is and how it is made. His observations on the human mind give an insight into how a brand can outlive a company, product or service.

He draws the analogy between the brand-building process in the human mind and that of birds building their nests (Figure 3.1): 'People build brands as birds build nests, from scraps and straws we chance upon.' Bullmore draws a number of key conclusions from this:

1. Products are made and owned by companies. Brands, on the other hand, are made and owned by people... by the public... by consumers.

Figure 3.1 Bald eagle nest, Missouri
Source: Photograph by Robert Lawton

2. A brand image belongs not to a brand – but to those who have knowledge of that brand.

3. The image of a brand is a subjective thing. No two people, however similar, hold precisely the same view of the same brand.

4. That highest of all ambitions for many CEOs, a global brand, is therefore a contradiction in terms and an impossibility.

5. People come to conclusions about brands as a result of an uncountable number of different stimuli, many of which are way outside the control or even influence of the product's owner.

6. Brands – unlike products – are living, organic entities: they change, however imperceptibly, every single day.

7. Much of what influences the value of a brand lies in the hands of its competitors (because they too are building competing 'bird's nests' in the brain).

8. The only way to begin to understand the nature of brands is to strive to acquire a faculty that only the greatest of novelists possess and that is so rare that it has no name.

9. The study of brands – in itself a relatively recent discipline – has generated a level of jargon that not only prompts deserved derision among financial directors but also provides some of the most entertaining submissions in Pseuds Corner, a regular feature in *Private Eye*, the UK's leading satirical magazine.

10. It is universally accepted that brands are a company's most valuable asset; yet there is no universally accepted method of measuring that value.

11. The only time you can be sure of the value of your brand is just after you've sold it.

12. It is becoming more and more apparent that, far from brands being hierarchically inferior to companies, only if companies are managed as brands can they hope to be successful.

13. And as if all this were not enough, in one of the most important works about brands, published in 2001, the author, Robert Heath, says this: 'Above all, I found I had to accept that effective brand communication... involves processes which are uncontrolled, disordered, abstract, intuitive... and frequently impossible to explain other than with the benefit of hindsight.'

Source: Jeremy Bullmore's Brands Lecture 'Posh Spice & Persil' to the British Brands Group 2001

One of Bullmore's key observations looms ever larger in the minds of forward-looking marketers: that brands are increasingly outside the control of marketers. We live in an era when *consumers*, in the chat rooms and social networking sites of the online world, increasingly mould brands, rather than their owners. In a sense this is nothing new: people have always overlaid their own thoughts and experiences on the marketing-created images of brands – sometimes with destructive consequences (remember how people ridiculed the Midland Bank when it called itself 'The Listening Bank', contrary to many of its customers' experiences?). It is just that now they are able to do so much more powerfully and publicly than before. Co-creation is a very real fact of life for brands. So wise marketers seek to influence rather than control public perceptions of their brands – they feed the online and offline buzz that shapes perceptions and hope to mitigate any adverse impressions.

This process is increasingly distant from the old-fashioned view that advertising alone builds brands – the 'what you tell them is what they will think' school of marketing. Instead, advertising is one of a number of influences that *may* condition consumer views of a brand, but is likely to work powerfully only if it works in tandem with those other influences. The realization of this has led marketing into the uncertain world of co-creation, and there have been mistakes along the way. The launch of the 2006 Chevrolet Tahoe provides a helpful illustration of the perils of co-creation. Chevrolet decided to provide online tools for consumers to create their own commercials for the launch of the vehicle. But the Tahoe is a sports utility vehicle (SUV), so what would you do if you were an environmentally responsible person given a chance to make a commercial for the latest gas-guzzling SUV to hit the showrooms? Chevrolet was soon inundated with commercials carrying some very unflattering messages – many could be viewed on YouTube. You will find no mention of this foolhardy experiment on its website now. Other brands that have embraced co-creation have been more successful, but nevertheless nervous. Sony's UK agency Fallon was initially distraught when bystanders' videos of its Bravia 'bouncing balls' shoot in San Francisco were posted on the internet before the makers had even seen the rushes of their footage (Figure 3.2).

Then when Sony set up a website to encourage video sharing of the making of its commercial, it was worried about a negative backlash following the company's assertion of digital music rights. In fact no backlash was mounted and the exercise was a great success. The consumer buzz created by internet pre-release has become an integral part of Fallon's subsequent 'Paint' and 'Play-Doh' commercials for the Sony Bravia. The lesson is that while co-creation is a fact of life, it is also unpredictable, and any brand that seeks to encourage it needs to be sure of its footing, to have contingency plans and to be ready to respond quickly to any unforeseen mishaps.

But, to return to Bullmore's bird's nest analogy, a clear corollary of his insight that brands exist independently of the corporations, products and services they derive from is that brands can therefore outlive them. If they are well managed they can be immortal. An important part of the management of brands over time is the development of brand architecture, so we will now take a brief look at how this can help.

Figure 3.2 Sony Bravia 'Balls', Fallon London
Reproduced by kind permission of Fallon and Sony

4 How brand architecture affects brand resilience

These are the key points in this chapter:

- Brand architecture is the strategic framework that companies use to think about the market sectors they operate in.
- There are four main types of brand architecture and each model brings different risks and rewards.
- The model has important implications and can affect the brand's chances of survival.

Perhaps the most important starting point for reviewing the strategic frameworks that companies use to think about the market sectors they operate in is the brand architecture that the business uses. Brand architecture has huge implications for the brands it governs.

In his book *Brand Leadership*, David Aaker lists four main brand architectures ranged along a spectrum, from where the corporation is an umbrella organization for operating companies that themselves offer a range of distinctive brands, to the other end where the company is itself the brand. These he calls: 'House of brands', 'Endorsed brands', 'Sub-brands' and 'Branded house'. Although he subdivides these further, the subdivisions are not importantly different and somewhat subjective, so it is sometimes a matter of opinion which subcategory a brand belongs in.

House of brands

First, then, there is the scenario where the corporation is an umbrella organization, often a publicly quoted corporation, beneath which usually unlisted subsidiary companies operate, which in turn market brands to customers (Figure 4.1).

An example of such a brand architecture is Unilever, which owns a series of company brands like Lever Fabergé and Unilever Best Foods, each of which in turn markets a range of strong brands with individual identities such as Persil and Hellmann's Mayonnaise. One of the attractions of this structure is the high degree of insulation between the frontline brands and the quoted holding corporation two levels above it.

Endorsed brands

Second, there is the architecture where the company markets a series of brands, which bear no obvious relation to the company itself, but where its name or logo is used as a 'house' endorsement to provide reassurance to the buyer (Figure 4.2).

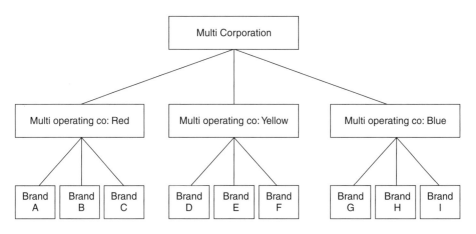

Figure 4.1 Multi corporation
Source: Butterfield (2003). Reproduced by kind permission of Elsevier, copyright holder

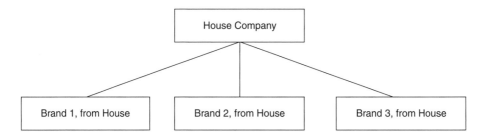

Figure 4.2 House company
Source: Butterfield (2003). Reproduced by kind permission of Elsevier, copyright holder

This is the situation with Pfizer with its Benylin, Sudafed and Viagra brands. And in recent years Unilever too has begun to migrate to this model. Usually these 'house' names are featured in a subsidiary manner on packaging and in advertising, with the main brand identity to the fore. The cumulative effect of billions of exposures adds up to a valuable reputation for quality, assuming of course that the individual brand performance is good. Thus the house name becomes a brand in its own right and can be a very effective endorsement in launching new products. However, there is clearly a growing risk in this second architecture of the negative publicity of any product problems affecting the 'house' name adversely and raising questions about its other products.

Sub-brands

Third, there is the case where the corporation is effectively the brand and sells a product range, which is essentially marketed under the same identity, but with sub-brands used to distinguish particular lines (Figure 4.3).

An example of this brand architecture is that of Virgin with its plethora of sub-brand extensions across disparate markets, from Virgin Atlantic and Virgin Trains to Virgin Mobile and Virgin Finance. In this case, the cross-market reinforcement of the brand franchise is at a maximum, but the exposure to risk is much higher in reputational terms, even if these entities are insulated from each other structurally and financially.

Branded house

Fourth, there is the instance where the corporation *is* the brand and where it is hard to discern much more than generic descriptors for the products or services it provides to its customers (Figure 4.4). An example of this is BP (and indeed most of the oil multinationals). Here there is no hiding place, and

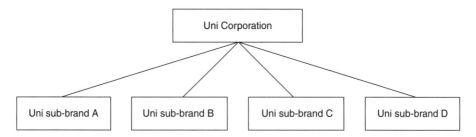

Figure 4.3 Uni corporation
Source: Butterfield (2003). Reproduced by kind permission of Elsevier, copyright holder

enormous care has to be taken with every aspect of the brand's behaviour in order not to allow even the smallest chink in the defensive armour to appear. Union Carbide was once a major chemicals brand until its plant in Bhopal, India exploded, killing many thousands of people. Much of what remains of the original company is now owned by Dow and branded as such.

Thus each choice of brand architecture brings with it a different risk profile that can have a material effect on a brand's chances of survival. At one end of the spectrum, an individual brand has to stand on its own two feet in the face of its customers with little or no halo effect, for good or bad. At the other end, the brand is indivisible from the holding company, whose fortunes can seriously affect the brand and its relationship with consumers. But there are examples of long-lived brands among all four of these brand architectures, so while some may make it easier to give birth to brands and others may make it more difficult for unfortunate events to kill a brand, on balance all are viable frameworks. Their importance lies in how they influence marketing and marketing investment as brands seek to grow and respond to their changing environment. But there is, of course, nothing to stop a company changing course and adopting a new brand architecture when it sees the need. David Aaker reminds us that when Black & Decker failed with its Professional sub-brand, it re-launched it as stand-alone DeWalt, with great success. Similarly, Toyota realized the need to launch Lexus in its successful assault on the premium car segment. The key learning is to remain flexible to consumer and category needs and to be prepared to reinvent architectures before it is too late. Perhaps Britain's Rover car business would still be alive if it had made more imaginative use of its brand assets via more flexible brand architecture.

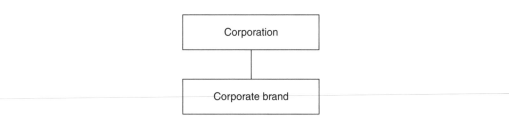

Figure 4.4 Corporation
Source: Butterfield (2003). Reproduced by kind permission of Elsevier, copyright holder

PART 2

Common business models: meaningful or menacing to brands?

5 Introduction to the dangers of some strategic thinking models

These are the key points in this chapter:

- Strategic thinking models can be useful tools if used appropriately.
- However, many have a category-centric perspective rather than a consumer-centric one, and so can be dangerous when applied to brands.

The following six chapters (6–11) are by way of a brand health warning. While there are many strategic thinking models that help prolong brand life (a number of which are discussed in these chapters), there are also models that, through misuse, ill-conception or simply being outdated, are potentially life-threatening; the most dangerous of these are examined in the following chapters. Some of these frameworks have been developed from a category-centric perspective, rather than from a brand-centric perspective, hence the dangers they can create if used.

Some of these models may make sense when applied to the issue of how a company should approach its markets, but rather less sense if applied to how it should develop its brands. As we have begun to argue, these can be very flexible and versatile assets if handled well. They have the capacity to transcend categories as well as to redefine them. Above all, brands do not have to be governed by the constraints of any one category or play by its 'rules', so it is important to distinguish between the category-centric and the brand-centric frameworks, or brands may be needlessly constrained or harmed. The following review of some very well-known and highly dangerous strategic thinking tools divides them into category- and brand-centric types. It is but a brief summary since each is the subject of dedicated books and many commentaries, and here they have been reviewed in the context of 'brand immortality'.

The next four chapters (6–9) will examine category-centric models that seek to help clarify the opportunities and challenges a company faces in its market-place. They aim to force some of the tricky decisions arising from whether a sector is dynamic or lethargic, earnings enhancing or diluting, and therefore whether companies are operating from a position of intrinsic market strength or weakness and need to revise their strategies accordingly. Used properly to assess the market opportunities, the start-points for the company's brand(s) are clearer, but the dangers often outweigh the increasingly marginal potential benefits.

The subsequent two chapters (10 and 11) will examine some of the more customer-centric strategic thinking models designed to help marketers and agencies structure their brand strategies around the changing nature of customers and their requirements. In each of them there may still be some potential for prolonging the life of the brand, even if these models were not originally conceived with this idea in mind.

Generally these tools fail to take account of category life stage – new, growth, maturity or decline – and the considerable impact this can have on strategy; allowance must therefore be made for this. As we shall show, the category life stage dimension is almost as important as the nature of the category and its consumers in determining the path a brand should take.

Examining the failings of these tools is not intended as a purely destructive exercise: in many instances better developments are discussed and the examination will hopefully help the reader achieve greater clarity and potency for their brand(s). We will see how many of the strongest, most enduring brands have a very clear sense of purpose and that fuzzy thinking is the enemy of immortality.

6 The Ansoff Matrix

These are the key points in this chapter:

- The Ansoff Matrix helps clarify thinking about the dimensions of the market and the brand position to help plot the appropriate strategy.
- Ansoff's focus is on the tangible aspects of products and services and there is little attention paid to the increasingly important intangible asset, the brand, which is often the passport to new markets.
- Another weakness of the Ansoff Matrix approach is that it doesn't really address the issue of entrenched brands or indeed of brand elasticity as a part of the strategic decision-making process.

The Ansoff Matrix, which was developed by Dr Igor Ansoff and first published in the *Harvard Business Review* in 1957, provides a rather blunt structure for thinking about the dimensions of market and brand position, and for plotting an appropriate strategy. Used with care, this matrix can help brand health by keeping minds and options open for the continuous development of brands. Again, the user needs to bear in mind that this tool is a category management one, originating in an era before it was fully understood that brands were rewriting the economics of business strategy. The matrix identifies four growth options for a business formed by matching up existing and new products and services with existing and new markets, as shown in Figure 6.1.

Market penetration

Starting in the bottom left-hand box of his matrix nearest the 'comfort zone', where the existing product or service offer is marketed at the existing

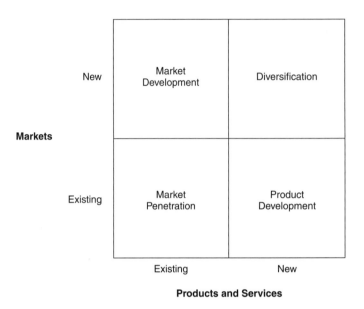

Figure 6.1 Ansoff Matrix
Source: Ansoff (1957)

customer base, it may well be possible for market penetration to be increased. Confusingly, 'market penetration' in the Ansoff Matrix does not mean the same as consumer penetration: it means selling more to existing customers as well as attracting more of the same *type* of customer. This quadrant is not about going after new customer segments, merely a greater share of existing target customers' category usage. So already this quadrant has raised two strategic approaches: trying to increase loyalty among existing customers and trying to increase penetration among 'similar' customers. Classically these two objectives would lead to very different marketing activity: some kind of relationship marketing or loyalty programme and a new customer recruitment programme, respectively. So already the model has begun to reveal its weakness and, as is typical of so many of these models, its naivety in the context of brand management: they often reveal a telling ignorance of the day-to-day practice of marketing.

Professor Ehrenberg's work on loyalty shows that in consumer markets building loyalty will not be easy: by and large, all brands in a category have very similar levels of loyalty, because it is extremely difficult to buck the norms of the category. So in practice this objective will most likely involve the cross-selling of existing products to customers of your other related products: perhaps a loan to a current account customer, or a product upgrade of some sort. This is more likely to be a task for direct marketing (online or offline) or sales promotion than advertising, but there are examples of brands where advertising has very successfully facilitated cross-selling via direct marketing. UK insurer Direct Line is one such example. Starting as a car insurer and using what was then a relatively novel distribution channel – the telephone – Direct Line has managed to diversify successfully across insurance categories, largely by cross-selling. The brand's advertising helped drive this with what has become an iconic mascot – the red telephone on wheels – and also to encourage use of the internet as a distribution channel to customers (Figure 6.2).

Figure 6.2 Direct Line red telephone and mouse
Reproduced by kind permission of Direct Line

CASE STUDY: Direct Line – How a Red Phone Grew a Super Product into a Superbrand

Nigel Robinson, Mortimer Whittaker O'Sullivan and Dom Boyd, Silver, IPA Effectiveness Awards, 2004

It's not often that communications can viably claim the credit for £1bn of incremental profit. But such is the potency of Direct Line's business and the iconic red phone device it has pressed into service for 15 years now – a device and business model that have both spawned a long list of copycats and generated a truly extraordinary return on investment for the brand leader.

In the low-cost insurance sector, salient advertising is not just an efficient way to drive sales (by their nature, direct insurers have few alternative sales channels). It is also a critical part of the business model: increasing operating efficiencies, which are then passed back to the consumer via low premiums and enhanced service.

Direct Line's advertising has not just given the brand a critical advantage in terms of awareness, consideration, cost of sales and market share; it has also broadened the brand footprint beyond price and towards a service proposition. Moreover, the campaign is judged to have dramatically reduced the cost and risk of entering new markets or establishing new channels: be it pet insurance on the one hand or internet presence for Direct Line on the other.

This case study demonstrates a return on investment of £4 profit to every £1 spent, and overwhelmingly makes the case for branding and communications in even this most price-sensitive and price-led of markets.

Ehrenberg's work also suggests that recruiting new users to the brand is a much more fertile strategy, so long as they exist in reasonable numbers. The marketing team will already know a lot about these prospects because they are similar to existing customers: tried and trusted recruitment tactics will be known, as well as the likely costs of acquisition. This is as low risk as marketing gets, and for that reason is often as far as many less adventurous brands seek to go. But sooner or later the aspiration to immortality will drive a brand beyond this cosy world.

More ambitiously, a competitor can be purchased and assimilated, as has happened in the US mobile telecoms market as it consolidates with maturity. According to Jeremy Fox of the University of Chicago, in 1989, 13 separate firms owned the 40 cellphone licences for the top 20 US geographic markets. By 2005, only 3 firms controlled them, and 2 of those 3, Verizon and Cingular, had 39 of the 40 licences! Acquisition of competitors is often viewed as a quick route to market penetration, and indeed it can be. But it usually comes at a price over organic growth, and unless significant operating synergies exist to enable costs to be cut considerably, it can prove to be a very expensive way to build market share.

Market development

Developing the market for the existing product or service on offer can provide plenty of opportunity at relatively low risk. The product can be introduced to new customers without altering it, in areas of the market not currently being addressed: new customer segments, new customer geographies or simply new channels to market. The mobile telecoms category also provides numerous illustrations of geographic market development in Europe, with Germany's Mannesmann being taken over by Vodafone, both Orange and Wanadoo being acquired by France Telecom, and O_2 by Spain's Telefónica.

Many retailers that once depended on their high street stores alone now also have out-of-town superstores, a catalogue and an internet business with home delivery. Tesco, the dominant UK food retailer, has branched out successfully into several Eastern European and Far Eastern countries and as of 2005/06 the *Guardian* reports that a quarter of total revenues come from outside the UK. In 2006, Tesco announced its assault on the United States with ambitious plans to open 100 outlets in the first year in Southern California, and at least 20 in the Las Vegas area. Unusually, the financial analysts in the City of London did not mark down its share price – a tribute to the retailer's management and brand strength, given how many UK companies have failed to make it in the United States. This is interesting, given Tesco's crucial decision not to use its existing brand, but to build a new one, 'Fresh & Easy', for the United States:

> We've taken the view that we want to have a light touch, rather than a heavy touch, and that what we want to export is the basic philosophy of the business. It's the basic philosophy that's important, more than it is the logo or the name. So whether we call ourselves 'Fresh & Easy Neighborhood Market' in America, or Tesco, you have to still build the brand in the country. Our reputation probably does slightly precede us, but it tends to be more in the business press than in the consumer psyche. You have to build a brand in every country you go into. They will judge whether the Tesco Lotus brand in Thailand is any good. (Richard Brasher, Commercial and Trading Director, Tesco)

Ansoff's focus is on the tangible aspects of products and services and there is little attention paid to the increasingly important intangible asset, the brand, which is often the passport to new markets – though as Tesco has wisely reminded us, when it comes to the development of new geographies it is dangerous to overestimate the potency of the brand as passport.

Market development can involve targeting new market segments with existing products: in essence this will require some 'repackaging' of the offer and a new presentation aimed at the needs of the segment. The UK financial services sector has provided many examples of different approaches as it developed into telephone and internet banking. In many cases the leading companies have chosen not to use their existing brands to pioneer these new distribution channels. This has been done for both internal and external reasons. For institutions heavily committed to a legacy branch network, it was less risky to develop radically new and potentially cannibalistic banking systems by setting them up as distinct businesses. For institutions heavily committed to third-party distribution channels it lessened the degree of conflict. And for staff used to traditional service delivery it clearly delineated the different offerings. On the customer-facing side, it was cleaner to shed the inherited imagery and, for some, the negatives associated with traditional financial services, and offer customers new, more accessible and more user-friendly services under a new brand name. And so Midland Bank established UK telephone-only banking with First Direct, and other established institutions followed a similar 'newco' strategy: Prudential with Egg, Halifax with Intelligent Finance and the Co-operative Bank with Cahoot. Now online banking has moved into the mainstream with services from all the major players. These early launches have produced pretty variable results, with Egg being a recent casualty and sold to Citibank in January 2007 following mounting losses. The sale raised a mere £575 million for Prudential: considerably less than the £1.4 billion the business was reputed to have been worth around two years earlier.

This is a graphic illustration of the challenges new brands face in unseating established players in a mature category. Even faced with attractive new offers from start-up brands, existing players usually enjoy considerable protection through emotional customer loyalties to their brands, while they work out their response. A weakness of the Ansoff Matrix approach is that it doesn't really address the issue of entrenched brands or indeed of brand elasticity as part of the strategic decision-making process. Brands with greater elasticity (the ability to stretch across segments and categories without losing their consumer appeal) are better equipped to take advantage of market development opportunities than inelastic ones. This alone makes the Ansoff Matrix a questionable all-round tool for strategy development in the modern world, but used as an input only, it can still help to structure thinking.

Product development

[Please refer back to Figure 6.1]

Moving further into the uncertain arena of product development, new products and services can be created to appeal to the existing customer franchise. To reduce risk, these new products may be able to rely on an existing brand's strength in terms of heritage and reputation to increase the likelihood of trial or repurchase, ie they are line extensions/new variants rather than new brands. Heinz used to claim to have 57 varieties, but nowadays, thanks to the strength of the brand, it's more like 5,700. While many of these products will have had intrinsic functional benefits in terms of flavour and appetite appeal, their successful introduction will have depended heavily on the trial-inducing reputation of Heinz. Thus, over time, Heinz (like Kellogg's, Campbell's, and many other fast-moving consumer goods brands) has migrated from its original core products to establish a presence in many other food and drink categories. The same process has occurred in many other markets. Starting with light bulbs in 1891, Philips has diversified its brand into durables as varied as electric razors, audio and video equipment and even defibrillators. The issues facing brand extensions are dealt with in greater depth in Chapter 16.

A radical example of product development can be found in the United States with General Motors' creation of an entirely new brand and dealer network in the shape of Saturn. Saturn was established as a radically different kind of customer-friendly, transparently priced car marque to appeal to a customer segment looking to avoid high-pressure sales techniques and decades of (to them) negative imagery associated with existing brands such as Chevrolet, Cadillac, Buick, Oldsmobile and Pontiac. Car buyers in this segment were increasingly attracted to Japanese marques, and GM judged it essential to launch a new brand against this threat rather than attempting to re-launch existing brands. Thus it could be argued that there was also an element of market development in the launch of Saturn: a defensive launch into an emerging customer segment.

It has been said that one of the ways to create innovative new product ideas is to juxtapose two different categories and, in conceptual terms, put them at right angles to each other as if a pair of doors, and then look at what might be created at the 'hinges'. We have already seen the convergence of mobile phones and photography, and, on a more parochial level, the combination of two of the most distinctive black food and drink products in the UK market – Marmite with Guinness (Figure 6.3).

Figure 6.3 Marmite with Guinness, promotional pack for St Patrick's Day 2007
Reproduced by kind permission of the Marmite brand

The taste of Marmite has always been polarizing for consumers and the brand has capitalized on this truth in recent years by positioning itself as the spread that you either love or hate:

> No one hated the *brand* Marmite, and no one loved the *brand* Marmite; it was the *taste* you loved or hated, so it was a subtle difference, but quite an important one. We'd written ads around Marmite being your best friend, where you might have it as your best man at your wedding, but it wasn't about that, it was about the sort of reactions to the taste that you loved or hated. So that realization made all the difference actually. (Lucy Jameson, Executive Strategy Director, DDB London)

Guinness too is regarded as an acquired taste for drinkers. Thus the genius of this partnership is that it has generated lots of newsworthiness around two long-standing and well-established brands and given customers a powerful new reason to reconsider and try. Originally conceived as a limited-production promotional item to be launched in the run-up to St Patrick's Day on 17 March 2007, only 300,000 jars were produced. Priced at £2.49 in UK supermarkets, over two-thirds of the quantity had already been sold by the due date. The power of the partnership between these two great brands and its novelty value has been confirmed on eBay where single jars were selling for in excess of £10 and entrepreneurial traders who have added a bit of green gift packaging and a touch of Shamrock blarney were asking double that! A combination of media coverage and viral 'word of mouse' has spread awareness of Marmite with Guinness around the world: Unilever, which owns the Marmite brand, found itself dealing with sales enquiries from the Americas, Middle Eastern and Asia-Pacific regions. Perhaps it will become a continuing line, rather as Cadbury's Creme Eggs used only to be available at Easter time, but are now on sale all year round.

Diversification

[Please refer back to Figure 6.1]

Of the four operational quadrants of the Ansoff Matrix, 'diversification' is the most risky. By definition, there is little relevant expertise or the potential to leverage the scale and resources of the existing business because you're embarking on the process of selling completely different products or services to unfamiliar customers. Cognizant of this risk and being wary of collateral damage, companies often create a completely new business to lead the charge.

Entrepreneur brands such as Virgin and Easy are prime examples of this. Diversification for Virgin often involves partnership with other businesses that have operational experience in the category but lack the strong brand appeal. Ideally a joint venture partnership is created in which operational and investment risks all round are minimized: a win–win situation for both parties. This model is underpinned by the extreme elasticity of these brands. They are able to stretch themselves a long way before they occasionally reach their breaking points, at which point a cola or a cinema chain fails to perform like the airline at the company's core. The crucial thing about these sorts of brands is that the 'glue' that holds them together is very clearly understood by the company, its employees, franchisees and agencies. 'Virgin' is a clever brand name for two main reasons, which can outlive its founder. First, it is still a provocative name, though clearly nothing like as controversial as when it was first used, and that provocative nature is intrinsic to its challenging character and its self-casting as David to so many corporate Goliaths. Second, its implication of youth and purity also translates into how it approaches markets, with a fresh unsullied eye and an innocence that means anything is possible. Here's how one of the most senior people in Virgin describes the brand:

> Consistent execution and the philosophy of what the brand really means to people are the important things in brand extensions. We alighted on what that was for Virgin, as it emerged from the research we were doing in the late 1980s, and which was mainly driven by Virgin Atlantic and Virgin Records. We had this reputation with the public of being what we did, and doing it with quality. However, we were also considered a value-for-money brand, an entrepreneurial company, and then it became very competitively challenging as a result of the airline. These ideas that Virgin stood for – 'competitive challenge', 'entrepreneurialism', 'quality' and 'value for money' – and doing it all with a sense of fun and style were so important. It just was incredibly consistent.
>
> Virgin also had something else: it had the personality of the single entrepreneur owner. Vance Packard had written in the 1950s about brands in America and the way the big American corporates work. He said one of the biggest problems for American businesses and American brands was the divorce of ownership from control. Quite clearly, Virgin doesn't have that divorce. So we went about our diversification with the number one thing in mind: that the Virgin ownership will always remain with Virgin, and the brand would only be licensed for whatever we did in the future. The brand is owned by Virgin Enterprises Ltd, and Sir Richard owns 100 per cent of that. (Will Whitehorn, President, Virgin Galactic and former Group Corporate Affairs and Brand Development Director, Virgin)

And that sense of 'brand' strongly pervades Virgin's communications advisors, as illustrated by the ex-CEO of Virgin Mobile's UK agency:

> The classic Virgin new product launch is all about challenging, and that challenge is against one of two things. They are either challenging a specific competitor in the market or the very status quo. So, for example, when Virgin Atlantic launched it was really all about attacking British Airways. BA had been the UK's national monopoly carrier, and though they'd been privatized they were able to exploit their near-monopoly situation. And so Virgin identified that and presented itself as a liberating competitor.

The other way that Virgin enters a market is by challenging the status quo, the tired, old-fashioned, confused way that things are, to offer a fresh alternative. That was the case with the Virgin Direct launch into financial services, where they talked about themselves as trying to clear the FOG. The FOG was the Financial Old Guard. The acronym and the analogy were perfect as it described what the FOG were peddling, which was confusion and complexity. What Virgin would bring was clarity and simplicity. (James Murphy, former CEO, RKCR/Y&R)

Although subsequently running into problems, NTL's 2006 purchase of Virgin Mobile for £962 million to create the first 'four play' provider of mobile phone, fixed-line telephony, cable TV and internet access is yet further evidence of the importance of the brand in diversification strategies. The premium NTL paid for the Virgin Mobile business reflected its desire to use the Virgin brand for its new integrated business – a property for which it will also be required to pay an annual 0.25 per cent royalty on revenues for *30 years* – with a *minimum annual payment of £8.5 million*. Such is the commercial value of risk reduction in diversification and the reassurance that a brand like Virgin can give investors.

7 The Boston Matrix

These are the key points from this chapter:

- The Boston Matrix was originally developed as a tool to help the allocation of scarce capital across operating companies or divisions.
- However, there is widespread misuse of the Boston Matrix when applied to the world of marketing.
- It can result in a self-fulfilling prophecy if applied to brands: growth falters so support is cut, so growth falters, and so on in a vicious downward spiral.

The Boston, or Growth-Share, Matrix was invented in 1970 by Bruce Henderson of the Boston Consulting Group. It was developed as a tool to help companies allocate scarce resources between competing lines of business in the days when capital was much less freely available through financial markets than it is today. The core assumption was that the growth potential for a given product or service could be judged according to individual market shares and market growth rates. The higher your market share, the higher proportion of the market you control and the more likely you are to make profits through market dominance and economies of scale. On the other hand, a brand with a low share operating within a high-growth market could have the potential for significant increases in business, if only it had the resources to do so.

However, as noted in the Introduction to this book, the application of the Boston Matrix to the world of *brand* marketing is a complete misuse of it and should never happen: it can so easily result in a self-fulfilling prophecy if applied to brands. The matrix quadrants of 'Stars', 'Cash Cows', 'Dogs' and 'Question Marks' were originally conceived to guide the allocation of financial resources to categories rather than brands, with investment funds being awarded to business units in growth categories rather than ones in steady state or declining categories. These quadrants are also commonly assumed to be sequential. Thus the application of the Boston Matrix to brands often carries with it the assumption that at some point, when growth falters, a 'Star' brand will progress to 'Cash Cow', 'Question Mark' or even 'Dog' status. As growth falters, so investment is withdrawn, often reducing the brand's competitiveness, and marketing support is cut, so growth falters further and so on. A spiral of decline sets in that is very difficult to pull out of.

So there are two important aspects of the Boston Matrix (Figure 7.1) that should always be borne in mind before applying it:

1. Since it is a category management tool and was never formulated as a brand management one, the question is: would the continuation of marketing effort behind new strategies have rejuvenated the brand, or would it have been folly to do so? It may be impossible to rejuvenate a brand within its existing category, but what about extending it to other categories or even creating new ones? There are many examples of mature brands that might be defined as 'Cash Cows' being refreshed profitably and reinvigorated by new investment. This should make any brand owner very wary of a disinvestment recommendation based on a Boston Matrix analysis.

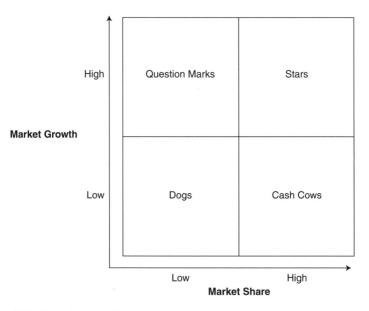

Figure 7.1 The Boston Matrix
Source: The Boston Consulting Group (1970)

2.   The model was created in an era before companies fully understood the intangible value of brands. Nowadays a company with a strong brand in a declining category might reach a rather different decision about the future of the brand than would be implied by the Boston Matrix. The brand is now recognized as an asset that should be protected since it is an important component of shareholder value. Informed businesses therefore no longer 'milk' their 'Cash Cow' brands in the unthinking way some once did.

So use of the Boston Matrix should be restricted to category management and never extended to the brand level. Given the much-increased availability of funding since the 1970s, it is arguable that the Boston Matrix has had its day and should be consigned to the history books. But it does still have some lingering value as a tool for prioritizing the categories served by a company or brand, so it merits a cautious review. Its terminology has become world famous, but nevertheless it's perhaps worth giving a brief description of the meaning of each.

'Dogs'

Where nobody really wants to be is in the bottom left quadrant of this matrix where market growth is low or declining, but so is your market share. It looks as if it could be pretty tough to fight your way out of this corner: it will use up significant resources and perhaps the potential simply isn't there. Right now, not many people want to be in UK regional newspaper publishing, the major operators having achieved the maximum economies and profits through consolidation, and are now facing serious losses of classified advertising revenues to the likes of Google, Yahoo and MSN. US newspapers are under similar pressures where key categories such as real estate advertising are migrating to the internet. Research in 2007 by ad consultancy Classified Intelligence indicates that nowadays 80 per cent of home sellers start their search online. So, according to the Boston Matrix, regional papers should be disinvested in and disposed of if possible, as the Daily Mail and General Trust tried and failed to do in 2006 with its Northcliffe division of regional and local newspapers. But what about the brand value and customer franchises represented by these titles? Would it have been worth reinvesting in them much earlier and migrating their customers to their online versions pre-Google? Is it too late now?

Sometimes, of course, one company's 'Dog' turns out to be another company's rising 'Star': thus in 2006 Unilever chose to exit from the mainstream frozen foods category by disposing of Birds Eye to Permira for £1.15

billion. Unilever had around 15 per cent share in the UK of a category that it judged was going nowhere fast because consumers are more interested in chilled foods these days. It had perhaps soldiered on too long with an outdated but famous Captain Birds Eye campaign that had done nothing to arrest the decline. Belatedly, it empowered a new marketing director, Jerry Wright, to try to breathe new life into the business. A stream of product innovations followed, backed up by a provocative new campaign highlighting the deterioration of chilled foods (Figure 7.2).

The business stabilized, but patience was in short supply at an embattled Unilever HQ, already taking heavy flak from investors about its ability to generate organic growth following the failure of its much-vaunted 'Path to Growth' strategy to deliver results. Under this plan the decision had been taken that Unilever could earn a better return on its shareholders' capital by investing its money behind 400 core brands, and this no longer included Birds Eye: the company was put up for sale.

Permira, on the other hand, with an impressive track record of improving the performance of failing businesses, judged that this was another one they could turn around. To Permira, the Birds Eye purchase was a value-building opportunity for its fund-holders' money. Time will tell whether Permira got a bargain, but there is a good chance that Birds Eye, a long-standing, famous and trusted brand, has a long and profitable life ahead both in and beyond the confines of the frozen food category.

Over the past few years a number of venture capitalists, like Permira, have bought up 'Dogs' from parent multi-brand corporations, like Unilever, seeking to focus resources behind their most powerful brands. By reinvesting in the 'Dog' brands they've acquired, these entrepreneurs have had some success:

- Princes bought the Napolina olive oil brand from Unilever in 2001 for £8.3 million and repositioned it as an Italian ingredients range. By 2004, it had overtaken Unilever's Bertolli share of the olive oil category.
- Premier foods bought Ambrosia from Unilever in 2003 and re-launched it in 2005, driving 12 per cent annual sales growth. Strong growth continued through 2006 at 5.5 per cent.

And Unilever is not alone in shedding non-core brands. Being well served by a number of leading toiletries and cosmetics brands, in 2005 Procter & Gamble divested itself of Yardley, a brand with total US sales of only $10 million. Lornamead has a track record of acquiring and building 'orphaned' brands and it bought the 236-year-old brand believing that through rebirth and reinvestment in 'luxury', Yardley could get back to the level of popularity it enjoyed 30 years ago.

Figure 7.2 Birds Eye against deteriorating food, BBH
Reproduced by kind permission of Birds Eye

As we have seen, 'Dog' status is very much in the eye of the beholder, and this is a huge weakness of the Boston Matrix. Like so many management consultant tools, it fails to acknowledge the potential of inspired brand thinking: what value do such tools really have in the era of the intangible asset? Who would have thought that the moribund UK cider market could have been revitalized by Magners' brilliantly simple expedient of selling the drink in big bottles and serving it poured over ice? How can Boston-style analysis explain the continued and massive investment in the unprofitable, low-growth, high-risk haute-couture market: a 'Chien' if there ever was one? The answer is that the fashion houses have been expert at exploiting the 'halo' of haute couture to protect and enhance their mainstream fashion 'Cash Cows'. Their annual investment in rarefied made-to-measure clothing to be worn only by a tiny number of women, and paraded before them and the world's fashionistas in catwalk extravaganzas, generates the aspirational publicity that fuels their extensive ready-to-wear, accessory and fragrance operations. Brands like Armani, Chanel, Gucci and Yves St Laurent are in fact complex mixtures of businesses one or other of which can be located in all the Boston Matrix quartiles, but each contributes to the overall strength of these perennial brands as they ride the waves of fashion trends (Figure 7.3). Over-

Figure 7.3 Chanel catwalk
Source: Image supplied by Corbis Corporation. Photograph by Olivier Hoslet

rational business analysis tools can't hope to handle the very human complexities of branded businesses operating successful models such as these.

'Cash Cows'

If they cannot have a portfolio entirely composed of 'Stars', then every company would like to have at least one 'Cash Cow' instead. This is a brand sitting comfortably with a high market share in a well-established category. The growth potential may not be great, but the profits should be good. The argument runs that returns on further investment in this category will be less than in other growing categories and so profits should be diverted to more rewarding areas of the matrix. This is true to a seductive degree, as we shall see: returns on marketing investment are indeed lower in mature categories than in new and growing ones. So far, so good. But there are two huge bear-traps in this seductive line of thinking that have done much to ensure the mortality of brands over the years.

The first bear-trap is that it downplays the investment requirement in any category of maintaining market share. In general, the zero investment condition is not stasis – it is decline. This is because the competition keeps spending. An insidious double whammy takes place of declining share as competitors take advantage of the brand's underinvestment in marketing, and increasing price sensitivity as the lack of investment in innovation and product upgrades starts to take its toll at the tills. The change is slow at first, but gathers pace and then before you know it, the 'Cash Cow' is no longer able to throw off buckets full of cream to fund other developments. Worse still, it may have lost the capacity to defend what is left of its profitability. The highly authoritative PIMS study of 3,000 business units teaches us that two key determinants of profitability for a contender in any category are their market share and their perceived relative quality (and hence the ability to hold firm on pricing). To lose one of these is unfortunate, but to lose both is disastrous. So the whole notion of the 'Cash Cow' when applied to brands is entirely false, since without competitive levels of brand investment, the profit stream will falter.

Even the most venerable of brands needs a steady succession of nips, tucks and facelifts to maintain its appeal. It can be challenging to come up with relevant innovation for long-established brands, and this is where real creativity earns its money. In this context, Arthur C Clarke has a few pithy words to say:

Every revolutionary idea evokes three stages of reaction:

1. It's completely impossible.
2. It's possible but it's not worth doing.
3. I said it was a good idea all along.

His words are especially true when it comes to long-established brands where there can be a strong sense of tradition verging on ossification. So it's worth noting how often it's a packaging idea that breathes new life into old brands – perhaps brand managers feel more certain in this most tangible of areas? The steady flow of new materials and technologies is a source of inspiration for every marketer; however, they should bear in mind designer Raymond Loewy's MAYA dictum: Most Advanced Yet Acceptable. Loewy believed that 'The adult public's taste is not necessarily ready to accept the logical solutions to their requirements if the solution implies too vast a departure from what they have been conditioned into accepting as the norm.'

Heinz faced the 'Cash Cow' problem with its iconic tomato ketchup product, first launched in the UK in 1876. One of its answers was its upside-down squeezable bottle: a brilliantly simple solution to the impracticality of one of its key brand strengths – its viscosity (Figure 7.4).

In the United States, Heinz has gone even further to breathe new life into its ketchup range, with a variety of excitingly coloured and flavoured products for a generation that has become accustomed to more choice. There's even a mystery colour variant for true thrill seekers...

A clever packaging innovation also transformed the fortunes of a product that was struggling in an un-differentiated mature category. This was achieved with SC Johnson's Toilet Duck by the simple device of a built-in directional squirter making it easy to apply the cleaning liquid under the rim of the toilet bowl, and giving the brand its name and considerable longevity (Figure 7.5).

But it's not just long-established brands that need continuous attention – the pace of technological change means that even relatively newly established 'Cash

Figure 7.4 Heinz Tomato Ketchup squeezy
Reproduced by kind permission of packagingdigest.com

Figure 7.5 SC Johnson's Toilet Duck
Courtesy of SC Johnson, A Family Company

Cows' cannot afford to chew the cud. Sony failed to move quickly enough with its iconic Walkman brand (Figure 7.6) when its one-way bet behind the removable minidisc format was rendered obsolete overnight by new developments in miniaturized hard discs and subsequently in flash memory. Look how quickly this once-dominant mobile music brand was usurped by Apple's iPod (Figure 7.7). But now even this iconic brand is under huge competitive attack. After three years' pioneering the concept, Apple had sold 4 million iPods, whereas in 2006 Sony Ericsson sold 17 million Walkman phones, plus a further 43 million music-playing mobiles rejuvenating the brand in the process. Meanwhile Nokia sold 70 million music-enabled phones, making it the world's biggest manufacturer of MP3 players – and Nokia's research shows that 60 per cent of its customers now use these music capabilities. No wonder Apple is now investing heavily in its new iPhone – after all, why carry around two devices instead of one?

Indeed, the new Apple iPhone, combining a cellphone, video iPod, e-mail terminal, web browser, camera, alarm clock and organizer, was launched on 30 June 2007 amid a frenzy of customer enthusiasm and media hype. Customers began queuing outside New York's Apple store at 5 am on Monday even though the product did not go on sale until 6 pm on Friday. Many successful buyers immediately put their purchase back on the market via eBay at a significant price premium. The screen displays touch-sensitive icons that can be accessed by fingertip rather than with a stylus and it features a touch-screen typewriter-style keyboard. This combination of technology and design (by Jonathan Ive) is typical of Apple's approach. It contrasts powerfully with rivals

Figure 7.6 Sony Walkman
Reproduced by kind permission
of Rodger L Carter and
DigicamHistory.com

Figure 7.7 Apple iPod
Courtesy of Apple

such as the BlackBerry, which tend to use more conventional approaches, such as real keyboards with miniature keys that are tricky to use: the art of spelling has never before seen such torment. The Apple magic is reflected in the price. The iPhone is significantly higher-priced than many other devices with a total cost of up to £1,500, comprising £250 to £300 for the device itself and the rest on a compulsory two-year service contract plus the cost of extra calls and texts. Thus in a few years the Apple brand has been evolved from a struggling computer brand, to a mould-breaking music internet site and MP3 player and now to a serious challenger in the mobile phone market.

The second bear-trap of the Boston Matrix is the imposition of investment guidelines relating to a category onto a brand. Brands are not restricted to a category, so why not let the brand earn its investment by stretching into (or creating) new and growing categories? That way there will at least be a halo effect of the new developments back onto the original core of the brand and there will be a stronger business rationale to keep the mothership afloat. More importantly, past investment in the brand will be safeguarded and launch costs will be reduced thanks to the ready-made brand equity available. As we have seen, Apple has stretched successfully from a personal computer company to market leader in mobile music. Mars has leapfrogged from confectionery to ice cream. Marks & Spencer has built a huge food business on the back of its original clothing franchise, while Tesco is going in the other direction from conventional grocery supermarketing to brown goods and homewares. Laura Ashley has added home furnishings to fashion.

Another good example of this strategy is that of Kellogg's Fruit Winders, the Kellogg Company's first significant non-cereal product launch. Fruit Winders succeeded in establishing a new fruit snack category while refreshing Kellogg's imagery among young children and their mothers at a time when the parent cereal brands were under intense pressure from competitive manufacturer and retailer brands.

'Stars'

[Please refer back to Figure 7.1]

Any management would like to own a portfolio populated from the top right-hand quadrant: twinkling with 'Stars'. These are businesses that are established with good shares in market sectors that are exhibiting high rates of growth. As a result, there are great opportunities for building business and consolidating positions – growth is not only easier to achieve, but usually earns a good rate of return. An excellent example of a current star is the BlackBerry mobile and e-mail device made by Research in Motion based in Ontario, Canada (Figure 7.8). As of September 2006, there were 6.2 million subscribers, and the number was growing at the rate of 1.5 million per year. Many of them are high net worth individuals from the worlds of business, law, politics and media, thus constituting an enormously valuable customer base. Investment bank Nomura estimates that the BlackBerry has about 65 per cent share of the corporate mobile e-mail market. Moreover, the company shrewdly allows competitors such as Motorola, Nokia and Palm to manufacture compatible devices and thus build the overall market in which it is the dominant brand. However, competition is intensifying, with the likelihood that BlackBerry will have to fight very hard to maintain its hefty price premium and market leadership as the category matures. Hopefully, Research in Motion are already well down the research and development road in developing new products that the BlackBerry brand can segue into.

'Question Marks'

Lastly, to the top left quadrant are the 'Question Marks', also sometimes known as 'Problem Children'. This is a market position that is difficult to know what to do with: market share is low, but the category is high growth so there should be potential. However, there is clearly something wrong with the product or service, its positioning or presence in the marketplace. Sometimes well-installed competitors have erected barriers to entry. Perhaps taking advantage of their greater profitability, they may be deliberately pricing at a level that makes it impossible for a smaller rival to make money. Or perhaps they may be investing in communications at a level that makes it impossible for new arrivals to afford cut-through levels of share of voice. The question is,

Figure 7.8 BlackBerry
Reproduced by kind permission of Research
in Motion/Blackberry

how much is it going to cost in time and resources to fix this problem and how feasible is it given the level of competition and profitability in the category?

DaimlerChrysler's Smart (Figure 7.9) looked so promising at one time: a space-efficient, fuel-efficient town car co-designed by Swatch and Daimler-Benz. The idea was to be able to park nose-in in a normal parking bay, thanks to its short length. Each car would use only half a parking space and with

Figure 7.9 Smart Car
Source: Photograph by Barbara Smith/Monceau on Flickr.com

Figure 7.10 Original Mini
Source: Photograph by Hamish Pringle

Figure 7.11 New Mini
Source: Photograph by Dave Elkington

average fuel consumption of around 60 mpg this would be the ultimate town car. But despite strong growth, the small car segment is fiercely competitive and margins are tight. The quirky appeal of the Smart car just couldn't make up for the expensive technology under the bonnet. Losses mounted and Swatch pulled out. DaimlerChrysler soldiers on, launching Smart into the US market, but has yet to turn the corner. And with growing competition from more environmentally friendly hybrid-fuel cars, things don't look good.

These 'Question Marks' are tantalizing because, of course, with the right treatment and appropriate investment they could potentially become 'Stars'. So it's always worthwhile thinking creatively to re-examine the possibilities.

The resurrection of the Mini brand has been a wonderful example of this, with the new model rising from the ashes of the Phoenix/BMW deal in 2000. A 'classic' car (Figure 7.10) that had been withdrawn from sale was resurrected, re-engineered and restyled. But BMW recognized that product excellence was not enough in a highly competitive category. The Mini was brought right back up to date (Figure 7.11) with brilliant communications campaigns around the world that capitalized on its fun-loving, individualistic personality (Figure 7.12).

Figure 7.12 Assorted MINI US campaign images, Crispin Porter and Bogusky
Reproduced by permission of MINI USA. © 2007 MINI, a division of BMW of North
America, LLC. All rights reserved. The MINI and BMW trademark, model, names and
logo are registered trademarks

So it is clear that the Boston Matrix not only is a dangerous tool to apply to
brands, but also completely fails to take into account the transformational
potential of inspiring marketing. It is the worst kind of 'painting by numbers'
tool – rooted in a world of pure logic, 'perfect' economics and tangible assets.

8 Porter's Five Forces

These are the key points from this chapter:

- Porter's Five Forces is a powerful analytical tool for weighing up risks and opportunities.
- If there is a single lesson that can be learnt from Porter, it is to 'be paranoid'.
- Companies must challenge constantly preconceptions of their competitive set and be alive to new technologies that could unseat their own.
- Legislation needs to be added to the list of Porter's Five Forces.

Porter's Five Forces model is potentially a more valuable aid to brands seeking immortality because it feeds the state of managed paranoia that is essential to long life. It prompts the kinds of questions that can prick the bubbles of complacency and overconfidence that bedevil successful brands. It can also arm younger brands with the forethought necessary to win the battles ahead. It is a useful analytical tool for weighing up risks and opportunities, but is incomplete and thus so dangerous if regarded as a definitive checklist. Michael E Porter, Bishop William Lawrence University Professor at Harvard Business School, introduced his 'Five Forces' concept in his article 'How competitive forces shape strategy' published in the *Harvard Business Review* in 1979. These forces are visualized in Figure 8.1.

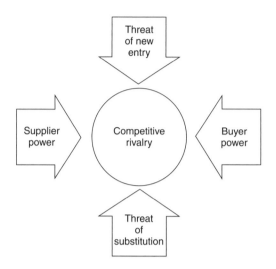

Figure 8.1 Porter's Five Forces
Source: Porter (1979)

Competitive rivalry

Understanding the extent of competitive rivalry, and the strength of it, is fundamentally important in assessing either the vulnerability of your own brand or its potential for increasing its share of market. How distinctive or unique is your offer to the market? Does your brand have the underpinning protection of a patent or the protective umbrella of a powerful brand image? Look how quickly the sales of drug brands collapse when their patents expire and they become generics, and how hard their owners fight in the courts to extend those patents. Bristol-Myers and its partner Sanofi-Aventis are striving to preserve the patent life of their top-selling heart pill Plavix; Pfizer's court victory protected its best-seller Lipitor, hiking its share price; and Cephalon may win several extra years of sales of its wakefulness drug Provigil. But one of the best-known patent battles has been by Pfizer against Eli Lilly and Icos over Viagra, originally developed at Pfizer's research centre in Sandwich, Kent. Pfizer lost its 1993 patent but retained its 1991 and 1997 ones and therefore retains rights over the molecular structure of sildenafil or UK-92480 (Figure 8.2), so that the basic product patent will remain in force until 2013. But its best long-term protection may well be the brand name and distinctive pill.

The same relentless competition is endemic in consumer markets: for example, Johnson's 'Holiday Skin' went on sale in May 2005 and was an instant hit. However, by 2006, major competitors had seen the opportunity Johnson's

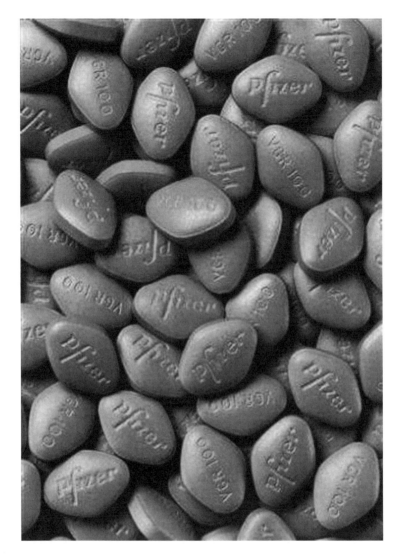

Figure 8.2 Viagra: sildenafil or UK-92480
Source: Pfizer. Reproduced by kind permission of Pfizer

had created and there were at least five tanning moisturizers from which the consumer was able to choose. Competitive rivalry can be most damaging in emerging categories: while there may be fewer competitors, there are also likely to be more casualties as the combatants strive to establish their positions, often taking fatal risks in the process. There are many salutary examples from the dot.com era: Webvan expanded very quickly from its inception in 1999 and at its peak was estimated to be worth $1.2 billion, but closed down in July 2001;

and Pets.com also lasted just two years. Boo.com, perhaps the most notorious dot.com of all, burnt $160 million of investors' money before liquidating in May 2000. But that investment has a residual value and the Boo brand may live on: it is currently being resurrected as a travel website.

Supplier power

Supplier power is a key factor in your and your competitors' competitive positions. Life stage can be an important factor here: a new company struggling to establish itself in a fast-growing new market with inherent volatility is likely to be more at the mercy of suppliers, which themselves are jockeying for position, than new companies in more mature sectors. Whatever your company's age and life stage, to what extent do your current suppliers have power over you? Are there alternatives to them who could deliver at a competitive price and in a timely manner? What would the consequences be if one of your suppliers switched to a competitor or went bankrupt? Do you have any real options and at what cost? Again the pharmaceuticals market gives us an example of supplier power, with Pfizer revealing its intention to negotiate its drug prices direct with UK pharmacists and employ UniChem, part of the newly formed Alliance Boots Group, as its sole distribution arm. With Pfizer's 15 per cent of the UK's £10bn annual medicines sales, and UniChem's ownership of the largest retail pharmacy chain with 2,600 stores, this move looks pretty threatening.

Buyer power

To what degree is your company beholden to its major customers and are there rather too few of them for comfort? In markets that have matured and been subject to consolidation, buyer power can have an enormous impact. Starting in Newport, Arkansas in 1962, the United States' Wal-Mart now has current sales of over $300 billion, and has enormous power over its suppliers, even though its dominance is finally leading to some significant reactions by both worker and consumer groups. In Finland, just three retailers have a combined market share of 91 per cent, and in the much bigger UK and Netherlands grocery markets, four major players now dominate, each with over 60 per cent combined share (Figures 8.3 and 8.4).

A key part of Marks & Spencer's recovery in the UK market has been a reappraisal of its suppliers, with devastating consequences for those who lost contracts. Lambert Howarth was until recently the most important shoe supplier to M&S, but after it lost its major contract for comfort shoes, sales fell from £46.2 million to £26.6 million, resulting in a half-year loss of £13 million

United Kingdom	% share 2005
Tesco	28.2%
Asda	15.7%
Sainsbury's	14.6%
Morrisons	11.2%

Figure 8.3 UK % market share of supermarkets 2005
Source: AC Nielsen Homescan Total Till. Reproduced by kind permission of AC Nielsen

Netherlands	% share 2005
Albert Heijn (Ahold)	26.9%
C1000	15.6%
Super de Boer	8.9%
Aldi/Lidl	9.3%

Figure 8.4 Netherlands % market share of supermarkets
Source: Information Resources Inc 2005. Reproduced by kind permission of Information Resources Inc

and the workforce having to be cut by 28 per cent. The company never recovered from this mortal blow and went into administration in October 2007.

Companies supplying to these customers, and fearful of losing valuable contracts, find themselves under pressure from every angle that a buyer's ingenuity can conceive. They face demands for ever-lower prices, bigger listing and display fees, larger promotional contributions to joint advertising and promotions, and the requirement to purchase from the retailer's own inventory of advertising media such as posters, customer magazines, statement inserts, and now in-store TV (Figure 8.5).

So the leading manufacturers' brands across a whole range of categories have been put under enormous pressure to reduce prices and profitability by being squeezed between the 'rock' of de-listing and the 'hard place' of competition from value brands and the retailer's own brand. How can your brand escape such pressures? Are there alternative channels of distribution that could be opened up? Does the internet enable a direct relationship with end users without threatening existing buyer relationships, perhaps through a new brand? What about wholly owned retail outlets such as Nike and Apple which

Figure 8.5 Tesco's in-store TV
Reproduced by kind permission of Tesco

have developed so successfully? The first Niketown was a sensation when it launched in Portland, Oregon in 1990 (Figure 8.6) and its successors have continued to be hugely impressive temples to sportswear and equipment.

The architect of Apple's retail strategy, Ron Johnson, made a key decision right at the outset. This was to eschew the idea of co-locating with the out-of-town computer 'sheds' and car dealers and instead establish its stores in town centres. As Johnson said in an interview with the UK's *Daily Telegraph* in 2007, 'The stores were as much about reinvigorating the Apple brand as they were about piling stuff on shelves in a big room. They're all in busy urban centres where there's substantial passing trade. Steve Jobs' view was they'll never drive 10 miles to look at us, but they will walk 10 feet.' Apple's upper-floor Genius Bars, where people can get trained in using their Apple equipment, are part of a fundamental shift in the role of retail outlets in the online era. As Johnson points out:

> Over half the space in London's Regent Street store is given over to people who have already bought Apple products. We want to make sure that they have such a great experience of owning them that they will stay with us for a lifetime and become promoters to their friends. It's basically another way Apple can increase its market share – not just with the products and software, but with the owner-ship experience. The front line of that is our store.

Figure 8.6 Niketown, Oxford Circus, London
Source: Photograph by Hamish Pringle. Reproduced by kind permission of Nike

Apple has innovated throughout its retail design: its award-winning glass staircase by structural engineer James O'Callaghan makes the upper floor much more inviting without the need to install a bulky escalator (Figure 8.7).

In both these cases and others like them, the brand is able to create the ideal environment in which to stock Apple merchandise. So not only is it displayed to best advantage, but it is also presented through the total retail experience in the context of the brand idea. Abercrombie & Fitch, the famous US clothing brand, took this to a new level when it opened its first-ever store outside North America in London, and garnered acres of media coverage with an aspirational line-up of beautiful staff who were all (or certainly looked like) actors or models.

Threat of substitution

[Please refer back to Figure 8.1]

In a sense, substitutability is a function of several of the other forces at work in Porter's model. How easy would it be for one of your buyers to find an alternative provider? To what extent is the component, process or software that you are providing able to be replicated or replaced? Could one of your major

Figure 8.7 Apple
staircase
Reproduced by kind
permission of Gary Allen at
ifoapplestore.com

business customers take the service that you provide and turn it into an in-house function? Dixons Store Group in the UK has been heavily dependent on press advertising for over 20 years, but is now encountering a sharp decline in its effectiveness, as its customers increasingly use the internet as a shopping tool. Quite suddenly, a cornerstone client of the national press is being undermined by new communications technology. In Venezuela in 1996, Coca-Cola pulled off a devastating commercial coup against perennial global rival Pepsi-Cola when it bought the latter's sole bottler and distributor out from under its nose, achieving market leadership almost overnight. Ten years later in 2006, Carphone Warehouse was taken unawares when Vodafone abruptly terminated the main part of its UK distribution deal in favour of Phones 4u, which thus became its exclusive third-party seller of phones on monthly contracts. More recently, in an apparent retaliation for its $9 billion takeover of Colombian brewer Bavaria, which it deemed detrimental to its interests, Heineken terminated SABMiller's licence to brew and distribute its Amstel Lager in South Africa. Given that the brand has around 9 per cent of that country's beer sales, this loss will reportedly cost SAB $80 million a year in profits.

And we should never forget the end-user's power in substituting one product or service for another – look how digital cameras usurped 35mm film and how mobile phones with integral cameras are now taking them over. In 2008, it is estimated that one billion mobile phone cameras will be in use around the world and that by 2010, no fewer than 228 billion images will have been captured on them. In the process, famous, but slow-moving, brands such as Kodak and Polaroid find themselves struggling to survive. Polaroid sales peaked in 1994 at $2.3 billion, but started to slip in 1996 and by 2001 the company had filed for Chapter-11 bankruptcy protection. Kodak fights on, trying to replace the rapidly dwindling profits of its legacy traditional film business (revenue fell 18 per cent in 2005) with profits from its fast-growing but, so far, less profitable digital business. Restructuring costs associated with this struggle led in large part to an operating loss of around $600 million in 2005. The company is not out of the woods yet: operating losses of $200 million were recorded in 2006 and a net loss of $600 million.

If these companies had applied Porter's Five Forces to their thinking, perhaps they would have recognized earlier the substitution threat arising from irresistible technological change in the category. It may seem inevitable that when a technology shift as fundamental as the move to camera phones takes place, it is bound to leave casualties in its wake, but this is simply not true. Brands always have escape routes if they act early enough while they still have a decent profit stream from existing operations. Les Binet makes the point that companies often confuse product life cycles with category life cycles, because they have a misleadingly narrow view of their category, and that this can lead them to make investment mistakes:

> There are life cycles for categories, and a lot of those are very long-term, and then within that there are life cycles for products, and those are often much more short term, particularly in any category where the technology is changing. I think the life cycles of categories are more about very long-term things to do with consumer needs, which actually don't change very much over time in a lot of categories. It's about meeting those consumer needs in different ways, and jockeying for position with competitors who are catching up with you. Brands are mental constructs that are attached to products within categories that they can change over time: they can attach themselves to different products. (Les Binet, European Director, DDB Matrix)

Hopefully, for the sakes of the many thousands of people who work for Kodak, the brand will belatedly find a way through its troubles. What is inconceivable is that the brand will die – it is simply too valuable for someone not to swoop to the rescue...

Porter does not include it as one of his five, but legislative change has become an increasingly powerful force with which companies have to contend. The Sarbanes–Oxley legislation passed in the United States in June 2002 has already had a far-reaching impact on many markets, including the advertising agency sector. Interpublic Group (IPG) declared a completely transparent business policy and promised multi-million-dollar refunds to clients of unbilled media and previously undisclosed volume discounts. 'The NatWest Three' were arrested and extradited to the United States to face charges and jail sentences related to the Enron debacle. The publicly quoted shares of Sportingbet, one of the pioneers of the burgeoning online betting market, were thrown into turmoil by the seizing of top executive Peter Dicks at JFK airport in September 2006. Shares then went into free fall when unexpected anti-gaming legislation was passed in October in the shape of the Unlawful Gambling Internet Act of 2006. The main sponsor of this US legislation was one Jim Leach, a Republican from Iowa, home to 13 casinos and 3 race tracks with slot machines generating $300 million a year in State revenues. This new Act made it illegal for banks and credit card companies to process online gaming payments from the United States, with devastating consequences – more than £3.5 billion was wiped off the value of Britain's leading internet gaming companies (Figure 8.8).

The European Commission has accused mobile phone operators such as Vodafone, T-Mobile and Orange of 'unfair and excessive' roaming charges in Europe and has promised to cut these fees, which are claimed to account for

© 2007 Interactive Investor Trading Limited

Figure 8.8 888 Holdings plc – fluctuations in share price 2006–07
Reproduced by kind permission of Interactive Investor Trading Ltd, www.iii.co.uk

up to 15 per cent of their profits. Food companies are being attacked relentlessly on both sides of the Atlantic for being the cause of obesity, despite all the evidence laying a large proportion of the fault at the door of modern sedentary lifestyles and poor parenting. One of the leading US food companies is already involved in the early skirmishes of a food equivalent of the anti-tobacco class action suits. In Europe, attention is on the UK, where Ofcom has ruled that broadcast advertising of high fat, salt and sugar foods and soft drinks must be curtailed by tougher regulatory codes governing content of advertising to primary school children, overlaid with scheduling and volume restrictions for under-16s. The definition of what products are high in fat, salt and sugar depends on the application of the Food Standards Agency's controversial nutrient profiling system. Among other things, the FSA system means that Marmite and cheese can no longer be advertised to children, and in a revealing *volte-face*, it has been forced to recalculate to allow milk to be promoted. Environmental concerns, especially over climate change, are increasing daily, with fundamental implications for brands across many categories. In the autumn of 2006, the State of California began a lawsuit against six major car-makers. General Motors, Toyota, Ford, Honda, Chrysler and Nissan are accused of accounting for a third of the State's carbon dioxide emissions, harming environmental health and costing it billions of dollars.

US-style litigation has spread to the UK and Europe, fuelled by aggressive 'no win no fee' client solicitation tactics. What would once have been regarded as laughable claims now have to be taken very seriously indeed, especially by successful, visible brands that look as if they're good for the money. In February 2007, it was revealed that not only was Tate Modern the UK's top attraction with a 21 per cent increase in visitors to 4,915,000 during 2006, but also that it was being sued by Kate Phillips, one of its visitors. One of the key contributors to building Tate Modern's great position has been The Unilever Series of spectacular sponsored installations in the massive turbine hall, including Carsten Holler's *Test Site,* a huge popular success in 2006/07. The artwork comprised several stainless steel slides reminiscent of fairground helter-skelters. These varied in height and speed from the short and benign to the 180ft tall and scary, so Southwark Council's health and safety experts were kept busy inspecting them before the exhibit could be opened to the public. The Council insisted that all users be given instruction leaflets and personal guidance by Tate Modern attendants at the top of each slide. They were also required to place their arms across their chest and to lie back on protective fabric sheets with a foot pocket before descending. In the early days of the exhibit, which opened in October 2006, the gallery even installed extra rubber mats at the bottom of the slides after the first people down the slides claimed they had suffered friction burns. These precautions were very elaborate, expensive and time-consuming. Visitors had to arrive as the Tate

Modern opened in order to buy a limited number of timed access tickets for the slides, which still suffered from long queues. Despite all these elaborate precautions, there were a few minor injuries and evidence of yet another nail in the coffin of personal responsibility. Kate Phillips, a charity worker in Glasgow, allegedly injured herself on the star attraction. She brought a legal action after saying she broke her hand on the exhibit, leaving her in severe pain and with difficulties working. Ms Phillips said she needed seven stitches after sliding down one of the helter-skelters: 'I am claiming for the loss of facility of my right hand... it's been a real problem,' she said. 'I couldn't type, write or drive for two months. I travel extensively with work but I couldn't even carry a suitcase. Only now, three months on, am I getting back to normal.' As a spokeswoman for Tate Modern said, the gallery had done all it could to ensure the safety of the slides: 'Our advice has been approved following a full inspection by the local health and safety department of Southwark Council. All of these injuries have been caused by visitors who have not followed the instructions for using the slides.' Unfortunately, even brands such as Tate Modern can become victims of this compensation culture – and ironically so, given that artist Holler claimed that his slides are a fusion of art and architecture that could be used to combat stress and depression...

Porter's Five Forces, although incomplete in the key area of legislation, can still be a useful stimulant to thought. If there's a single lesson that can be learnt from Porter, it is to 'be paranoid'. Companies must constantly challenge their preconceptions of their competitive set and be alive to new technologies that could unseat their own. Too often successful companies become inward-looking and simply don't spend enough time, energy and resources antici-pating and then pre-empting the potential sources of their brands' future morbidity.

9 The 4 Ps

These are the key points from this chapter:

- Despite being published over 40 years ago, the simple idea of addressing the 4 'P's of Product, Price, Place and Promotion still has utility.
- But marketers should consider how these tangible aspects of production and service delivery translate into the long-term asset of intangible brand value.
- Using a newer tool and thinking about Solutions, Information, Value and Access (SIVA) is a much more customer-centric approach.
- In continuing to use the 4 Ps, an additional 'P' should be included, that of 'People'.

'The 4 Ps' is another strategic framework that has had a significant influence on marketers over the years, but has perhaps also begun to outlive its usefulness. 'The 4 Ps' were originated by Professor Richard Clewett, modified and published by Jerry McCarthy in *Basic Marketing*, but made famous by Philip Kotler in his seminal 1967 book *Marketing Management: Analysis, planning and control*.

The increasingly simplistic idea of addressing the 4 'Ps' of Product, Price, Place and Promotion has struggled to keep up with the developments and realities of the modern business world. As Kotler has written in a recent article, 'Alphabet soup', in the March/April 2006 issue of *Marketing Management*, many attempts have been made, including by himself, to refine the framework and, most importantly, to shift its orientation from a seller's to a *buyer's* one. Figure 9.1 summarizes a few of the variations on the theme, but doesn't go so far as to include the many other Ps that might also feature, such as 'packaging', 'personal selling', 'process', and even company 'passion', which is rated highly by some.

4 Ps	4 Cs	4 As
Product	Customer needs and wants	Acceptability
Price	Cost to customer	Affordability
Place	Convenience	Availability
Promotion	Communication	Awareness
Source: Jerry McCarthy, *Basic Marketing* (Richard D. Irwin, 1960)	*Source:* Robert Lauterborn, 'New marketing litany: 4Ps passé; C words take over', *Advertising Age*, 1 October 1990	*Source:* Jagdish Seth and Rajendra Sisodia, 'Iridium's 66 pies in the sky', August 1999

Figure 9.1 4 Ps, 4 Cs and 4 As chart

From the point of view of ensuring the longevity of brands, the 'P' that is most glaringly omitted in the 1960s supply-side thinking enshrined in the 4 Ps would denote 'purchasers' – ie the customers who are the heart of the business. These are the people in whose minds the brand promise resides and who decide the all-important level of *demand* for the brand. In an article in *Market Leader* in 2005, eminent academics Chekitan Dev and Don Schultz argue that it is time to kill off the 4 Ps entirely because they are fatally bound up with outdated supply-side thinking. The need to move on from the 4 Ps is perhaps most clearly illustrated by the growing absurdity of the idea that marketers can dictate pricing. The best they can usually do in the modern world is to try to shift the demand curve for the brand by adding perceived value to it, so that customers are prepared to pay more for the brand than for its competitors. But this falls a long way short of controlling pricing.

Dev and Schultz argue for a new customer-centric framework that they label with the acronym SIVA: Solutions, Information, Value and Access. Their framework is somewhat rational, as will become clear, but nevertheless represents a quantum leap forward from the 4 Ps. Their premise is that in the modern over-supplied message-cluttered world, consumers have progressed beyond the quest for products that meet their needs in clearly defined ways to the quest for *Solutions* to their problems that meet their needs in whichever ways work. They then seek *Information* to direct them to the appropriate solution. This is arguably where the framework becomes naively rational – consumers are more powerfully influenced by their emotional feelings towards the solutions, so wise marketers would seek to create positive feelings as well as disseminate relevant information about the solution. Perhaps a better 'I' would be for *'Inspiration'* rather than *Information*. Customers will not purchase unless they perceive that the *Value* offered to them is fair. At this point, Dev and Schultz caution wisely that value is not primarily about price: it is more important to the bottom line that a brand adds value through the quality of the brand experience and its ability to motivate customers to pay more, not less. And so to *Access*, for which Dev and Schultz argue that customers now require what they want, when, where and how they want it. So multiple overlapping delivery mechanisms are the order of the day, perhaps best epitomized by Coca-Cola's famous 'arm's reach' mantra of availability (see the third of the following sections – 'Place'). Providing this level of access requires innovative thinking that goes way beyond traditional notions of distribution.

Whether or not you fully accept the SIVA framework, it undoubtedly high-lights the fatal weaknesses of the traditional 4 Ps framework. So the following review of the 4 Ps should be seen as a challenge to think more deeply, rather than merely accept its structure.

Product

The term 'product' is used here in its widest sense to cover service and corporate brands as well as physical ones. The key question is how your product or service is unique, different from or better than the competition – or is it not? Increasingly important in the era of the elastic brand is 'how do you *define* your product or service?'. This may sound a dumb question, but ever since Theodore Levitt published 'Marketing myopia' in the *Harvard Business Review* in 1960, companies have known of the benefits of defining their product space more broadly. In his paper, Levitt famously pointed out that the oil companies (as they then saw themselves) were really in the energy business, a much more fertile territory for development. Even more inspirationally, Steve Jobs, CEO of Apple, has placed his brand not in the business of hardware (very limiting in a fast-changing technology sector), but in the business of *changing the world*. And at some level many Apple products do actually deliver against this. But most importantly, by redefining the nature of his product in such a stimulating way, Jobs has liberated the creative talents of his people to great effect. In November 2001, Apple was a $5 billion company and just six years later it is forecast to achieve $23 billion in revenues, with more than half coming from iPods and iTunes while having only a 5 per cent market share in its original PC sector.

Other product-related questions include:

- 'How closely do you scrutinize your competitive set?'
- 'Are comparative product tests or mystery shopping an integral part of your continuous improvement programme?'
- 'How innovative is your brand?'

The innovation question is *not* to ask how much money you throw at R&D, but rather how successful it is in delivering a stream of successful ideas and how quickly it can respond to new challenges. As Mark Snyder, Senior Vice-President of world-wide brand management for the Holiday Inn family of brands, has said *'Holiday Inn is 54 years old and the fastest way to kill a legacy brand is not to innovate. Watch out if there's too much of "what used to be" still there!'* An early casualty of the internet was the Encyclopaedia Britannica. This once-great brand was founded in 1768 and has let slip away its 223-year heritage by failing to anticipate, and then deal effectively with, the threat to its once-invincible position. It has been decimated by Wikipedia and the like. The record industry also learnt this lesson to its cost when it reacted too slowly to the threat origi-nally posed by Napster and KaZaA, whose idea for digital file-sharing tech-nologies undermined the historical pre-eminence of analogue 'hard copy' music delivery systems such as audio cassettes and CDs (Figure 9.2). The tradi-tional music industry players tried, Canute-like, to stem the tide by legal means and it took an outsider, Apple, to lead the way forward with iTunes.

And how extraordinary that the movie business has been caught out by exactly the same downloading alternatives provided by the likes of YouTube and BitTorrent. While other studios dithered, Disney sold 1.3 million down-loads on the iTunes platform in the first three months of sale. And Disney's conclusion about the much-feared cannibalization of DVD sales that has frozen the other studios into inactivity? 'The pie is getting bigger.' The benefit of taking advantage of the new distribution opportunity is to *increase* overall consumption. The alternative is piracy – and who knows more about pirates than Disney?

	2005	2006	Change
Broadband lines	209	280	34%
Song catalogue online	2	4	100%
Single tracks downloaded	420	795	89%
Subscription service users	2.8	3.5	25%
Mobile subscriptions	1,817	2,017	11%
3G mobile subscriptions	90	137	52%
Portable player sales	84	120	43%

Figure 9.2 Global digital music market in figures (millions)
Source: Digital Music Report 2007. Reproduced by kind permission of the IFPI

Price

The caveats about price as one of the 4 Ps have already been mentioned. But, broadly speaking, this P is about how your pricing is relative to the competition: super-premium, premium, mainstream or value? Its importance is obvious: for very significant proportions of the population price has always been, and is likely to continue to be, a fundamentally important motivator. AC Nielsen reports that in the UK, discounted goods account for about 25 per cent of all purchases and that 80 per cent of shoppers go out looking for price promotions. It has often been said that the word 'free' is one of the most powerful in the advertiser's language, and if proof were necessary, the recent offer of a 'free broadband for life' service by the UK's Carphone Warehouse has been pretty definitive. Just seven weeks after the April 2006 'TalkTalk' launch, *Marketing* magazine reported that subscriptions had reached 340,000, double the number expected, according to Chief Executive Charles Dunstone. By July, it had recruited 596,000 broadband customers. This massive response caused the company major logistical problems and severe delays to customer installations, resulting in the first negative PR Dunstone had ever experienced. His high-minded words about 'right' and 'privilege' at the launch came back to haunt him: *'Today we are cutting more than 60 per cent off the cost of the average UK residential telephony and broadband bill, and additionally providing unlimited calls to 28 international destinations. The residential telecoms market in the UK will never be the same again. From today, broadband is a right, not a privilege.'* Subsequently it emerged that more than 10 per cent of the new TalkTalk customers had deserted as a result of poor service, and Carphone Warehouse posted a £4.6 million loss for the half-year to September 2006.

'Free' isn't the only motivating price positioning in the marketplace and highly generous sales promotions can induce a buying frenzy, as Swedish furniture company IKEA found to its cost in February 2005. The midnight opening of the UK's largest store in Edmonton, north London attracted a crowd of 6,000 shoppers – over three times the size anticipated – because 350 sofas, usually priced at £325, were on sale for just £49 each. Mayhem erupted immediately the doors opened, with people diving on sofas and lying on them while others were fighting for possession. The store was closed just 40 minutes later, leaving 20 bargain hunters in need of hospital treatment. Tragically, only five months earlier on 1 September 2004, three people were crushed to death in Jeddah, Saudi Arabia when a crowd of 8,000 gathered for the new IKEA store opening, lured by the handout of $150 vouchers. Perhaps the lesson should have been learned?

Fortunately, it's also well established that there can be an inverse relationship between price and demand, and not just in the obvious area of luxury goods where certain logos are tantamount to wearing $10,000 bills as accessories. Take the case of the beer brand Stella Artois (Figure 9.3), whose long-running campaign has built a workaday lager into one of the great brands in the market and has supported a highly profitable price premium (albeit a rather more modest one than that implied by the campaign!). They have evolved from a print campaign featuring such great headlines as '"My shout," he whispered', underpinned by the strap line 'Reassuringly expensive', into mini epics on TV and in cinemas. These commercials, exuding premium positioning, are engaging tales of drinkers prepared to sacrifice anything, and anyone, to get their Stella.

Figure 9.3 Stella Artois, CDP (top) and LOWE London (bottom)
Reproduced by kind permission of Stella Artois

In most markets, the strength of the brand in terms of its *perceived* quality is a key component in justifying its price premium, as blind versus branded tests of market leaders against lesser brands and retailer own labels have proven. The UK's Andrex toilet-tissue brand continues to fend off own label in a market that could so easily become completely commoditized. It has around 34 per cent value share versus 42 per cent for own label and much of its resilience is attributable to its long-running campaign featuring adorable Labrador puppies. In playing with the Andrex toilet paper these cuddly creatures convey the brand benefits of softness, strength and length of roll, all wrapped up in warm family values (Figure 9.4).

Ideally, a virtuous circle of perceived product superiority and reduced price elasticity can be established that, with careful fine-tuning of pricing, can drive profitability in a strong manner. It will also help the brand avoid the trap of reliance on promotional pricing, which has been demonstrated to be a very short-term tactic. Extensive market analysis by Andrew Ehrenberg and other academics from the London Business School, UCL and elsewhere has shown that price promotions rarely attract new customers or lead to extra subsequent sales. They merely bring forward sales to existing customers at a lower price and without increasing their loyalty to the brand. All in all, a massive own-goal for a brand, but one seen scored daily by too many brand managers and increasingly penalized by their shareholders. Witness the wild fluctuations in

Figure 9.4 Andrex puppy
Reproduced by kind permission of
Kimberly-Clark

low-cost airline stock market prices as tiny changes in load factors raise or diminish the prospect of discounting to fill seats.

But this is a lesson some have learned in the United States, where a Banc of America Securities report in 2006 (Figure 9.5) showed that while sales volume had fallen across a number of important markets, this had been more than offset in many cases by inflation-busting price increases. These marketers have realized that shifting the demand curve can generate significant improvements in margins and thus profitability.

Significant competitive advantage can also be achieved by the fine-tuning of price points and the balancing of full-price trading with on-sale or promotional periods. In the mid-1980s, Smiths (now Walkers within PepsiCo) introduced a new generation of snacks based on an innovative 'pillow' technology, which was introduced initially with hollow products like Scampi Fries, and latterly with filled ones such as 'Cheese Flavoured Moments'. When research was conducted using a random pricing technique, it produced consumer preference clusters at two possible price points, one at around 15p and the other around 20p. Both were pretty exciting given that the average price of a conventional bagged snack was under 10p at the time! The wise decision was taken to test-market at 20p in the South West region of the UK. Success was assured when it was learned that within a few weeks of the launch, enterprising wholesalers were buying in bulk and transporting the Scampi Fries to the North West, where they were discovered on sale in pubs and clubs at up to 25p a pack, and selling fast. In a more recent example of fine-tuning a price point, Orange scored a key victory in its UK heyday by moving to per-second billing when its competitors were still

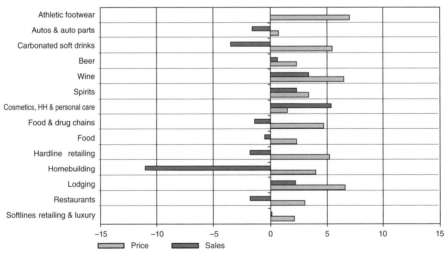

SALES GROWTH
While sales declined in many categories, prices rose in almost all.

Figure 9.5 Banc of America Securities
Data provided and reproduced by kind permission of Banc of America Securities

charging to the nearest minute. Not only did this reinforce the brand's modern, open, honest and friendly image, it saved its customers money and positioned its competitors as expensive, and perhaps even devious.

Maintaining the balance between full-price trading and sales is always difficult and in many eyes the UK's retailers have lost the battle, with the traditional January sales now beginning in December. But for many years the annual Harrods post-Christmas sale was deliberately started much later than those of all the other department stores, and promoted with the headline 'There is only one sale', thus making it the one to wait for. The queues on opening day were legendary and while there were undoubted bargains to be had, they managed to deliver years of record profitable sales. The John Lewis Partnership has also been very successful in the long term by delivering on its brand promise of being 'Never knowingly undersold'. This promise works in combination with its wide range, good quality and keen prices, and is supported by a high standard of customer service provided by employees who are all partners in the business. Only rarely is John Lewis taken up on its offer to pay the difference on the same product purchased elsewhere.

Place

[Please refer back to Figure 9.1]

'Place' is a beguilingly short and simple word to encapsulate the daunting complexities of modern distribution. In the United States, Wal-Mart stocks a total of around 3 million stock-keeping units (SKUs) with an average per store of about 300,000 different product lines. The logistical issues involved are mind-boggling, let alone the negotiations on terms of business. Distribution clearly does matter: in market after market, customers buy from a portfolio of favoured products or services and very rarely are they 100 per cent loyal to a single brand. This means that substitutability is an inherent fact of life – if your product is not on the shelf then the customer will simply buy another, or if your outlet is not open, they will go elsewhere. However, David Cowan has shown that in certain fast-moving consumer goods markets, distribution and market share do not operate in a linear relationship, but in one that is closer to exponential, as shown in Figure 9.6. The implication here is that an improvement in distribution from *85 per cent* up to *90 per cent* could mean an additional *30 to 35 per cent* in market share!

Indeed, distribution can be so powerful that Doug Ivestor, CEO and Chairman of Coca-Cola, was quoted as saying that his goal is 'for everyone on earth to be within an arm's length of a Coke' (Figure 9.7).

But sometimes 'place' is about exploiting new distribution opportunities or responding to threats posed by them. As we have seen, the music industry

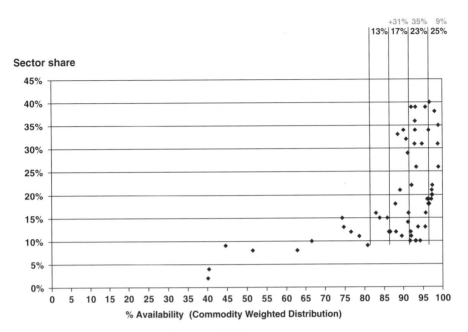

Figure 9.6 Brand share against availability
Source: David Cowan, FORENSICS. Reproduced by kind permission of David Cowan, Founder of FORENSICS, a marketing detective work consultancy

Figure 9.7 Coke in the Third World
Source: Photograph by A J Pate

reacted very slowly to the threat originally posed by Napster and KaZaA, and simply had no answer to the new download distribution channel being created by popular demand. 'Only the paranoid survive,' proclaimed Andrew Grove, CEO of Intel, in the title of his 1996 book about how companies need to keep abreast of potential transitions in their marketplaces. A little paranoia among the established music distributors would have done no harm in the face of such complacency. Embracing new distribution channels is not only a way of generating more sales opportunities – it can also build brand values. Mass availability of broadband and much faster internet connections are making the user experience much richer. And so the internet is offering more and more distribution opportunities and fuelling a renaissance of the home delivery service pioneered by the likes of Amazon. GAP or agency Leo Burnett opening up a virtual store on Second Life may not actually result in much immediate business, but it produces an instant result in terms of PR coverage and a sense of a brand that's right in touch with contemporary culture (Figure 9.8).

But there's also a danger in too much distribution of the wrong kind. Starbucks is a case in point, as revealed in Chairman Howard Schultz's notorious leaked memo. The expansion into airports, hotels and other stores lost

Figure 9.8 Leo Burnett's Second Life Tree House.
Reproduced by kind permission of Leo Burnett

much of the original brand ambience, and a series of changes to the original proposition to facilitate this wider distribution further undermined the brand: flavour-locked packaging instead of the smell of freshly ground coffee; plastic chairs instead of sofas and comfy armchairs; automatic espresso machines instead of handmade by a barista; pre-packaged, date-coded foods and pastries instead of freshly made ones. Perhaps like McDonald's before it, Starbucks has relied too much on growth by extension of distribution and lost sight of what made it such a powerful consumer proposition in the first place.

As companies seek opportunities to interact directly with their customers, there has been a boom in the use of promotional events, field marketing, sampling, exhibitions and shows. Specialist agencies, such as Iris Experience, iD Live Brand Experience, Sledge, TRO, BEcause, Cake, Evoke, RPM, Fitch Live!, Jack Morgan and Imagination, all loosely clustered under the banner of 'brand experience', have become increasingly sophisticated in either utilizing existing venues and events such as motor shows, or creating entirely new ones tailored to the brand. Perhaps one of the best examples of the latter is 'Fruitstock', created by Albion for innocent drinks in 2003. This summer music festival, evoking the spirit of 'Woodstock', reinforces their natural, youthful, slightly alternative brand image and creates a great opportunity for people to sample new Innocent smoothies and juices (Figure 9.9).

Innocent provides yet another illustration of the limitations of the original 4 Ps framework. The brand's early distribution strategy was in fact much more the kind of thinking that would be prompted by Schultz and Dev's thoughts on *Access*. If the brand had relied on a traditional 4 Ps analysis of distribution opportunities it would likely have died very shortly after birth, instead of becoming category leader.

Promotion

This is another increasingly vague catch-all word to encompass a huge range of ways in which a company can communicate with its customers. These include advertising, public relations, direct mail, packaging, sponsorship, sales promotion, customer magazines, exhibitions, loyalty cards, special events, sponsored programming, websites, e-mail, SMS, blogs, RSS – the list is long and still growing. That said, the IPA TouchPoints research shows that the average UK person claims to be only aware of being exposed to an average of just over four different media each day (Figure 9.10). Given the oft-quoted figure of between 3,000 and 4,000 commercial impacts daily being made on consumers, this is perhaps an indication of how deft people have become at screening out messages at a conscious level.

Figure 9.9 Fruitstock
Reproduced by kind permission of innocent drinks

In the right hands, these channels of communication, which are increasingly interactive, can provide a company with what many regard as 'the last remaining means of unfair competition'. This is because a brand's speed to market is accelerating, but so is the time to produce a competitive 'me-too'. It is hard to sustain a competitive differential based on tangibles, such as intrinsic product performance or other qualities in use. On the other hand, intangibles such as brand reputation and emotional and psychological values are enduring, and gaining an increasing share of importance in customer decision-making. As markets become more cluttered and messages proliferate, competing for a finite amount of mental space, inspiring brands act as magnets for customers. Strong brands can also offset unforeseen problems by

Medium	Percentage Reach (%)
TV	95.5
Posters	78.3
Radio	69.4
Addressed DM	49.5
Internet	36.8
Unaddressed DM	36.0
Daily newspapers	32.5
Telemarketing	20.1
Commercial SMS messages	8.5
Local directories	8.2
Weekly magazines	7.6
Monthly magazines	5.7
Sunday newspapers	Between 0 and 6
Cinema	1.6
Average number of media a person is exposed to on an average day	**4.5**

Figure 9.10 A typical weekday (Wednesday) percentage reach figures
Source: Roger Ingham, Data Alive/IPA TouchPoints 2006

establishing the 'benefit of the doubt' in favour of the company while they are addressed. Public relations agency Weber Shandwick has identified the major triggers of corporate reputation failure, as shown in Figure 9.11.

Financial irregularity	72%
Unethical behaviour	68%
Executive misconduct	64%
Security breaches	62%
Environmental violations	60%
Health and safety product recalls	60%

Figure 9.11 Major triggers of corporate reputation failure
Source: Weber Shandwick Safeguarding Reputation™ Survey/KRC Research 2006

Clearly, even the best-managed companies can fall prey to any one of these failings. Cadbury Schweppes in the UK is a recent example, with the Health Protection Agency and the Food Standards Agency requiring a major precautionary product recall of several brands following a salmonella Montevideo contamination at its factory in Marlbrook, Herefordshire in 2006. This recall is estimated to have cost the company £26 million, of which just £6 million will be covered by insurance. Half of the total related to the recall and the balance to one-off manufacturing improvement costs and increased media investment. However, the strength of the Cadbury and Dairy Milk brands is such that long-term damage is unlikely to be great.

In summary, the 4 Ps framework is well past its sell-by date, but so long as it is reinterpreted for the modern world (as in the SIVA framework), it can still be useful by prompting continuous reappraisal of many of the defining conditions for business success. But it is not a sufficient framework to guarantee success and should only be used alongside other strategic thinking tools.

PART 3

The evolution of advertising industry models

10 The FCB grid

These are the key points from this chapter:

- Agencies often use customer-centric thinking models and this is clearly a step in the right direction.
- However too often these separate the 'rational' from the 'emotional' imposing unproven 'rules' on communication strategy.

Many leading agencies have customer-centric models to help structure the thinking around brand communications strategy, and there are too many to review them all here. Many of these are benign or better, such as Young & Rubicam's Brand Asset Valuator. However, this cannot be said of all such models and there is one very authoritative model that can be dangerous from the perspective of brand immortality: the FCB grid. To be fair, it was developed a while back in 1980 and there have been attempts since to revise the grid to bring it more in line with current thinking, as we shall see. It was developed by Richard Vaughn of advertising agency Foote Cone & Belding (FCB) as a way of identifying the most appropriate broad approach to advertising for a given category. The grid divides categories along two dimensions: whether the purchase decision is chiefly rational or chiefly emotional ('think' or 'feel' in the original terminology) and whether the decision is highly involving, or not (Figure 10.1).

Thus there are four quadrants to the FCB grid. Typically Quadrant 1 will contain products such as cars or computers, which are purchases of high importance (largely because they are expensive but also because making the wrong choice could make a considerable difference), and which is a very technical/functional purchase and thus worthy of detailed pre-purchase research and rational consideration. Quadrant 2 also contains expensive purchases,

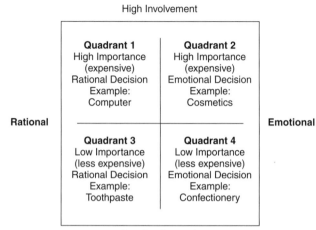

Figure 10.1 FCB grid
Source: Richard Vaughn, FCB 1980

but these ones have a higher emotional component of decision-making (usually because choice is highly subjective), such as cosmetics or fragrances. Quadrant 3 is populated by lower-priced, less considered items of routine consumption like toothpaste, shampoo or other household supplies. Quadrant 4 has similarly inexpensive products, but these are less essential and more impulsive (and subjective) in purchase terms. A confectionery bar popped into the supermarket trolley at the checkout would be a typical example. Each quadrant is accompanied by a number of communications 'rules' derived from the nature and depth of the decision-making process: eg long factual copy for rational, high-involvement categories. These are beginning to look rather dated now in the digital age, but more importantly they are not supported by new learning. In particular, the IPA dataBANK suggests that emotional communications work more powerfully even in 'high think' categories – although the advantage is less than in 'high feel' categories. So the FCB grid's general rules are wrong and are widely broken by successful brands: the toilet tissue called Andrex whose appeal is built by an adorable Labrador puppy; a computer brand called Apple that has the power to generate real passion among its many devotees; L'Oréal toiletries and cosmetics marketed to women because they're 'worth it'; chocolate sold under the 'Fair Trade' scheme; and the Red American Express credit card designed to help cure HIV.

Another potential downside of the FCB grid is the forcing of the divide between rational and emotional decision-making. In practice it is now widely accepted that most decisions include elements of both and that emotions feature much more strongly than Richard Vaughn gave them credit for. In particular, Quadrant 1 was often typified by 'choosing a new car'. Few marketers these days would regard the choice of car marque or even model as a rational one: practical considerations may well determine what segment of the category consumers are choosing from, but the brand choice is anything but rational.

In 1991, academic John Rossiter and consultant Larry Percy attempted to breathe new life into the grid by refining the 'think–feel' dimension to a 'negative–positive' motivations one, characterized essentially by whether the product fulfils a consumer need or want (although the motivations were spelt out in greater detail than this). The resulting so-called 'Rossiter–Percy grid' also acknowledged that brands may engender different motivations as compared with categories. This is an important improvement, but one that clearly undermines the general universality of the original grid: every brand in a category may be different. Nevertheless, the same fundamental weakness of the FCB grid persists: the idea that communications must be matched in some way to the nature of the purchase decision.

Users of either grid would be wise to regard the quadrants as tendencies rather than absolutes – and ignore the rules altogether for the sake of the health of their brands.

11 Maslow's Hierarchy of Needs

These are the key points from this chapter:

- Maslow argued that human beings have a series of needs which they seek to fulfil, starting with the most basic ones of subsistence.
- He believed that as these basic needs were satisfied, people would gravitate to 'higher order' needs, which were more to do with their relationships with others and their standing in the community.
- We can see that brands have responded to these changing needs and have evolved in a similar manner, with rational and functional benefits being supplemented with emotional, psychological, ethical and political ones.
- Marketers need to reappraise their brand promise regularly to ensure that it is evolving in line with their customers' needs, and continues to satisfy them.

Maslow's Hierarchy of Needs is a much-used framework for understanding the evolution of society over time, and, by extension, consumers' developing requirements of brands. A H Maslow was an academic working at Brooklyn College in the early 1940s when he produced his now famous 'Hierarchy of Needs', represented graphically in Figure 11.1.

It proposes a hierarchy of human needs, from basic survival through to spiritual enlightenment, which over time mankind has successively met, moving ever onwards and upwards to the next level. This was parodied amusingly by Douglas Adams in the second book of the *Hitchhiker's Guide to the Galaxy* trilogy – *The Restaurant at the End of the Universe* – in which he suggested that every civilization progresses through three phases characterized by the questions: 'How can we eat?', 'Why do we eat?' and 'Where shall we have lunch?'

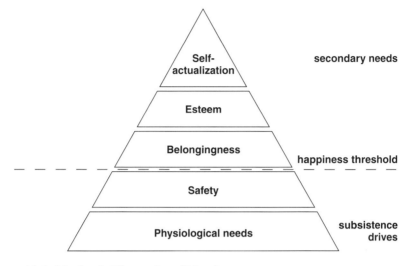

Figure 11.1 Maslow's Hierarchy of Needs
Source: A H Maslow (1940)

Maslow argued that the most basic needs that human beings seek to fulfil are 'subsistence drives'. These are to do with survival itself and the requirements for food, shelter, warmth and sex. He believed that as these basic needs were satisfied, people would gravitate to needs that were more to do with their relationships with others, and their standing within the community. Maslow hypothesized that once a person had achieved a sense of 'belonging', they would then move on to higher-order concerns. These are to do with the degree to which they enjoyed 'esteem' in society and, beyond that, whether they might achieve 'self-actualization' in a spiritual sense.

At the time, it seemed to be a rather fanciful theory, but it now appears uncannily accurate in forecasting the evolution of consumer behaviour. Consumers have indeed followed the path set out by Maslow. For example, there is now relatively little difference between upmarket and downmarket consumers in terms of the durable goods that they own. As populations in Westernized economies have moved up Maslow's Hierarchy of Needs, having fulfilled the 'basics', they have become much more concerned with issues of self-esteem and self-actualization. Thus their requirements of brands have also evolved such that the functional or rational aspects, while still essential as 'hygiene factors', have become of less interest to the customer than emotional and psychological attributes. More recently, it is on the basis of 'higher order' issues of corporate social responsibility, ethical and political standards that many people discriminate between brands. While Maslow provides a fascinating explanation for why successful brands have evolved the way they have, the Hierarchy is rather less useful for predicting the future or for providing guidance for brands that already operate at this 'higher order'. Its best use is perhaps to explain to less enlightened business people why brands need to operate at the emotional level – most smart brand owners know this already.

Maslow's Hierarchy of Needs suggests that brands ought generally to have evolved over time as the societies in which they traded, in the way summarized in Figure 11.2. But one flaw in the application of Maslow to the modern world is the inbuilt assumption that society is homogeneous. We live in an era when disparities of affluence even within prosperous Western economies have widened considerably, and although most have moved up the hierarchy, there are growing and commercially important groups of the disadvantaged that do not necessarily operate exclusively at the level of self-actualization. Overlay onto that the disparate populations of the rapidly developing Indian and Chinese markets and you can very quickly see how the use of Maslow's Hierarchy as a marketing tool could lead to false conclusions. Clearly, it's essential to establish the evolutionary stage of each of these developing populations.

A further danger arises from the simplistic misuse of Maslow, which has led some marketers to believe that all they need do is create a higher-order 'veneer' around their brands and the business will roll in. They forget that the concept of a hierarchy implies the satisfaction of lower-order needs *as well*: if brands do not deliver fully at the functional, lower-order levels, then no amount of higher-order veneer will compensate.

Generally, there has been a change in the nature of the 'propositions' that competing brands have put to their users in response to the growing sophistication of their needs. While it's a little artificial, it's possible to break down the evolution of these propositions since the 1950s, in terms of the kinds of brand values they enshrine – though it is easy to find 1950s thinking still in use today, often for the wrong reasons.

The unique selling proposition

While it is something of a simplification, it's possible to typify the early 1950s as the era of the Unique Selling Proposition, developed by Rosser Reeves of the Ted Bates agency. Products and services were scrutinized in order to discover their most competitive and distinctive functional consumer benefit – their USP – which became the single-minded focus of their advertising. As Robin Wight, co-founder of UK agency WCRS, has said memorably about developing brand positionings and communications ideas: *'You've got to interrogate the product until it confesses to its strengths.'* Many famous brands were built using this approach, and slogans such 'Persil washes whiter', 'Minstrels, the chocolates that melt in your mouth, not in your hand' and 'You'll wonder where the

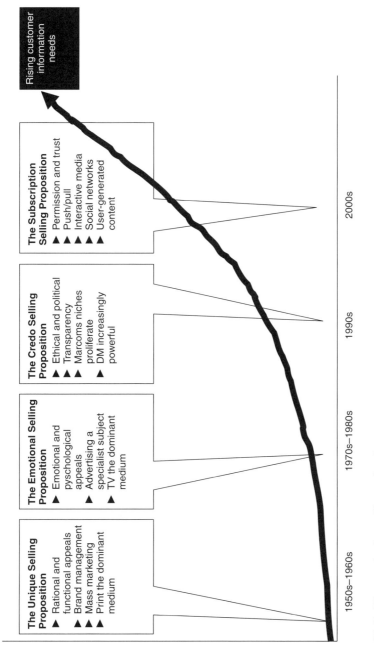

The Unique Selling Proposition
▲ Rational and functional appeals
▲ Brand management
▲ Mass marketing
▲ Print the dominant medium

The Emotional Selling Proposition
▲ Emotional and psychological appeals
▲ Advertising a specialist subject
▲ TV the dominant medium

The Credo Selling Proposition
▲ Ethical and political
▲ Transparency
▲ Marcoms niches proliferate
▲ DM increasingly powerful

The Subscription Selling Proposition
▲ Permission and trust
▲ Push/pull
▲ Interactive media
▲ Social networks
▲ User-generated content

Rising customer information needs

1950s–1960s   1970s–1980s   1990s   2000s

Figure 11.2 The evolution of brand values

yellow went when you brush your teeth with Pepsodent' were embedded in generations of minds, often with the help of music (Figure 11.3).

But by the 1970s, competition became much more cut-throat and technological advances rendered functional differences more fleeting. Brands that just relied on a functional point of difference soon found that competitors had copied it and so the writing was on the wall for the USP as the pre-eminent model for a brand that wished to have a life beyond this year's technical advantage. That said, as we shall see later, attaching a brand to a unique *idea*, as opposed to a fact, can be very effective.

The emotional selling proposition

Building upon Freud's ideas about the subconscious mind during the 1960s and 1970s, the new science of behavioural psychology inspired marketers and advertisers to add a whole new dimension to their brands. Using qualitative research and the 'focus group', they discovered that most buying decisions are far from rational, and began to overlay the functional benefits of their products and services with powerful emotional and psychological appeals. New York agency Doyle Dane Bernbach was pre-eminent in its effective use of the 'soft sell' and humour in advertising, while London's Boase Massimi Pollitt similarly dominated the field in the UK. In 1974, BMP produced the famous Smash 'Martians' campaign, which was voted best TV commercial ever by ITV viewers in 2005, three decades after it was first aired (Figure 11.4). It owed its effectiveness – and its enduring appeal – to its charming and humorous way of getting across the time and labour-saving benefits of instant mashed potato, rather than just by using a rational selling proposition.

Conceptually, the brand image can be seen at this time as an inverse pyramid, with a core fact at the tip supporting an edifice of personality and imagery. Later on, in the 1980s, Bartle Bogle Hegarty were to excel in the use of music and fashionable imagery in landmark advertising for brands such as Levis and Häagen-Dazs. Jeans, those most functional of garments, became a fashion item. Ice cream was no longer just a frozen food and Häagen-Dazs's sexually charged ads (Figure 11.5) anticipated Marks & Spencer by some 20 years in portraying 'food porn'.

BBH referred to their approach as the ESP – the Emotional Selling Proposition. These emotional and psychological benefits can give brands temporary protection against 'me-too' competitors who copy their functional advantages, and in effect buy them time to come up with their own innovations in order to stay ahead. In addition, the lessons of engagement learnt during this period by advertisers are even more relevant today as brands seek survival paths through the growing banks of message filtration placed between them and the consumer.

Figure 11.4 Smash Martians, Boase Massimi Pollitt
Reproduced by kind permission of Cadbury's Smash

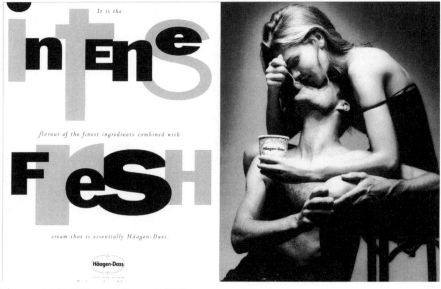

Figure 11.5 Häagen-Dazs, BBH
Image provided by The History of Advertising Trust (HAT Archive), www.hatads.org.uk

The credo selling proposition

Employed by a few early-adopter brands such as American Express in the early 1980s, then with others recognizing its potential during the 1990s, the 'credo' is now much more widespread as a way of responding to consumers' 'self-actualization' needs. In this model, brands seek to be noticed, trusted and followed for the beliefs they espouse. Not beliefs merely in the sense of cause-related marketing, ie the linking of a brand to a charity or good cause, though this can be a very effective approach, but beliefs in the sense of powerful human 'higher order' motivations or aspirations that the brand can credibly claim to espouse. Apple was one of the earliest brands to adopt a 'cause' with its famous 1984 commercial by agency TBWA. This mini-epic captured the anti-establishment, anti-IBM mood of the times and positioned Apple as a personal computer for the independent and creative individual.

The 60-second commercial was created by advertising agency Chiat/Day, with copy written by Steve Hayden and directed by RSA's Ridley Scott, who had just finished filming *Blade Runner*. The commercial was shot in London and involved the powerful sequence of a sledgehammer being thrown through a giant 'PC' screen: it took Anya Major, a discus thrower, to pull it off. Famously, the spot was aired only once for a mass audience – in the third-quarter break of the Super Bowl – and perhaps did more than any other commercial to establish the importance of that time slot. Arguably, Apple's

'1984' was the ancestor of 'virals' in that the film has been shown countless times since in TV documentaries and on awards show reels, achieving massive audiences and global fame despite no further paid-for media being involved. The latest extension to its long life has been as a pro-Barack Obama attack on Hillary Clinton. This pastiche has Hillary Clinton's visage superimposed over the brainwashing 'Big Blue' face on the giant screen, with the liberating athlete a clear metaphor for Obama. Published on YouTube in March 2007, it caused a flurry of concern on Capitol Hill as the new 'internet democracy' found its voice in the run-up to the Democratic Party nominations.

This 'higher order' trail was also blazed by Nike with its brand named after the Greek goddess of victory, 'Just do it' strap line, and 'swoosh' logo espousing the can-do determination, grit and passion necessary to win at sport: the sportsperson as demigod. CEO Phil Knight was an early and expert user of sports celebrities, building his Nike brand from its grassroots in US sports events and leading eventually to the Michael Jordan 'Air' product range. Indeed, Nike's sophisticated usage of aspirational star endorsements gave the campaign credibility and momentum long before Nike embarked on paid-for advertising.

'Cause-related marketing' (CRM) became an increasingly important tool in adding new sorts of 'credo' values to brands over this period. American Express was one of the originators of CRM in the modern era and indeed it trade-marked, but never enforced, the term 'cause-related marketing' – perhaps a good example of 'credo' in action! Its card-related fundraiser for the repair of the Statue of Liberty was an early success. Indeed, the wider concept of corporate social responsibility (CSR) and the idea of the 'triple bottom line' (economic profit, environmental impact and social contribution) have continued to rise up the consumer agenda with the result that for many a 'credo' has become an essential part of a brand's make-up.

Perhaps one of the most innovative CRM campaigns yet seen is the (RED) concept originated in 2006 by Bono and Bobby Shriver, who summarized it as follows: *'(RED) is not a charity. It is simply a business model. You buy the (RED) stuff. We buy the pills and distribute them... It's easy. All you have to do is upgrade your choice.'* The mechanics of (RED) are that its trademark, a pair of red parentheses symbolizing the 'embrace of solidarity', is licensed to partner companies that use it on specific products (Figure 11.6). In return, the licensees donate an agreed part of their revenues or profits to the Geneva-based Global Fund to Fight Aids, Tuberculosis and Malaria, and an annual fee to (RED) to cover its own marketing and administration costs. Early sign-ups included Gap, Armani, American Express, Converse, Motorola and Apple, with donations varying from Amex's 1 per cent of spend on its (RED) credit card to Gap's 50 per cent of profits on sales of its (RED) clothing. Bono and Shriver's involvement of high-profile figures such as Oprah Winfrey and Steven Spielberg

Figure 11.6 Images from (RED) campaign
Reproduced by kind permission of (RED)

generated massive publicity around the launch, and spending by licensees has reportedly reached $100 million in year one. This activity has enabled these brands to link themselves with a powerful ready-made cause-related marketing programme and add 'credo' very effectively. The only fly in the ointment is the relatively small sum of $18 million so far donated to the Global Fund, but it could be argued that the campaign has reinforced the support of the US Congress, which approved an additional $724 million on top of the $1.9 billion already allocated to the Fund, and encouraged the $650 million donation from the Bill & Melinda Gates Foundation.

In a number of cases, CSR has haunted the very brands that prospered by proclaiming their credos to the world. Nike's treatment of the people in the developing world who made its shoes is perhaps the best-known example. And more recently the (RED) business system has been criticized for the high promotional costs involved in relation to the modest sums actually donated to the relief of AIDS. BP, so recently lauded worldwide for its repositioning from an oil to an energy company as symbolized by its 'flower' logo, has run into serious trouble over its safety record in the United States. Clearly, those brands that live by the credo need to make sure that they will not die by it.

The subscription selling proposition

[Please refer back to Figure 11.2]

As the new century has unfolded, technological development and the rise of digital media have been rapid. These have enabled a massive increase in two-way communication and have spawned a whole new phenomenon of enormous online social networks such as MySpace, YouTube, Bebo and Facebook. Facilitated by the increased availability of broadband internet access, there has been extraordinary growth of user-generated content (UGC) through blogs and uploads to these community websites. Meanwhile, millions of users are opting out of various forms of advertising communication through registration with the mailing, telephone, fax and e-mail opt-out preference services and the use of anti-spam and pop-up software programs on their computers. This means that increasingly brands need to secure the permission of customers to communicate with them. We have moved from 'interruption' to 'engagement', from 'push' to 'pull', and brands now need to motivate customers to allow or 'subscribe to' brand communications on their terms rather than the brand owner's.

The agency, Ogilvy, has had a huge international success with its client Unilever in repositioning its Dove toiletries brand around its 'Campaign for Real Beauty'. This is what Rory Sutherland, executive creative director and vice-chairman of Ogilvy Group UK, would describe as a 'big ideal', rather than just a 'big idea'. He suggests the latter has a weakness in that individuals in marketing and agencies often have difficulty in building on someone else's idea, because the work has already been done. However, he believes that an 'ideal' is a more open concept that people can interpret and build upon with their own ideas. Certainly this has happened with Dove as an original concept created by agency Ogilvy with key input from influential feminist author and psychologist Susie Orbach. This inspiring campaign is now global, with original contributions and iterations from many other markets. Indeed, Ogilvy's Toronto office won the Grand Prix at Cannes in 2007 with its Dove 'Evolution' film. Intrinsic to this big ideal is that it asks people to sign up to the campaign, either literally or metaphorically, and thus it creates a deeper level of engagement and commitment among those consumers who subscribe to it (Figure 11.7).

AOL in the UK followed the 'subscription selling' model with its campaign designed to create a dialogue with users about the issues raised by the internet. And *The Times* has been asking its readers to 'Join the debate' with its current campaign strap line. David Magliano, a key figure in London's winning bid for the 2012 Olympics, reports how the campaign to build public enthusiasm to the level required by the IOC only really took off when people were given the opportunity to express their support in practical ways such as texting, registering online or walking through a 'people-counter' archway. We can expect many more brands to seek customer interaction and engagement in this way. Getting people to sign up, either literally or metaphorically, is a very powerful way to embed the brand in their minds and ensure its longevity.

Figure 11.7 Wizened/Wonderful image from the Dove Campaign for Real Beauty, Ogilvy
Reproduced by kind permission of Rankin and Dove

The brand promise system

The brand promise system is an attempt to correct the simplistic application of Maslow to marketing, resulting in brands that are founded on nothing more than higher-order emotional dimensions. As we have seen, in order to survive and prosper, brands in the advanced economies of the world have had to evolve and become more sophisticated. If a brand represents a promise made by the company to its customers, then these promises have consequently become more complex. In managing the modern brand for immortality there are three aspects that must be carefully considered: first, the creation of the promise itself; second, how it is to be conveyed; and third, how it is to be kept. Thus, a company should manage its relationship with its customers by analysing its performance in terms of the rational, emotional and ethical dimensions of its promise. This approach can be summarized as the 'brand promise system' (Figure 11.8).

Most brand promises are a cocktail of these three ingredients, and brands have different 'centres of gravity' in terms of where the weight of their consumer promise lies. Thus there are still many successful brands that trade predominantly on their rational or functional benefits – some leading detergents such as Ariel and cleaning products such as Flash are prime examples.

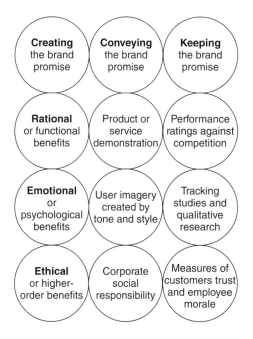

Figure 11.8 Brand promise system
Source: Hamish Pringle, Brand Beliefs Limited, 2000

Typically these functional brands convey their brand promise through a product or service demonstration. The long-running and highly effective 'half head test', which featured in the commercials of P&G's anti-dandruff shampoo Head & Shoulders, was a classic of its kind, though even this has now been superseded by a more emotional approach. The performance of this type of brand is measured by rating it against its key competitors through comparative tests, both blind and branded, to see to what degree it's keeping its promise to customers. For functionally defined brands, huge pressure is placed on relentless innovation to keep the brand competitive – Gillette has now predictably gone one better than Wilkinson Sword's four-bladed razor by offering men a five-bladed razor (Figure 11.9). What next from Wilkinson Sword? Please surprise us!

Those personal products such as clothing, fashion accessories, watches, cars and other purchases that customers use as an expression of their personal identity make promises that are heavily laden with emotional and psychological benefits. While there nearly always needs to be a grain of product or service truth to support the brand's emotional edifice, be it quality of materials, skill in manufacture or pleasure in usage, it is the brand image that is the core of its appeal. The user is promised variously an aspirational lifestyle, an enhanced self-image, or some emotional and psychological reinforcement. This is conveyed by brand naming, identity, packaging, advertising style and tone of voice, sampling, pricing, and purchase experience in appropriate surroundings that establish the desirability of the brand's personality. Celebrities may be used as an executional device to bolster the cachet of the brand (Figure 11.10). Successful delivery of these sorts of brand promises is very difficult to measure quantitatively because emotions are notoriously difficult to gauge in structured

Figure 11.9 Gillette Fusion razor
Reproduced by kind permission of Gillette

interviews. For that reason, marketers often turn to qualitative research, with all its statistical uncertainties. Ultimately a leap of faith is required between communication and observing the hard sales results. And herein lies the challenge for this approach: modern business practice is heavily focused on risk reduction. Leaps of faith do not sit well with those more accustomed to discounted cash flow projections.

Figure 11.10 Rimmel London, JWT
Reproduced by kind permission of Rimmel. Photographed by Dusan Reljin

Many brands have decided they need to acquire ethical values in order to add another Maslowian higher-order dimension to their brand promise. Market research has shown repeatedly that most consumers are not primarily motivated by altruism and will not sacrifice product or service performance or other lower-order benefits in exchange for saving the planet: they want both washing efficacy and environmental responsibility. Thus a brand like Tide Coldwater sends a clear signal to the customer, but has to deliver in terms of performance. Many companies are enhancing their brand promise through corporate social responsibility programmes. In Figure 11.11 we see a clever linkage of leading UK retailer Marks & Spencer to a cause of great relevance to millions of their customers, the Breakthrough Breast Cancer Charity.

Club Med has gone one better than the 'save the environment, please reuse your towels' notices that have become generic in the hotel industry by providing highly visible, indeed decorative, opportunities for guests to take positive action to protect their planet (Figure 11.12).

Two of the longest-running UK CRM programmes have been Tesco's 'Computers for Schools' and Walkers' 'Books for Schools'; however, both came under consumer attack on grounds of poor value and exploitation of families

Figure 11.11
M&S lingerie
advertisement,
RKCR/Y&R
Reproduced by kind
permission of RKCR/Y&R
and Marks & Spencer

Figure 11.12 Recycling pots
Source: Photograph by Hamish Pringle

and kids, despite their best intentions. Conveying an ethical or CSR brand promise is a minefield, as companies often get accused of 'greenwashing' when they try to help tackle complex social issues. Despite these challenges, the leading companies still strive to achieve a balance in their 'triple bottom line' of delivering profits to shareholders, mitigating environmental impact and putting something back into society. They measure the keeping of their promise through stakeholder surveys gauging key measures such as trust and employee morale.

With global warming now topping the UK public's list of concerns for the future, according to a 2007 Millward Brown ReputationZ study, we can expect to see a strongly growing influence of carbon-related issues on the CSR activity of companies and their brands (Figure 11.13).

The same study illustrated some strong commonalities with US consumers, though global warming, despite reports of rapidly growing US consumer awareness and the success of Al Gore's movie *An Inconvenient Truth*, failed to make it into to the top 10 concerns (Figure 11.14).

The key point is that brand managers need to be reassessing on a regular basis the constituent parts of their brand promise. They must ensure that it not only remains compelling and competitive within its market sector, but also reflects the wider shifts in sentiment within society that could in turn affect their customers. Longevity for a brand comes from being adaptable in

UK ranking	UK issue	Level of concern %
1	Climate change	85
2=	Obesity	84
	Irresponsible drinking	84
4	Risks of smoking	81
5	High crime rates	74
6	Personal debt	67
7=	Heart disease	61
	Fair trade	61
9	Advertising to kids	59
10=	Dieting issues	58
	Making poverty history	58

Figure 11.13 UK public's list of concerns
Source: Millward Brown/ReputationZ 2007. Reproduced by kind permission of Millward Brown

US ranking	US issue	Level of concern %
1	Obesity	77
2	Risks of smoking	69
3	Oil supplies	63
4	High crime rates	59
5	Heart disease	58
6	Diet matters	55
7	Offshoring jobs	54
8	Corporate corruption	54
9	CEO salaries	54
10	Irresponsible drinking	51

Figure 11.14 US public's list of concerns
Source: Millward Brown/ReputationZ 2007. Reproduced by kind permission of Millward Brown

response to changing circumstances, but so often this manifests itself as a tactical activity rather than a strategic process. Clearly, marketing people have the primary responsibility for the guardianship of their brands, but in reality a good deal of that duty falls to agencies. In fact, given the relatively short job tenure of the key decision-makers in key markets such as the United States and UK, it often turns out that the agency has longer and deeper experience of the brand than their client. In 2007, research by recruitment consultancy Spencer Stuart found that the average tenure for chief marketing officers (CMOs) in 100 leading US consumer branded companies in 2007 was 26.8 months. Less than one-third of the companies (29) had CMOs who had been in their posts for three years or more. In addition, 16 per cent of the companies had a vacant CMO position or have no such role in their organization. The situation is a little better in the UK, where similar research carried out on behalf of magazine *Marketing Week* shows that the average tenure is about three years. It is worrying, therefore, that the arrival of a new CMO or marketing director often leads to a competitive review and change of agency. A change of agency nearly always means a change of campaign direction, sometimes with disruptive or damaging implications for the brand promise. Too many brands are damaged rather than enhanced by changes of agency brought about for change's sake, rather than to build shareholder value.

PART 4

The customer context for brands

12 The influence of customer life stage

These are the key points from this chapter:

- The human life-cycle is the eternal context within which marketers must navigate, and each life stage presents its own challenges and opportunities.
- Older consumers in Western economies are increasing as a proportion of the population and have growing spending power.
- In the UK, these older consumers are much less likely than younger ones to be interested in new brands, whereas they're more open to them in the United States.
- Either way, marketers are going to have to work harder to persuade these numerous and wealthy older consumers to switch brands, or consider new ones.

People's reactions are influenced by their own age and relationship to the marketplace. But is it true that older people are intrinsically less interested in commercial communications, or is this a prejudice of a youth-obsessed marketing industry? And how selective is human perception and to what extent and why do certain messages get through when others do not?

There is a fine Shakespearean soliloquy that encapsulates a 16th-century man's life in just 28 lines:

The Seven Ages of Man
All the world's a stage,
And all the men and women merely players:
They have their exits and their entrances;
And one man in his time plays many parts,
His acts being seven ages. At first the infant,

Mewling and puking in the nurse's arms.
Then the whining school-boy, with his satchel
And shining morning face, creeping like snail
Unwillingly to school. And then the lover,
Sighing like furnace, with a woeful ballad
Made to his mistress' eyebrow. Then a soldier,
Full of strange oaths, and bearded like the pard,
Jealous in honor, sudden and quick in quarrel,
Seeking the bubble reputation
Even in the cannon's mouth. And then the justice,
In fair round belly with good capon lined,
With eyes severe and beard of formal cut,
Full of wise saws and modern instances;
And so he plays his part. The sixth age shifts
Into the lean and slipper'd pantaloon,
With spectacles on nose and pouch on side,
His youthful hose, well saved, a world too wide
For his shrunk shank; and his big manly voice,
Turning again toward childish treble, pipes
And whistles in his sound. Last scene of all,
That ends this strange eventful history,
Is second childishness and mere oblivion,
Sans teeth, sans eyes, sans taste, sans every thing.

Source: William Shakespeare's *As You Like It*, 1599. Jacques' soliloquy in Act 2, Scene 7.

Shakespeare's lines still have relevance now and remind us that if a brand is to last for ever, it needs to bear in mind that its customers can't. Each human life stage presents its own challenges and opportunities. And in many categories (eg financial services), products are segmented according to life stage. Children and young people are incredibly open to new ideas and we marvel at their apparent ability to multi-task: homework is accompanied by music from an iPod and counterpointed by TV and text messaging. Marketers have long recognized the potential for recruiting customers from this generation and wholeheartedly subscribe to the Society of Jesus' (Jesuit) motto: 'Give me a child until he is seven and I will give you the man.' The 'baby boom' of the post-Second World War era coincided with the advent of modern mass marketing and an explosion of consumer goods and services largely driven by the United States. This buoyant period for both population and economies was mirrored in Western Europe and in parts of Asia Pacific such as Japan, Hong Kong and Australia. Now we're witnessing the extraordinary growth of the so-called BRIC nations – Brazil, Russia, India and China, with their massive, relatively young and still increasing populations (Figures 12.1 and 12.2).

Another set of happy hunting grounds for marketers undoubtedly, but there's a spectre at this feast of unsustainable consumption: the accelerating effects of industrialization on climate change will have to be addressed.

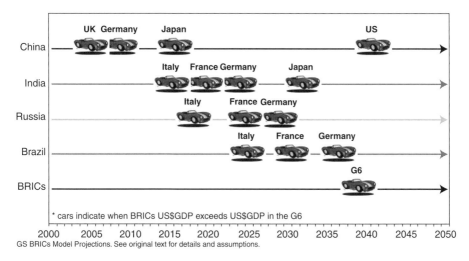

Figure 12.1 Overtaking the G6: when BRICs' US $GDP would exceed the G6
Source: Goldman Sachs, Global Economics Paper No 99, *Dreaming with BRICS: The path to 2050.* Reproduced by kind permission of Goldman Sachs

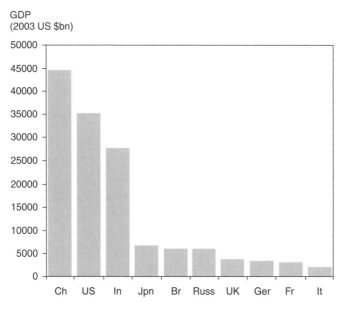

Figure 12.2 The largest economies in 2050
Source: Goldman Sachs, Global Economics Paper No 99, *Dreaming with BRICS: The path to 2050.* Reproduced by kind permission of Goldman Sachs

Meanwhile, in some of the more developed economies, as we can see from Figures 12.3 and 12.4, populations are ageing and older people are becoming very significant in terms of their spending power as a proportion of the total.

For example, L'Oréal's Pro-Calcium Age Re-Perfect line, advertised by 68-year-old actress Jane Fonda, helped create one of the fastest-growing sub-sectors within the cosmetics market. Sales rose 99 per cent between 2001 and 2005 to reach US $12.7bn, according to Euromonitor International. While this ageing process suits incumbent brands with existing customer franchises, these older customers are making life much harder for marketers who are trying to introduce new products and services, or compete for increased share. 'You can't teach an old dog new tricks' as the saying goes, and we do seem to become creatures of habit as we age. In childhood, new thought processes create fresh connections in the brain, but as the openness of youth peaks and then gives way to adulthood, repetition has turned these familiar connections into channels that become the well-ploughed furrows from which it is hard to deviate. In brain chemistry terms, the learning process seems to be one of establishing pathways or neural networks that constitute 'trains of thought'. The more we think upon similar lines and use the same sequences of neural connections, the easier and quicker it is for a 'thought wave' to travel.

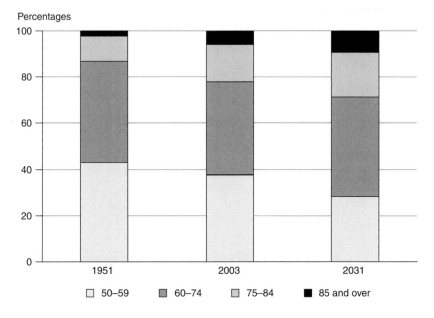

Figure 12.3 UK population: 20.0 million aged 50 and over
Reproduced by kind permission of National Statistics Online

Country	% population over 65 2000	% population over 65 2007
Germany	16.4	19.8
Russia	–	14.4
United Kingdom	–	15.8
USA	12.4	12.6
World	7.1	7.5

Figure 12.4 Population aged 65 and over: a comparison
Source: CIA World Factbook 2007/OECD database 2007

Younger people, on a voyage of self-exploration, are not only wide open to new ideas and experiences, but actively seek them. Older people whose identities, lifestyles and behaviours are more settled into a comfortable familiarity are much less inclined to novelty. For example, personal tastes in music acquired during the formative 'courtship' years can persist for a lifetime. On the second day of a conference we return to the same seat we occupied on day one. People on holiday quickly establish their preferred table in the hotel restaurant and favoured sun-loungers by the pool. They then spend a fortnight defending these 'territories' against all-comers. Some people, such as top-level sports stars, take their routines to extreme levels of precision. The New Zealand All Blacks are famous for their pre-match ritual, the Haka. This powerful tribal dance manages to convey passion, testosterone, menace and national pride all in a few grimaces, gestures, steps and shouts (Figure 12.5).

They have performed it before kick-off since 1905 and it has contributed hugely to their fearsome reputation and frequent successes on the rugby pitch. New Zealander Jonah Lomu has an individual ritual of his own – he always eats mashed potato, spaghetti and six egg whites before a rugby match. Ritualistic behaviour is not confined to the sphere of rugby either: Scots tennis player Andy Murray always listens to the Black Eyed Peas on his iPod before a match. Clearly, there is sense in habitual behaviour: first, it is easier and less risky in every aspect of life to use a tried and tested approach that works. Second, it takes more effort to do things differently, to drive a new route to work, to stand at a different part of the platform, or even to walk down an unaccustomed path in the park. It takes a strong conscious effort to break a habit.

Figure 12.5 The New Zealand rugby team performing the 'Haka'
Reproduced by kind permission of allblacks.com

The same is true with customers' relationships with products or services: the majority of frequent purchases are highly repetitious, with the choice being made from the same limited portfolio of brands over a period of many years. New market entrants, offering a product or service innovation, have to fight very hard to break through the barrier of routine put up by the person who is committed to their current range of brands and overcome their habitual inertia to achieve an initial trial, let alone a repeat purchase. By the same token, existing brands enjoy the benefits of this habitual behaviour and can sustain it by the judicious use of key elements of the marketing mix such as advertising and loyalty rewards (Figures 12.6 and 12.7).

This essentially defensive activity can appear to be 'running fast to stand still', according to Andrew Ehrenberg, but nevertheless is crucial to maintaining the status quo by protecting brand share and profitability against the threat of challengers.

Clearly, this progressive settling into habits and patterns of behaviour as people age has a profound implication for the advertising and marketing communications of brands. In order to get a sense of the significance of this factor we can draw upon the new IPA TouchPoints survey and look at the three questions that most closely relate to people's propensity to consider new products and services. The results suggest consistently that older people are significantly less likely than younger people to consider new brands: in the case of new technologies this may be by as much as three times!

Figure 12.6 Sainsbury's
Nectar card
Reproduced by kind permission
of LMUK

Figure 12.7 Saks Fifth
Avenue card
Reproduced by kind permission
of Saks Fifth Avenue

The first TouchPoints question that is relevant is: 'Friends ask my advice on new products or brands' (Figure 12.8). Clearly, this is a reflection of two factors that relate to experimentation by the respondent: first, the extent to which the respondent's peer group are experimenting (and by extension the respondent); and second, the extent to which the respondent's opinion on new brands is valued by others. Those that agree with this statement are therefore more likely to be responsive to new product launches. The TouchPoints data shows that while 60.7 per cent of 15- to 24-year-olds agree with this, the degree of agreement declines with age to a low of 30.5 per cent among those aged over 65.

The second question that gives us another insight into people's reactions to newness is: 'I am willing to try new products from companies I trust even if it is in an area in which they have no previous experience.' Here it's interesting to note that while younger people are more experimental than their elders, the gap is not as marked as with the last question (Figure 12.9). This suggests that older people's relative lack of enthusiasm for new brands is not necessarily the result of an inherent unwillingness to experiment, but rather a need for more convincing, *trustworthy* justification for trial. They are more sceptical, having had more experience of life, and for them the

Age	% agreeing with statement
15–24	60.7%
25–34	44.6%
35–44	35.9%
45–54	34.9%
55–64	31.3%
65+	30.5%
Overall average	39.2%

Figure 12.8 'Friends ask my advice on new products or brands'
Source: IPA TouchPoints 2006

maxim 'all that glitters is not gold' is a cautionary counterbalance to the desire for new experiences.

Interestingly, evidence from communications tracking company Millward Brown suggests that older people are no less interested in launch advertising for new brands or products than their younger counterparts, but that they generally find them less persuasive, hence they need more convincing (Figures 12.10 and 12.11). Consequently, average levels of achieved brand appeal are slightly lower for older people, but the difference is not great (Figure 12.12).

IPA TouchPoints does not examine the desire to try new brands, but it does look at attitudes to new technology via the attitude statement 'I like to keep up with new technology'. Here there is a marked reduction in enthusiasm for technological innovation: an area that is producing many of the most exciting new products and services (Figure 12.13). This is clearly a 'torture test' for experimentation since older people often face greater physical as well as psychological barriers to usage with new technology products than with non-technology ones, but nevertheless illustrates one of the big problems facing these sorts of innovators.

If we then combine the three TouchPoints measures ('friends seek my advice on new products', 'willing to try new products' and 'keep up with technology') by adding up those who agree with all three, you can see how the cumulative effects of these factors can build into a challenging pattern for older target consumers (Figure 12.14).

From this, we might crudely infer that 15–24-year-olds are twice as likely as the average to be responsive to new technology product launches and three

Age	% agreeing with statement
15–24	61.2%
25–34	58.3%
35–44	45.8%
45–54	48.7%
55–64	47.5%
65+	50.1%
Overall average	51.7%

Figure 12.9 'I am willing to try new products from companies I trust even if it is in an area in which they have no previous experience'
Source: IPA TouchPoints 2006

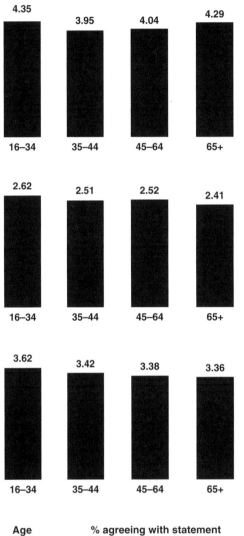

Figure 12.10 Involvement with Launch Ad
Source: Millward Brown 2006. Reproduced by kind permission of Millward Brown

Figure 12.11 Persuasion by Launch Ad
Source: Millward Brown 2006. Reproduced by kind permission of Millward Brown

Figure 12.12 Average brand appeal – Launch Ads
Source: Millward Brown 2006. Reproduced by kind permission of Millward Brown

Age	% agreeing with statement
15–24	69.5%
25–34	50.7%
35–44	42.6%
45–54	45.3%
55–64	33.4%
65+	37.7%
Overall average	46.2%

Figure 12.13 'I like to keep up with new technology'
Source: IPA TouchPoints

Age	% agreeing with all three statements
15–24	32.2%
25–34	22.4%
35–44	12.6%
45–54	13.9%
55–64	10.7%
65+	10.2%
Overall	16.7%

Figure 12.14 % agreeing with all the statements above by age
Source: IPA TouchPoints 2006

times as likely as people over 55. Given that in the UK the 55+ segment represents 28 per cent of the total population and is forecast to rise by a further 2 per cent by 2014, and that the over-50s account for 40 per cent of the country's annual disposable income, marketers need to rise to the challenge posed by older consumers.

For the sake of brevity, we can compare the impact of age on experimentation with that of socio-economic grouping (SEG) by adding up those who agreed with all the same three questions. As you would expect, SEG has a less marked effect than age and in general it is a decreasing factor in differentiating attitudes (Figure 12.15).

So experimentation generally increases as you move up the social scale, but Millward Brown data suggest this has more to do with higher disposable income than attitudes. People from lower down the scale are if anything *more* interested in new brands, judging by the appeal of launch ads for them (Figure 12.16).

We can also look at relevant questions on the UK's Target Group Index, produced by BMRB through their massive annual survey of 26,500 people. There are two statements of particular interest, one affirming a respondent's openness to new products and one that covers the opposite (Figure 12.17). Here we see that younger people are about 25 per cent more likely to claim greater interest in trying new things than their elders. And while the differences are less in terms of loyalty, it also seems that older people do tend to stick to brands a bit more than the young (Figure 12.18).

However, it's not impossible to introduce older people to new things. UK JICIMS (Joint Industry Committee for Internet Measurement Systems) data shows that while there are still marked differences in internet usage according to age, the 'silver surfer' phenomenon is already significant and growing (Figure 12.19).

Class	% agreeing with all three statements
A	**24.2%**
B	**23.9%**
C1	16.1%
C2	15.3%
D	11.4%
E	14.9%
Overall average	16.7%

Figure 12.15 % agreeing with all the statements above by class
Source: IPA TouchPoints 2006

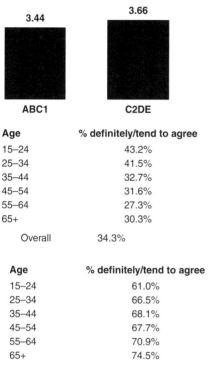

3.44   **3.66**

ABC1   C2DE

Figure 12.16 Average brand appeal
by class. – Launch Ads
Source: Millward Brown. Reproduced by kind
permission of Millward Brown

Age	% definitely/tend to agree
15–24	43.2%
25–34	41.5%
35–44	32.7%
45–54	31.6%
55–64	27.3%
65+	30.3%
Overall	34.3%

Figure 12.17 'When I see a new brand
I often buy it to see what it's like'
Source: GB TGI Q3 (April 2005–March 2006)

Age	% definitely/tend to agree
15–24	61.0%
25–34	66.5%
35–44	68.1%
45–54	67.7%
55–64	70.9%
65+	74.5%
Overall	68.3%

Figure 12.18 'Once I find a brand I
like I tend to stick to it'
Source: GB TGI Q3 (April 2005–March 2006)

	Total %	Any internet last month %
Men	48.5	52.8
Women	51.5	47.2
Age 15–24	15.8	22.7
Age 25–34	15.6	19.9
Age 35–44	18.7	22.8
Age 45–54	15.8	17
Age 55–64	14.5	12
Age 65+	19.6	5.7
Social grade ABC1	55.1	67.5
Social grade C2DE	44.9	32.5

Figure 12.19 Internet demographics
Source: NRS: JICIMS July–December 2006

The picture seems pretty clear-cut in the UK, but what about a major market like the United States? Here the over-50s have 70 per cent of the total disposable income, and at 119 million strong, the so-called 'Baby boomers' (the generation born during the period 1946 to 1964), plus 'Matures' (born before 1946), represent one out of every two adults in the United States. This group controls more than 90 per cent of the wealth and is responsible for 55 per cent of all consumer expenditures, some $3 trillion a year. So the market potential is truly massive, but we get conflicting data that seem to contradict the UK finding that older people are more inert than younger.

According to the Focalyst View Study, a joint initiative between AARP Services and Millward Brown, 'Boomers and older consumers are different from those that went before them in their diversity, in their "attitude", and in the values that guide their lives. They appear to be independent, demanding, information-hungry, experience-seeking and most importantly open to new ideas, products, and brands.' The Focalyst research shows that across product categories like cars, computers, televisions and home appliances, and service categories such as airlines, hotels and banks, fewer than three in ten say they buy the same brands they grew up with. This is of course in part explained by the mortality of the brands they grew up with, but not entirely. These US consumers are also very active in product categories that didn't exist when they grew up. Seventy-two per cent own a cellphone and one-third own five or more technology products such as PDAs, DVDs and MP3 players. They have also taken to the internet: 82 per cent of 'Boomers' (born between 1946 and 1964) and 49 per cent of 'Matures' (born before 1946) are online. And when it comes to trying new products, this group is just as likely as the younger cohort to experiment. In fact, according to an AARP/Focalyst Brand Loyalty Study, six in ten 'Boomers' (61 per cent) agreed that 'In today's marketplace, it doesn't pay to be loyal to one brand', virtually the same as those between the ages of 18 and 41 at 62 per cent. Interestingly, the research also showed that the older group (60+) were actually slightly more likely to agree with the statement 'When I see a new brand, I often buy it to see what it is like.' Moreover, this group has the financial power to trade up for quality. Nearly eight in ten (77 per cent) agreed that 'If a manufacturer can show me why their brand has more benefits than the one I normally use, I'm likely to switch, even if it's a little more expensive.' There was other evidence of a group that values experimentation and even adventure: when planning a vacation, 46 per cent of the 42+ population prefer taking vacations off the beaten path while 45 per cent try to go somewhere different each time.

It may be that these important differences in attitude among older people on either side of the Atlantic are attributable in part to differences in their relative discretionary income, population mobility, degree of being demanding and adherence to tradition. Marketers and their agencies have always paid very special attention to the issue of targeting when constructing communications plans. What these data evidence is the need to adjust the message when targeting older consumers: they are interested, but will need more careful convincing, especially in the UK. This is particularly true when launching new product or service brands.

But no matter what their age group, consumers will always respond to a powerful new product proposition. Steven Barton and Stewart Long, biologists specializing in dermatological research, have worked for Boots since 1989, heading the R&D teams. No 7 Protect & Perfect Beauty Serum was launched in 2004 after an extensive R&D programme in skincare and had been selling about 10,000 bottles a month at £16.75 for 30 millilitres (Figure 12.20).

Then, in March 2007, Professor Chris Griffiths of the Manchester University Dermatology Centre appeared on the BBC's *Horizon* programme. He reported the results of tests his team had conducted and said, '*At both basic science and clinical levels, No 7 Protect & Perfect has been shown scientifically to repair photo-aged skin and improve the fine wrinkles associated with photo-ageing.*' Despite

his technical language, the short 10-day timescale of the test and only 15 test volunteers, the effect on women was electrifying. The Boots.com website sold out overnight and Boots stores were emptied of the product in days. Production has now been increased to an astonishing 720,000 bottles a month. This is a telling indicator of the economic power of the growing number of older women and how they can be drawn to try new products specifically targeted at them. Brand immortality perhaps secured by human mortality?

Figure 12.20 No 7 Protect & Perfect Beauty Serum
Reproduced by kind permission of Boots

13 The influence of customer mindset

These are the key points from this chapter:

- There are some important aspects of customer 'mindset' and consequent behaviour that must be taken into account when developing a brand marketing and communications strategy.
- The human facility for low attention processing helps explain the power of emotional communications as opposed to purely rational ones.
- However, its long-established counterpart, high attention processing, is a stronger force and both can work together to maximum effect.
- 'Selective perception', 'cognitive dissonance', 'the herd instinct', the implications of 'double jeopardy' and the degrees of 'customer commitment' are all powerful influences on consumers which marketers need to take account of.

We have seen how a customer's age can affect their relation to and their interest in brands and brand communications, and that this must be taken into account in establishing an effective dialogue. There are also some important aspects of customer 'mindset' and consequent behaviour that should be considered when developing communications. These include 'selective perception', 'cognitive dissonance', the 'herd instinct', the implications of 'double jeopardy', and degrees of 'customer commitment'. Despite the fact that these phenomena are well documented in academic circles, they seem to have had relatively little impact on marketing communications practitioners. Many marketers continue to operate on a simplistic view of human psychology as exemplified by mechanistic and linear models of commercial communication such as AIDA – Attention, Interest, Desire, Action. While there have been many challenges to this sort of thinking which have tried to show that the communications process is much more complex in reality, there was no coherent alternative view, based on science, until Dr Robert Heath's came along.

Low (and high) attention processing

Heath first put forward his new theory of how advertising works and his ideas on low involvement processing (subsequently renamed low attention processing and referred to hereafter as LAP) in an *Admap* article in March 1999. He pointed out that

> traditional theories of how advertising works were based on the hypothesis that it must be processed cognitively by consumers to be effective – in other words, it must capture your attention and interest, and make you 'think' about and remember the ad and the message within it. Advertising that does not 'cut through' in this way is deemed to be largely wasted.

Heath's theory set out to challenge this received view, which has underpinned the vast proportion of communications strategy and its associated market research. His theory stated that:

- We process advertising on an almost continuous basis, along with other brand impressions, with great efficiency, but at low levels of involvement.
- This processing takes place passively and instinctively, predominantly using the subconscious brain.
- Because this does not involve conscious analysis, data are collected as complete sets of sensory associations, and transferred directly into long-term memory. It is these sensory associations that comprise most of the information we have about brands, and that therefore effectively *define* brands in our minds.
- When we come to make a purchase, these associations can exert a powerful influence on the decision about which brand to choose, even if we are not consciously aware of them, do not 'think' about them or do not actively analyse their meaning.

Heath's theory was welcomed with enthusiasm, especially by those yearning for an explanation of why effective ads often did badly in quantitative pre-tests and tracking studies. At last, here was a rationale to support 'creative' advertising, ie emotional not factual; use of analogy and symbolism rather than product demonstration; less emphasis on brand name mentions, large logos and mnemonic devices. However, many remain unconvinced and his theory has provoked much debate and many articles, both for and against.

One of the more robust challenges has come from leading research company Ipsos ASI. It has accumulated a database of metrics covering the performance of tens of thousands of commercials from around the world using its Next*TV test. In its methodology, respondents are not aware initially that they are participating in advertising research, but believe they are evaluating a new 30-minute TV programme in which a commercial break containing the test ad (and others) is embedded. It is as close to a natural viewing environment as market research is likely to come. In day-after interviewing, Ipsos can confirm that viewers have watched the show before asking both recall and recognition of the test ad. This allows them to segment respondents into the groups that Heath recommends for seeking evidence of LAP, namely:

1. those who demonstrate proven recall of the ad (for example, they can describe it in an identifiable manner);
2. those who cannot spontaneously recall the ad, but are able to recognize it from a description;
3. those who neither recall nor recognize the ad, but who are known to have been exposed because they have taken part in the test.

Those in the first group might be said to have been high attention processors (HAP) of the advertisement, while those in the second group can be considered to have processed it with low attention (LAP). Further, Ipsos have the added benefit of being able to analyse the third group of respondents, who might be termed as ultra low attention processors (ULAP).

The Ipsos analysis was based on responses from 97,083 respondents, 512 ads covering 65 categories, and 47 different client companies. All the test ads were for established US brands in FMCG categories. Their key findings can be summarized as follows.

1. Advertising has a significant effect on brand choice, regardless of whether it is processed with high or low levels of attention.
2. Ads processed with ultra low attention also have a significant impact on brand choice.
3. Ads that succeed in being processed with high attention are over two and a half times more impactful than ads processed with low attention, and six times more impactful than ads processed with ultra low attention (see Figure 13.1).

Ipsos applied a similar analytical approach to look into variances attributable to the creative content of the advertising being tested. The results suggest that LAP is a slightly more potent force for information-driven ads than for the less

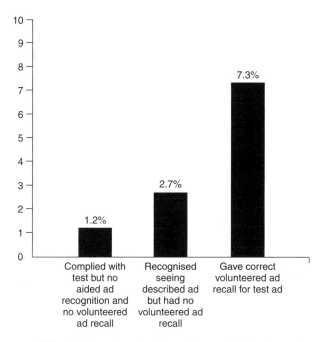

Figure 13.1 Net shift (%) for advertised brand – established products only
Source: IPSOS ASI 2006. Reproduced by kind permission of IPSOS

informative, more fun, and emotionally driven ads. While current brain research indicates that these processes are not mutually exclusive, and that 'affective' (ie emotional) response is not always strongest for ads that consumers or practitioners might assume to be most 'emotional', it's interesting to see the relative power of HAP across all creative genres (Figure 13.2).

Thus, as is so often the case, both schools of thought are right. There is an impact on brand choice and purchase behaviour resulting from low attention processing of communications that had not previously been identified. However, its long-established counterpart, high attention processing, is a stronger force. To the extent that marketers can continue to generate HAP in an increasingly message-cluttered environment, it will remain pre-eminent, but clutter is a big issue. However, HAP has been given a new lease of life in the digital world, in which tools for generating brand 'buzz' and online 'word of mouth' are numerous and increasingly vital.

The relatively new theory of low attention processing perhaps has more radical implications for how we measure marketing communications' effects than for how we develop those communications – since it confirms what many other research studies have already established, namely that communications that establish strong emotional brand associations or 'markers' are more likely

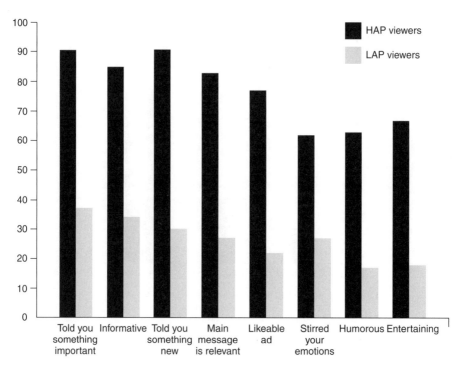

Figure 13.2   Net choice shift (%) for advertised brands
Source: IPSOS ASI 2006. Reproduced by kind permission of IPSOS

to be effective. However, there is already a great deal of learning about how to go about engaging customers in high attention processing mode, and within this body of knowledge it's worth focusing on some of the more powerful drivers of the human psyche.

Selective perception

First, there is the human phenomenon of 'selective perception', whose power we're recognizing increasingly as the media and commercial messages multiply. The American Marketing Association defines selective perception as:

1. The conscious or unconscious increase in attention for stimuli and information consistent with a person's attitudes or interests, or conscious or unconscious discounting of inconsistent stimuli.
2. The ability of the individual to protect himself or herself from the chaos and confusion of excessive and conflicting incoming stimuli. By selectively perceiving and organizing these stimuli, order is created. The needs, values, beliefs, opinions, personality, and other psychological and

physical factors are brought into play leading to selective attention, selective exposure and selective retention, along with the ability to distort and add information to meet the needs of the perceiver to cognitively reorganize reality.

The practical implications of selective perception were demonstrated by the classic experiment conducted in 1954 and documented in Hastorf and Cantril's 'They saw the game: A case study', published in the *Journal of Abnormal and Social Psychology*. In the test, a violent Princeton v Dartmouth American football game was shown to supporters of both teams. The viewers who were Princeton fans reported seeing nearly double the amount of rule violations committed by Dartmouth players than the Dartmouth supporters had done: allegiance to the different teams directly affected what their respective supporters saw. People seem to see what they want to see.

For example, how often have we observed people flicking through pages of advertising in the newspaper or magazine that they are reading in favour of the news? Many would argue that this screening or filtering ability is becoming ever more finely tuned as the explosion in media continues apace around us. At a subconscious level the customer selects which communications to be interested in: a person 'in the market' for some product or service will selectively perceive relevant brand messages when considering their purchase. Also, a regular purchaser of a particular brand will tend to preferentially perceive messages for that brand. This editing process comes naturally to all of us and very few of the thousands of commercial messages we receive daily are consciously allowed in.

This self-reinforcing trait in humans is why we see market research data for all sorts of product categories across the world showing that the buyers of Brand A are much more aware of A's advertising and more favourably disposed to it than non-buyers who favour Brand B. This is despite the fact that from an objective standpoint, the two brands and the quality of their advertising may be remarkably similar. Over 40 years ago, Rosser Reeves, then head of the Hobson Bates agency, but ignorant of this phenomenon, proposed a method of evaluating the effectiveness of advertising that involved measuring the different levels of brand purchasing among recallers of its advertising and non-recallers. He showed that consumers who were aware of the advertisements that his agency did for its clients were more favourably disposed towards those clients' brands across a range of measures, including likelihood to buy. Unfortunately, this did not mean his advertising was more effective, because the brand's buyers are more likely to be aware of that brand's advertising than non-buyers, through the process of selective perception. So in fact, those who buy the brand are more aware of the ads, rather than those who are aware of the ads being more likely to buy the brand. This mistake subsequently became known as the 'Rosser Reeves fallacy'; it still catches many people out today.

The barrier of selective perception is being exacerbated as we enter the era of permission marketing wherein unwelcome brand messages are consciously filtered out: communication is increasingly 'by invitation only'. We have already seen dramatic growth in consumer enrolment in preference services such as the United States' National Do-Not-Call Registry. This was announced on 27 June 2003. Within the first three days of the registry's operation, consumers registered more than 10 million telephone numbers. The number of registered telephone numbers had grown to over 88 million by September 2005. In the UK, there has also been a significant increase in the numbers of people registering for the Mailing, Fax, E-mail and Telephone Preference Services, which take their names off the lists that direct marketers use to target customers (Figure 13.3).

This potential for customer filtering is especially strong in the online arena, where the security technologies for screening out viruses and unwanted banners, pop-ups and e-mails are routinely included in a computer's original software installation. In this new environment, brands will have to engender sufficient customer confidence and trust to ensure that they are on the 'approved list' and make their communications timely and relevant or sufficiently attractive to be invited in.

So, using selective perception, the human brain is capable of screening out a vast proportion of the incoming communications that could potentially be absorbed but would result in overload if they were allowed in. We saw earlier how IPA TouchPoints research shows that the average UK person claims to be exposed to an average of just over four different media each day despite being bombarded by 3,000 to 4,000 messages through dozens of different media

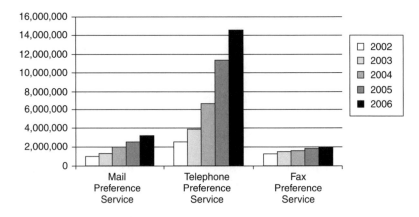

Figure 13.3 Number of new registrations each year
Source: DMA Preference Service Report. Reproduced by kind permission of the DMA

channels. Generally speaking, our minds are more open to useful, interesting, engaging, attractive, newsworthy communications that are relevant at that time, but are largely closed otherwise. From the point of view of marketing, this means that messages about products or services that the customer is already interested in are much more likely to get through.

At its most basic, there are only two kinds of advertising: 'display' and 'classified'. Display advertising can be typified as 'advertising that goes to people', whereas classified advertising is 'advertising that people go to', ie when they're actively interested in a company, product or service. Currently there's a dramatic increase in the volume of classified advertising owing to the rise of online search or pay-per-click. In the offline world, classified advertising is roughly one-third the size of display, but in the online world it's completely the other way around. It seems highly likely that when offline and online are added together in future, classified will be the dominant form of advertising by volume and value. Certainly this is the 10-year forecast by the Future Foundation in its 2006 report for the IPA, 'The future of advertising and agencies'. With new technologies, classified advertising, or 'search', is going to get better and better, with increasing utility for customers. What this means is that it's likely to get harder and harder for advertisers using 'display' advertising to engage their customers. Not only will selective perception screen out untimely, uninteresting and unrewarding messages as it has always done, but customers may have less interest in display advertising because they know where to look for brand information when they need it.

On the one hand, this represents great opportunities for brands when customers are in the mood to buy because they will be able to 'pull' useful content when, where and how they want it. We can imagine a future scenario where creating the 'point of search' for a brand becomes the focus for the whole range of marketing communications. On the other hand, the power of classified will put increasing pressure on display advertising. Greater demands will be put on the creative allure needed to achieve customer engagement and interest them in a brand which they are not currently in the market for. This is driving the current growth of 'brand experiences', in which the company creates exciting or enticing environments, entertainments or events that are imbued with the brand's attributes and values, and thus engage customers directly with them. Clearly, top-end department stores such as New York's Bergdorf Goodman and London's Selfridges have always provided great showcases for designer fashion. As we have seen earlier, there's been the development of flagship outlets for brands to showcase their complete range and philosophy. These include Niketown, the first of which opened in Portland, Oregon in 1990; the Absolut Icebar, a collaboration between the owners of Icehotel and the vodka brand Absolut, which opened in Jukkasjärvi, Sweden in 1994;' and early in the new century the Apple stores with their interactive demonstration theatres. Each time these showcases open they create massive media exposure for the brand as well as creating an intense customer experience (Figures 13.4 and 13.5)

In addition to these experiential tools, display advertising will always have a role, and perhaps even more so in the era of the internet search. It will remain vital in creating the brands to search for amid the plethora of competition and then influencing what the customer does with those search results. As we know, the decision will be driven by emotions, not the facts gleaned by a search. Indeed, just at the time when the death knell of the TV spot is being sounded by many pundits, we continue to see many examples of TV-driven effectiveness. The IPA dataBANK confirms that TV is not getting less effective – in fact it is getting more so. Most of these great commercials operate more at the emotional and psychological level than the factual and rational level and, as per Robert Heath's theory of 'low attention processing', we are taking in much more at a subconscious level than hitherto realized. However, there's no doubt that at a conscious level our brains are very effective in screening out irrelevant or untimely messages using selective perception.

Figure 13.4 Apple store opening, Fifth Avenue, New York
Source: Photograph by Ed Uthman

Figure 13.5 Absolut Icebar, Tokyo
Source: Photograph by Charles G Logan

Cognitive dissonance

Closely related to selective perception is another innate human mental process at work, 'cognitive dissonance', first identified by psychologist Leon Festinger in the 1950s. Festinger argued that we find it uncomfortable to hold contradictory positions because of the tension this creates and so we seek to resolve them wherever possible. For example, we are unlikely to say negative things about a product or service that we continue to purchase – either our opinion changes or we cease buying. In the same way we are much more prepared to take on board information, opinions and views that reinforce the positions we already hold, rather than challenge them, as Hastorf and Cantril's 'Princeton v Dartmouth' experiment proved. How often do we buy something – a new car for instance – and suddenly see the same model and its advertising everywhere we go? Our intense interest in our acquisitions, both current and past, sensitizes us to directly relevant information as we are often still in the mode of justifying to ourselves the correctness of our buying decision.

This is why it's so important when conducting evaluative research on a brand or its communications to be very specific about the recruitment criteria for respondents. As we have seen, if in the research you talk to the brand's fans you'll get a very different response than if you engage with its critics. Andrew

Ehrenberg reinforces this key point by showing that while all the buyers of all brands in a category may rate their brands similarly, the differences occur because bigger brands simply have more people voting for them. He also points out that it is often more useful to talk to the critics of a brand than fans in order to find out how to mitigate negatives and improve positives to encourage trial.

The practical implication of 'cognitive dissonance' for advertising and marketing communications is that it is hard to change attitudes and thus change behaviour, because the existing behaviour is so powerful in shaping attitudes and screening out any contradictory or challenging information. This is why direct contact between companies and potential customers through sampling, face-to-face communications programmes and live 'brand experiences' can be so effective. While these activities are often relatively expensive and need close monitoring to ensure payback, the brand 'widgets' or 'artefacts' that can be distributed online to customers to achieve 'virtual trial' are much lower cost. The increasing availability of the internet via fast broadband connections, and now WiFi, and the engaging nature of these free 'brand artefacts' hold out the possibility of changing attitudes through behaviours very cost-effectively.

Herd instinct

There is another powerful factor at work, which is the human tendency to seek reassurance by following the crowd. Research company MORI has for years tracked the relationship between familiarity and favourability and has shown that there is a clear correlation: better-known companies are generally better regarded. To a degree this may be due to the phenomenon just discussed, but not entirely. We see the same herd instinct at work in the stock markets, the music charts and in fashion. The phenomenon has been described by Mark Earls in his book *Herd* in which he puts forward a convincing argument that 'we do what we do because of other people', and the concept has been popularized by James Surowiecki in his book *The Wisdom of Crowds*. A mathematical twist on the business advantage of 'mass' and being bigger is provided by Andrew Ehrenberg's notion of 'double jeopardy'. Being tried twice for the same offence is prohibited by the Fifth Amendment to the US Constitution – the Double Jeopardy Clause. However, this is not the case in marketing. Ehrenberg has shown, with mathematical precision, that brands with higher market shares have not only higher penetration, ie more people ever buying them, but also invariably higher average frequency of purchase, ie their buyers buy them more often. Thus the brand leader in a given market sector will 'win' twice over and, all other things being equal, will not have to spend as much money as lesser brands to maintain its position. This means that smaller brands are punished twice for not being brand leader. Many find this a confusing and even counterintuitive concept, so perhaps a quote from the article by Neil Barnard, Andrew Ehrenberg and John Scriven, 'Differentiation or salience' in the *Journal of Advertising Research* (November/December 1997), will clarify the double jeopardy rule:

> In brief, for two brands – a big A and a small B, whose customers have the same overall levels of category consumption – proportionally more buyers of the small brand B also buy the big brand A and therefore have to buy the small brand B less often. That is compared with fewer buyers of the big brand A also buying the small brand B (because few people in general buy B, since it is small). They therefore have to buy A itself more often to satisfy their category demand.

Clearly, 'double jeopardy' is powerfully self-reinforcing, and has a massive knock-on effect in terms of retail distribution and display, as well as reducing the overall cost of marketing for brand leaders, and has kept the likes of Kellogg's Corn Flakes in pole position for decades.

In his book *Eating the Big Fish* Adam Morgan identifies this problem and suggests a number of ways that smaller 'challenger' brands can attempt to restack the odds more in their favour. Principal among his eight 'challenger credos' are:

- The development of powerfully emotive 'lighthouse identities' that create more intense consumer responses and buzz among those who connect with the brand.
- The assumption of 'thought leadership' of the category as a way of creating authority in the category out of proportion to the brand's size.
- The creation of symbols of re-evaluation that force consumers to rethink their attitudes to the brand.
- A focus of resources on the smaller number of 'plays' that can really make a difference to the brand.
- And finally the use of communications as an unmissable high-engagement asset.

He illustrates his argument powerfully by references to many successful challenger brands that have achieved more than brand leaders with less resource. And many of his ideas are also evidenced convincingly in the case studies of the IPA dataBANK. Unsurprisingly, his book has proved a bestseller among marketers.

Customer commitment

Jan Hofmeyr and Butch Rice have drawn these threads of customer mindset together in their Conversion Model™ described in detail in their book *Commitment-Led Marketing*. Using a large number of market research studies globally, they have produced a powerful analytical tool that can be used to establish the mindset of the customer and their propensity to consider an alternative brand. They classify users of a brand in four ways to define their level of commitment (Figure 13.6):

1. 'Entrenched' – these are users of the brand who are unlikely to switch to another brand in the foreseeable future.
2. 'Average' – these are users of the brand who are unlikely to change in the short term, but have some possibility of switching in the medium term.
3. 'Shallow' – these are users of the brand who have a lower commitment than average, some of whom are already actively considering an alternative to the brand that they are buying.
4. 'Convertible' – these are the users of the brand who are most likely to defect to another one.

In a similar way they also classify non-users of the brand into four segments:

1. 'Available' – these are non-users of the brand who prefer the brand to their current brands though they have not yet switched, and have been identified as psychologically ready to switch.
2. 'Ambivalent' – non-users who are as attracted to the brand as they are to their current brands. Hence, they are 'open' to the brand.
3. 'Weakly Unavailable' – non-users whose preference lies with their current brands, though not strongly.
4. 'Strongly Unavailable' – non-users whose preference lies strongly with their current brands. These people are the least likely to switch to the brand in the near future.

Applying this framework to many markets in many countries, Hofmeyr and Rice have established that there are significant variations in the degrees of commitment and availability for a given product category across different countries. This is typified by their example of claimed commitment levels in the beer category by most frequently bought brand in different countries (Figure 13.7). Clearly, this would be useful information to factor in if one were considering launching a brand of beer into a new country and had the option of either South Africa or Australia. Using this analytical tool to establish

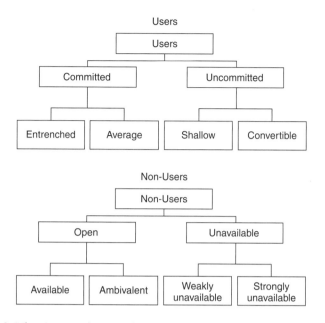

Figure 13.6 The Conversion Model segments
Source: Hofmeyr and Rice (2004)

Figure 13.7 Global commitment norms for most frequently used brands: beer
Source: Hofmeyr and Rice (2004)

degrees of commitment and availability is potentially useful to marketers whether they are considering launching a new brand, repositioning an existing one, or simply managing one in maturity. That said, they should always be a bit wary of *claimed* behaviour in any national market and certainly across markets!

So it is evident that all these key aspects of customer mindset must be borne in mind when developing communications. However, there are many other more important considerations in developing marketing strategy – and there is no better source of learning to examine these than the IPA dataBANK. So from here on, this book will mine the wealth of learning residing therein.

PART 5

The broad rules for longevity – insights from the IPA Effectiveness Awards

14 Broad rules for longevity – introduction

These are the key points from this chapter:

- The core samples for detailed analyses are the 880 case studies in the IPA dataBANK from the biennial UK national and international 'open' competition.
- The focus will be on the 'effectiveness success rate' – the likelihood of a brand behaviour resulting in any very large business effects, across a wide range of metrics from sales to profitability.
- The analysis teaches us that the life stage of the category a brand is in has a very important influence on which strategies are most likely to work.
- Brands of all types and sizes have demonstrated the ability to prosper in just about every category, whether or not the category is growing or declining.

The constant battleground of brands provides us with an ever-renewing laboratory of how to defy brand mortality. By studying brands that have prospered despite the competitive odds stacked against them, we can draw conclusions about how to stay fit. So the next chapter will examine the general lessons of brand fitness that apply to brands no matter what may be happening to the particular category in which they operate. The data we will use teaches us, though, that the life stage of the category has a very important influence on which strategies are most likely to work and what expectations can be had of them. So subsequent chapters of this book will examine how brands are affected and how their ideal strategies evolve, as their category progresses along the spectrum of development from the first flush of youth through growth and maturity to the threatening infirmity of decline.

Our primary source will be the IPA dataBANK of effectiveness case studies. This invaluable source is the product of 26 years of the IPA Effectiveness Awards and contains the accumulated learning of 880 case studies from the biennial UK national and international 'open' competition (plus many others that we will not examine here). Each paper submitted has to be accompanied by a questionnaire completed by its author as a condition of entry. This records the circumstances of the brand and its category at the time of the campaign, the marketing activity that constituted the campaign and, crucially, its results in detail. In all, 216 data fields covering over 30 topics can be used to search for common patterns of cause and effect: it is an enormous body of data that permits reliable conclusions to be drawn about how brands can thrive. But also, because of the double-vetting by industry experts (including academics, researchers, consultants and econometricians) and senior clients to which every paper is subjected, it is an enormously *rigorous* body of learning that has achieved a worldwide reputation for credibility.

So the best way of looking at the IPA dataBANK is as a collection of data that illustrates how brands can successfully defy competitive and market challenges. However, across the industry still far too little is known about how marketing can be deployed most effectively. Remarkably few people have delved into the extraordinary learning that resides in the IPA Effectiveness Awards. For example, the business bestseller by Rex Briggs and Greg Stuart, *What Sticks: Why most advertising fails and how to guarantee yours succeeds*, doesn't refer to them at all. Perhaps that's hardly surprising, given that each case history is between 4,000 and 5,000 words long and is densely populated with market research, sales data and payback analyses, sometimes supported by sophisticated econometric modelling. So one of the core purposes of this book is to extract the learning from these outstanding cases, make it as easily accessible as possible, and thus encourage others to make more use of it. Gary Player, the famous South African golfer, is quoted as saying, 'The more I practise, the luckier I get', and in a sense this book enables practitioners to get in plenty of practice, courtesy of all the people who have done the hard yards by collecting the data and writing the cases to create this gold standard of proof of effectiveness.

Most important from the point of view of brand health are the data fields recorded in the dataBANK relating to the scale of effects resulting from the campaign: they permit a clear distinction between the *most effective* campaigns and the *merely effective* ones. It would be simplistic to define effectiveness purely as whether or not a campaign achieved pre-set objectives, since this would take no account of other valuable effects that may have been achieved, but were not envisaged at the outset – marketing communications remain both an art and a science. The case studies in the IPA dataBANK reflect this reality and in many instances campaigns are evaluated against wider criteria than those stated as objectives by their authors. Largely because of this, effectiveness is measured in the following chapters as the 'effectiveness success rate' – the likelihood of a brand behaviour resulting in any very large business effects, across a wide range of metrics from penetration to profitability. A relatively high effectiveness success rate indicates that the behaviour is associated with the most effective campaigns. In this way, it is possible to see which brand behaviours lead to a healthier brand life and should therefore contribute to immortality. This measure has nothing whatsoever to do with whether the case won a prize in the IPA Effectiveness Awards, although prize-winners generally achieve larger business effects than non-winners. Quite rightly, the prizes are mostly influenced by the quality of the evidence, rather than the scale of the effect – but inevitably the larger the effect the easier it is to evidence, so the two are linked. The effectiveness success rate nevertheless remains a measure purely of business effectiveness.

Of course, brand managements come and go, and with them sometimes the wisdom that drives success, so not all the brands looked at have necessarily enjoyed the same high levels of success enduringly. But that doesn't undermine the lessons that can be learnt by examining those periods during which they were doing the right things and prospering: these key periods are what the case studies record for those who wish to learn the secrets of brand immortality.

Analysis of the IPA Effectiveness Awards supports the view that brands need not die. Brands of all types and sizes have demonstrated the ability to prosper in just about every category you can think of – whether or not it is growing or declining. Numerous brands have successfully defied the pressures of mature and declining categories by 'sticking to the knitting' of investment in innovation and marketing. They are not, in general, beneficiaries of aberrational strokes of luck or radical genius – they just refused to accept that there was no growth to be had, and went out and found it, either in the same category or in another.

15 The 'law of returns'

These are the key points from this chapter:

- The sobering truth of marketing is that what you get back in terms of market share growth is related to what you put in, in terms of share of voice.
- If share of voice is smaller than market share and the brand is not the brand leader, then it is likely to be in decline.
- It is in the interests of all brands to reinvent themselves in some way from time to time, so innovation is key.

One of the first things to realize about the IPA Effectiveness Awards is that proving effectiveness is a minority sport. Since the competition's inception in 1980, only 880 national and international cases have been submitted and there have been only 303 that met the more demanding standards of proof meriting an award and subsequent publication. The conventional explanation for this is the sheer difficulty for authors in writing a case history while holding down their day jobs, to say nothing of the intellectual and logistical challenge involved in marshalling the arguments and the data to support them. However, another more routine and realistic explanation is that there are simply not many campaigns where there is a demonstrable commercially valuable effect for the brand. We know from a huge body of research by Professor John Philip Jones, as well as by Millward Brown and others, that, all other things being equal, a brand that spends above its par share of voice, ie a larger percentage than its brand share, should increase its market share. The opposite is also true, of course: those brands that spend less than their par share are likely to decline. Given that in many markets most brands spend in line with their share and do not take an investment stance by spending ahead of it, nor employ above averagely effective creative work, it follows that few brands achieve notable growth.

So the first lesson of brand health – the backdrop to all the other life-enhancing brand behaviours – is a very straightforward one. The sobering truth of marketing is that, broadly speaking, what you get back in terms of market share growth is related to what you put in, in terms of share of voice (SOV). This is defined as the brand's percentage share of all the marketing communications (marcoms) delivered by all the brands in the market category. Clearly, there is a measurement issue in terms of capturing all marcoms deployed by brands, hence most calculations of SOV are based upon main media advertising expenditure as recorded by the likes of Nielsen Media, the broad assumption being that this is pro rata to the other monies being spent across the many other channels available, including sales promotion, direct marketing and public relations. There are various ways of setting a communications budget for a brand, but several of them tend to lead to an investment level broadly in line with the brand's share of market (SOM). So communications budgets for brands are often set to deliver an SOV equal to their SOM.

However, the dataBANK demonstrates that the *driving force* of share growth is the difference between SOV and share of market (SOV – SOM). Share growth is proportional to this difference in an apparently straightforward way. In fact it is slightly more complicated than this because bigger brands can get away with a lower share of voice, as John Philip Jones has shown. And, of course, truly outstanding marketing and creativity in commercial communications can help beat the odds imposed by a below-par media budget. But the relationship holds as a general rule, and the dataBANK confirms it for the 127 brands where there is detailed information on SOM, SOV and market share growth. This key finding reaffirms the analyses of J P Jones, Millward Brown and others, which have shown the same relationship between SOV, SOM and growth (Figure 15.1).

Therefore, the first and most obvious factor to influence a brand's health is whether its SOV is smaller than its market share: if it is smaller and if the brand is not the brand leader, then it is more than likely to be in decline. At the very least it will need to deploy the full range of other life-enhancing behaviours (that follow) to offset its underinvestment in SOV and hopefully help it hang on in there. But for most brands in most situations, if they are not investing adequately in marketing share of voice then the future doesn't look bright. The oft-quoted exception to this rule – Google – achieved its 'share of voice' in ways other than using paid-for media, but for many very obvious reasons will remain atypical of the vast majority of brands. According to Les Binet, the implications of the relationship between SOV

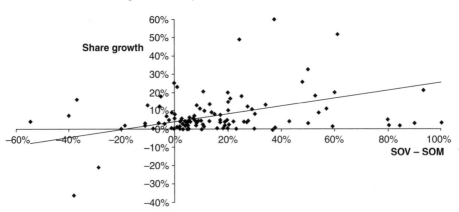

Figure 15.1 How SOV drives growth
Source: IPA dataBANK

and growth are widely misunderstood by marketers with brand life-threatening results:

> I think that most clients think that if you have sustained advertising you have sustained growth. When I ask the question of clients 'what happens if you keep advertising?', about two-thirds of them will say, 'well, it keeps the demand growing', so they're surprised when this doesn't happen. They tend to think it's easy to justify expenditure in the launch phase of a brand's career because they know you've got to invest in the brand to break into the market and you see really obvious paybacks, you see strong growth, so everyone feels happy. But later on it becomes much harder to justify continued expenditure because it looks like you're not getting anything back, and so it's very tempting at this point to start cutting the marketing budget. People are constantly looking for growth in profit and the obvious thing to do at this point is to say, 'well, we don't seem to be able to create any more demand, so the thing to do is to cut out the cost side of the business. Advertising is a cost, so we'll reduce it'. But when you reduce marketing expenditure what happens is you only get decay. And then when you've got a declining brand it's actually even harder to justify expenditure. Because people say, 'well, we're in the declining phase, we'll just treat it as a cash cow' and that's how brands die. They don't realize that the true ROI is not the change in profit, it's the difference between your profit as it was and as it would be. (Les Binet, European Director, DDB Matrix)

There are some other important observations to make about Figure 15.1 that are not necessarily immediately obvious at first glance. The first is that the gradient of the line is twice as steep as other researchers have shown to be the case for 'ordinary' campaigns and brands. That is to say, the brands featured in the IPA dataBANK enjoy on average twice as much growth per point of surplus SOV as a typical brand: their campaigns are twice as effective as the norm. Correcting for this leads you to the same conclusion as others: that as a rough rule of thumb you need SOV to exceed SOM by 10 percentage points for every point of annual SOM growth you wish to achieve. Much of this chapter is given over to observing how the IPA cases achieve this double effectiveness, and highlighting the key factors that underpin it. But no brand manager can afford to assume they will achieve these high levels of effectiveness, so the rule of thumb is a sensible guide for all brands.

The second observation is that while the data correlation is good, statistically speaking, there are nevertheless a fair number of cases (points on the chart) that have beaten the 'law of returns' line by a considerable margin. Even by the super-effective standards of the dataBANK, these cases have been doing something extraordinary and therefore warrant closer inspection. It turns out that the major common factor among what are otherwise a very diverse group of cases is that they were mostly cases where there was *major* change to the marketing mix: typically a brand extension or a complete brand re-launch, or alternatively the case was a brand launch. In such cases there is significant 'news' and other interest for the consumer, and not just new information but novel ideas and representations too. This makes campaigns work harder and is one of many reasons why innovation is good for brands.

Clearly, it is in the interests of brands to reinvent themselves in some way from time to time: consistency of brand vision may be a good thing, but this is not necessarily true of the way that vision is expressed to consumers. The human brain has been attuned by Darwinian evolution to notice change at both conscious and subconscious levels because it can be life-threatening or advantageous. Thus relevant innovation can be very effective in lodging in our brains, helping to reinforce the brand promise and its saliency.

So innovation is rightly at the top of most marketers' brand agendas. And a survey in 2007 of CMOs' use of innovation-related marketing strategies, published by *Advertising Age*, revealed that line extensions (a particular type of brand extension) are the key innovation strategies in use to meet next year's goals. But the whole area of brand extension is a complex one and failure rates are famously high at over 90 per cent (also according to *Advertising Age*). So this key stepping-stone to brand immortality is fraught with risk and danger. The whole of the next chapter is therefore dedicated to reviewing brand extensions and extracting the key lessons from brands that have extended successfully. Not all of these are to be found in the IPA dataBANK, but there are many that are.

16 The use and abuse of brand extensions

These are the key points from this chapter:

- There are three types of brand extension: range extensions, line extensions and brand extensions. Each has its own risks and potential rewards.
- Brand extensions can be an essential part of brand longevity as well as a way of beating the 'law of returns' by creating innovation and news for the brand.
- If a brand extension is the means of maintaining the vitality of the parent brand then the rationale for diverting resources to the extension is strong.
- From time to time, extensions can enable a brand's orderly transition from a declining category to a new growing one.

The term 'brand extension' is a dangerously vague one, so this exploration must start with a definition. Brand extensions, in the most general sense, are of different types and of different degrees. Although some researchers have postulated more complex categorizations, there are in essence only three types of brand extension and there are good examples of each in the IPA dataBANK:

1. **Range extension** – usually a new flavour or format of the existing brand. For example, the launch of Guinness Draught in cans.
2. **Line extension** – typically a new product or service occupying a different subcategory within the parent brand's category. For example, the launch of Hovis White bread. (Line extensions account for the majority of launches.)
3. **Brand extension** – the launch takes the parent brand into a completely different category. For example, the launch of Kellogg's Fruit Winders.

Range extension

The first of these, the range extension, is simply part and parcel of good brand management. It ensures the brand takes advantage of as many means of delivery within the category as is sensible. But range extension to the point of consumer bewilderment does happen: Crest toothpaste in the US market includes a dozen functional variants and nine different flavours. Not only can this level of range extension actually inhibit purchase by giving customers too many choices, but also the costs involved in supplying and maintaining over 80 stock-keeping units (SKUs) can be uneconomic. It's worth bearing in mind that while a major UK supermarket grocer such as Sainsbury's will stock around 16,000 lines, most of its customers will buy only about 100, and often many of the same ones on each shopping trip.

It is perhaps indicative that the successful case studies in the Effectiveness dataBANK that feature range extensions are largely about simple 'uncluttered' ones. The Lynx brand (also known as Axe) is perhaps one of the most well-extended brands to feature in the dataBANK hall of fame. The range includes five fragrances and covers deodorant body sprays, shower gels and aftershave. However, the highly successful launch of the Pulse fragrance was accompanied by the withdrawal of the weakest fragrance, Atlantis, in an annual cycle of brand refreshment, thereby maintaining disciplined innovation without the clutter. Range extension generally poses the fewest threats to the parent brand as it is unlikely to undermine the customer relationship or dilute the brand's values, unless wildly ill-disciplined or logistically inept.

In 1978 Ben Cohen and Jerry Greenfield opened their Ben & Jerry's Homemade ice cream scoop shop in Burlington, Vermont (Figure 16.1). In 2000, the business was acquired by Unilever for $326 million. The corporate website sets out the company's product mission: 'To make, distribute & sell the finest quality all natural ice cream & euphoric concoctions with a continued commitment to incorporating wholesome, natural ingredients and promoting business practices that respect the Earth and the Environment.' But nowhere among these and other good words about Ben & Jerry's social and environmental commitments is there anything much said about one of the key drivers of their business. This was the use of their jokey sense of humour to create flavours with amusing and distinctive names, which became the brand's distinctive discriminator and consumer motivation to try.

The company has generated dozens of these funny, punny ice cream varieties, as can be seen from the Flavour Graveyard for their 'dearly departed' varieties, which include such gems as 'Cool Britannia', 'Pulp Addiction' and 'Root Beer Float My Boat'. Here's the list of their current 'top ten', which is perhaps beginning to show some signs of conservatism:

Figure 16.1 Ben & Jerry's
Reproduced by kind permission of Ben & Jerry's

1. Cherry Garcia® Ice Cream
2. Chocolate Chip Cookie Dough Ice Cream
3. Chunky Monkey® Ice Cream
4. Chocolate Fudge Brownie™ Ice Cream
5. Half Baked™ Ice Cream
6. New York Super Fudge Chunk® Ice Cream
7. Phish Food® Ice Cream
8. Coffee Heath Bar Crunch® Ice Cream
9. Peanut Butter Cup™ Ice Cream
10. Vanilla Ice Cream

Elsewhere Unilever has safeguarded the founders' populist sense of fun: Ben & Jerry has committed to reducing its 'carbon hoofprint' by changing the diet of the cows from which it sources its milk so they belch less methane. Each day the average cow releases 400 grams of methane, which is a greenhouse gas 23 times more warming to the environment than carbon dioxide. Ben & Jerry's spokesperson Anniek Mauser said, 'We can't stop cows from doing what comes naturally, but we can work on methane emission reduction by changing animal feed to increase animal digestive ease.'

Peter van Stolk recognized the potential of 'mass customization' in the beverage industry and his Jones Soda was launched with six flavours in January 1996 (Figure 16.2). The brand's 'hook' is its unique packaging, which features constantly changing labels generated and submitted by its consumers, allied to wacky flavour names *à la* Ben & Jerry's.

Jones built street credibility with an initial distribution strategy that targeted skate, surf and snowboarding shops, tattoo and piercing parlours, as well as fashion and music stores. Having achieved cult status, the Jones brand has gone into mainstream retail outlets and by its 10th birthday in 2006 Jones Soda Co had achieved annual revenues of $36 million. Clearly, millions of soft drink consumers love the possibility of seeing their label on sale one day.

Coca-Cola is a mature brand that has sought to breathe new life into itself through the use of limited-edition variants. However, while there may be a short-term lift in sales, this particular tactic often does little for the long-term health of the brand and in the process tends to alienate retailers, who have to deal with the logistical problems involved. There is also a significant cost to the manufacturer in producing relatively short runs and distributing them. The associated marketing communications have to concentrate of necessity on the 'news value' and novelty of 'Coke with Lime' or 'Coke Orange', but in the process may well miss the target in terms of building core values. While endless label variation is a core brand virtue for Jones Soda, it isn't for Coke.

Figure 16.2 Jones Soda

Reproduced by kind permission of Jones Soda Co

Another soft drink that has used the idea of special edition packaging is PepsiCo's Mountain Dew brand. PepsiCo commissioned a dozen artists to provide individual designs on a limited edition of aluminium bottles, only to be distributed at special events featuring the artists in local communities across the United States. Mountain Dew has also used this as the platform for a competition for consumers to submit their own designs with a prize of $10,000 and the opportunity to be one of the brand's featured designs for 2008. However, compared to the genuinely grassroots feel of Jones Soda, or the funkiness of Ben & Jerry's, the Mountain Dew activity doesn't quite resonate as strongly.

Line extensions

Line extensions call for a higher level of care. The risk of conflict with established brand–consumer relationships is greater, and the potency of the parent brand in the new subcategory may not be as compelling as might be hoped. The risk of dilution of brand equity is also greater. When Hovis (a famous UK brand of wholemeal bread) first launched a white loaf in 1991 to take advantage of a fast-growing premium white subcategory, it failed to appreciate fully the potential complications. Although early growth was more or less guaranteed by widespread distribution thanks to Hovis's strong retailer relationships, by 1993 decline had set in. People simply found it difficult to associate the brown whole-meal Hovis brand they knew from before, with *white* bread. A focused advertising campaign restored the variant to growth and for a while all was rosy, albeit with considerably more investment behind the line extension than had originally been intended (Figure 16.3). Fast forward to 2001 and after a three-year period of dramatically reduced advertising expenditure, during which

Figure 16.3 Hovis heritage TV, CDP
Reproduced by kind permission of British Bakeries

pricing pressures had become acute, the new brand team found it necessary to re-launch the entire Hovis brand to restore profitability. The new agency, DDB London, immediately came up against a very familiar problem: how to divorce the brand from deeply ingrained associations with early *wholemeal* advertising (Figure 16.3).

A highly successful root and branch reinvention of the brand followed, driven by iconic new packaging that put about as much clear water between the new Hovis brand and its roots as it is possible to do. The brand is now more broadly defined – *more elastic* – and consequently better able to encompass a range of bakery products going well beyond loaves of bread. But with hindsight, line-extending the original Hovis brand was not the quick and easy route to extra sales and profit that was anticipated in 1991. The evidence we will examine shortly suggests that marketers often underestimate the hurdles and costs associated with successful line extensions. Hovis White was far from being unusual or indeed half-baked – it typifies the problems faced by line extensions.

The ready to drink (RTD) category within alcoholic drinks is a good example of how difficult it is to launch line extensions, especially when subject to increasing regulatory controls. In the UK, Mintel reported that RTD beverages were worth £1.2 billion in 2005, down 7.5 per cent on 2004. Diageo, one of the world's largest and most expert operators in this category, has had to fight very hard to sustain successful innovation in the face of this decline. According to *Marketing* magazine, between 2005 and 2007 the company launched 13 drinks in the UK and trialled as many, claiming to have added £86 million in incremental sales in the beer, wine and spirits sector. While there have been successes such as Baileys Flavours, Pimms Winter and the imported Bulleit Bourbon, there have been more failures. For example, Diageo withdrew Archers Vea, a low-sugar variant of its peach schnapps brand, and this followed the 2003 failed launches of Gordon's Edge, an RTD line extension of Gordon's gin, and Bailey's Glide, which debuted in 2003 and lasted only until 2006. It must seem a long time ago that Smirnoff Ice was a blazing success at its launch in 1999, establishing the market for mainstream spirits drinks brand extensions as RTDs in the UK and fomenting the explosive growth of 'malternatives' in the United States.

Brand extensions

If line extensions can face unforeseen problems then full-blown brand extensions can be doubly afflicted. The product development graveyards are littered with unfortunate examples, from BIC underwear to Harley-Davidson perfume. Clearly, marketing teams are sometimes unaware of, or turn a blind eye towards, the full set of brand associations in the minds of customers. What seems logical viewed from one perspective becomes laughable when viewed in the round. Sometimes the parent brand simply doesn't cut any ice in the new category. Thus Frito-Lay, a brand associated with thirst via salty snacks, found that it could not successfully exploit this by launching a lemonade. The 'logic' simply didn't work in the minds of consumers. Similarly, Virgin has learnt that its brand-defining characteristic style of delivery works well in service categories but not in packaged goods ones: the Virgin brand simply doesn't mean anything significant there.

Perhaps this explains the failure of Virgin Cola, which entered a clearly defined category where product innovation was either unnecessary or impossible. Worse still, the two other pre-conditions for a successful Virgin launch were missing: there wasn't a dominant bad guy in the market, nor was there a consumer sense of terrible injustice. So there was nothing to fight against and Virgin Cola couldn't make a differentiated offer that represented easily perceived added value:

> The Virgin kind of personality can't live with an FMCG brand because you can't get enough real differentiation. When it comes to buying a product like that, the public only really care about availability and price. (Will Whitehorn, President, Virgin Galactic and former Group Corporate Affairs and Brand Development Director, Virgin)

However, Kellogg's were able to rely successfully on the trust of mothers in matters nutritional when launching Kellogg's Real Fruit Winders at kids. They were able to create an entirely child-focused, fun and cool brand extension (as research had demonstrated would be necessary), safe in the knowledge that mums would trust the brand to deliver a healthy product. Just as important, the extension has helped to strengthen the relationship between the brand and mums – it is used as a treat that's better for their kids than ordinary confectionery.

There is another self-defeating illusion at work in brand extensions: the 'category definition'. Page and Farr at Millward Brown have suggested that marketers' views of the categories they operate in do not always agree with consumers' perspectives. Les Binet has tangled many times with misleading category definitions:

> The thing to do is to always bear in mind that any category definition which you do choose is not God-given, it's arbitrary and there are other ways to think about it. So, certainly MP3 players are part of mobile music, and they're part of music, but also part of things you do with your leisure time. We should think about it not from the point of view of categories of products or goods and services, but as categories of consumer needs if you like. So orange juice is part of the category of fluid consumption, which is one basic consumer need, but it's also part of the category of calorie delivery, so that you can think of it as a food as well. Or one could think of it differently again if you moved it into 'nutraceuticals'... (Les Binet, European Director, DDB Matrix)

So a marketer's view of a logical brand extension may be very different from a consumer's. If your hypothesis, as a brand with a range of salty snacks, is that you operate in some putative 'snack occasion' category, and that your product's saltiness creates a thirst, then the logic of launching a lemonade extension seems clear. If, however, the consumer sees you firmly as just a snacks brand then the logic is somewhat strained and a lot of brand redefinition will be necessary before the soft drink extension can fly. It may be easier and safer to launch under another brand. The important observation is that any category definitions used to justify a brand extension must have real currency with the target customers.

To a degree the critical factor in the success of a full brand extension is the elasticity of the parent. Some brands can, by their very nature, be stretched to cover other categories much more easily. In general, brands that are closely associated with a particular competence or product functionality are much less elastic than those associated with broader values. Some researchers have suggested that the strength of the brand in its core category has little effect on its elasticity and might even reduce it. As part of their BrandZ study, Page and Farr have developed elasticity scores for some global brands that illustrate this neatly. These are based on consumer research into the acceptance of 40 brands in categories outside their own. The elasticity scores relate to the average of the brands and categories studied. Their top three most elastic brands were:

1. Virgin (+25%)
2. Ford (+15%)
3. Body Shop (+11%)

while their bottom three least elastic brands were:

38. Amazon (–11%)
39. McDonald's (–13%)
40. KFC (–16%)

Virgin, their number one, is defined more by its approach to servicing customers than by its experience in any one of the many categories it operates in. It therefore has a highly elastic brand, but one that conveys real, positive expectations in any category it enters. That said, delivery is crucial. NTL:Telewest and Virgin.net merged and re-branded as Virgin Media in early 2007, offering customers a so-called 'quadplay', bundling together fixed-line telephony, broadband internet, on-demand cable TV and mobile phone services (Figure 16.4). This has presented some big challenges, while putting Richard Branson's personal reputation on the line again. The Virgin brand's 'gung ho' corporate culture and its desire always to seek out a Goliath to play David to may well be the undoing of Virgin Media. It is burdened by £6 billion worth of debt, a languishing share price and the loss of 46,900 subscribers in the first three

Figure 16.4 Richard Branson at the Virgin Media launch
Reproduced by kind permission of Virgin Media

months of 2007 despite a £25m spend on its Uma Thurman-led campaign. First, the ambitious 'quadplay' is very hard to deliver in practice. The poor service legacy of NTL (and its constituent cable companies) is difficult enough to deal with on its own, but then there's the considerable challenge of cross-selling TV, broadband, fixed-line telephone services and mobile phone contracts to households that more than likely have already got existing supplier relationships within each of these individual channels. On top of this, Virgin got involved in a distracting and expensive legal battle with BSkyB over programming supply and allegations of anti-competitive behaviour. In June 2007, seeing the tax management potential of its debt and the benefits of strong cash flows, the US Carlyle Group made a £4 billion bid approach and, for once, intervention by a private equity firm may be welcomed by both government and shareholders.

At the bottom of the BrandZ elasticity list, McDonald's and KFC are by contrast highly associated with excellence in the particular signature food categories served in their restaurants. This degree of product specialization conveys little elasticity to the brands, to the extent that it even inhibits their abilities to operate successfully in each other's closely related signature product areas.

It is increasingly true that taking a brand into a new category or subcategory, with all the attendant innovation that it requires, can be a critical element of maintaining the vitality of the brand. Apple is perhaps one of the most celebrated and successful examples of this. But the evidence suggests that brand extensions are rarely made in order to strengthen the parent brand. A survey by Brandgym found that only 2 per cent of marketers regard new brands as their main launch method for new products: brand extension is the much preferred route, regarded as a much more certain prospect. Brand extension for most marketers appears to have little to do with invigorating the parent brand and much to do with seizing new sales opportunities with a largely prefabricated branding. As with most things of this nature, construction is relatively cheap and easy. Research International has corroborated this suggestion – only 15 per cent of the volume forecasts they have produced for new products have been made for new brands. Such is the strength of belief by marketers in brand extensions that cautionary forecasts are also often ignored. The truth is, brand extensions are more likely to fail than new brands: a smaller proportion live long enough to see their first birthdays. With brand extensions, as with many things prefabricated, the results are often less durable.

So, apart from the cost and ease of launching (as if these weren't reason enough), why do marketers turn a blind eye to the failings of brand extensions? Helen Wing at Research International suggests that they are also misled by research findings. Brand extensions tend to score well on purchase intention measures versus new brands (12 per cent above average versus 19 per cent below average). But this reflects their immediate familiarity to consumers in the research situation rather than their enduring appeal in real life. Consequently, this research pattern doesn't reflect real-world success rates. She observes that the usual reasons for failure of a new launch are that it was not distinctive enough, not good enough or not effectively supported. Herein lies the rub for brand extensions in particular. On average they receive half the support of new brand launches and there is over-reliance on the parent brand to provide the differentiation needed. Consequently, brand extensions usually suffer from much lower advertising awareness and inadequate distinctiveness from the competition, which may enjoy bespoke branding and support. So the very reasons why marketers may favour brand extension over a new brand launch are often the causes of failure: you cannot defy the laws of gravity in underpowered flight.

But perhaps these failings are not inevitable if the underlying problems of underinvestment and inadequate distinctiveness are put right. Of course, this might undermine any false economics used to justify the launch. But if a broader perspective is taken of the role of brand extensions to include the reinvigoration of the parent brand, and if more discerning criteria are used to select those extensions, then these problems may not be insuperable. Experienced and successful brand extenders such as Unilever and Virgin have long held the view that the extension should not just borrow from the parent brand equity but feed back into it, strengthening the parent over time. Virgin has learnt from earlier failures and now has very clear and demanding requirements of the brand extension joint ventures it enters into:

> We developed a series of precepts which became the Virgin Charter. So that's the charter of how we do business. How we treat people, how we treat financial issues, how we treat company structuring, how we treat legal and fiduciary management, and all of the related reputation issues, so basically the companies have to live by that. They also have a brand licence, which is pretty strict in its terms; I mean we've withdrawn it once from a company.
>
> What's very clear to us is a lot of people have unrealistic expectations of this brand, who want to do business with us as a company, and what they will often have is the expectation that the brand will make the business work. The brand will never make the business work. We have this little thing called the 10 per cent advantage. Using the brand as Virgin as opposed to something else, gives us a 10 per cent advantage as to wherever you'd be if you'd have done it from scratch, which is always a nice place to start, but... (Will Whitehorn, President, Virgin Galactic and former Group Corporate Affairs and Brand Development Director, Virgin)

Similarly, Tesco has a very disciplined approach to extending into new categories and geographies:

> There are two things when deciding whether to take the brand into new areas. One, does it add value to customers and the second, clearly, does it add value to Tesco? Given since the war you've seen a gradual decline in the proportion of disposable income being spent on food consumption, and a reduction in the average price paid for a calorie, to see yourselves purely as a food grocer doesn't paint a massively attractive growth picture. We've therefore taken a policy to follow the customer and follow the money. By looking at what customers spend their money on and who is providing that service, then we can determine whether we can add value for the customer and, as I have outlined, for Tesco. Through this you open your mind to the possibility that you don't have to be restricted by your past. Many brands have got a tremendously strong heritage, but it sits like a millstone round their neck and actually stops them actually going anywhere. The more I look back, the more I kick myself that we could have done more, earlier. Take telecoms for example.

Companies like Carphone Warehouse did a fantastic job opening up this market, but we could have done more earlier. We didn't open our mind to the possibility that if you've got a strong brand that's not restricted, a brand that stands for fundamental principles, rather than one that's boxed in, as long as your brand is trusted, as long as your brand can give people great value for money, as long as it can give people great service, and as long as it can be conveniently accessed, then within reason, you can extend your brand. (Richard Brasher, Commercial and Trading Director, Tesco)

So if the extension becomes a means of maintaining the vitality of the parent brand then the rationale for diverting resources away from the parent to the extension is strong. In this way, not only is the extension more likely to succeed, but also the parent brand is less likely to suffer from the diluting effects of ill-disciplined extensions. Perhaps the guiding principle of brand extension should be, to paraphrase John F Kennedy in his inaugural presidential address: 'Ask not what your brand can do for your launch, but rather what your launch can do for your brand.'

Brand extensions should therefore be viewed as an essential part of brand longevity as well as a way of beating the 'law of returns' by creating innovation and news for the brand. But from time to time extensions will prove the life-blood of brands, enabling an orderly transition from a declining category to a new, growing one. Snopake was the world's first correction fluid used to correct errors typists made using the old 'golf ball' typewriters. These machines have long been usurped by word processors, but, building on its heritage, Snopake continues in a wider incarnation as a stationery brand (Figure 16.5).

So much for exceptional innovation: but what of the day-to-day brand practices that can help to ensure rude brand health? This tour of life-enhancing behaviours will continue with some more basic health advice.

Figure 16.5 Snopake
Reproduced by kind permission of Snopake Ltd

17 Setting the right objectives and strategy

These are the key points from this chapter:

- Setting hard business objectives, like market share, price sensitivity and consumer penetration, is good for brands.
- Campaigns with soft objectives such as brand loyalty enjoy considerably less success than campaigns with hard objectives.
- 'Fame' campaigns are particularly effective.
- TV is still at the top of the communications channel shopping list.
- Brands should not spread their money across too many advertising channels – three to four appear to be optimal for most.

When it comes to setting aims for marketing, the IPA dataBANK has one very obvious but often overlooked lesson: setting clear (ideally quantified) hard business objectives is good for brands. Hard business objectives include things like market share, price sensitivity and profitability. This lesson seems so obvious that one might almost exclude it from a book such as this, were it not for the fact that, even among the cases in the dataBANK, over 20 per cent of campaigns were developed without clear business goals. And if the IPA case studies (which are on average twice as effective as the average campaign) often lack them, then it is a fairly safe assumption that the average campaign is even less likely to have them. The overlapping pattern of business goals among those that set them is shown in Figure 17.1.

So, not surprisingly, campaigns without clear business objectives tend to be less effective than campaigns with them (Figure 17.2).

It goes without saying that the campaign objectives should fundamentally influence the communications strategy. If the objective of a campaign is to

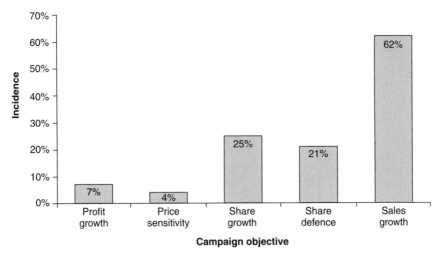

Figure 17.1 Incidence of primary business objectives
Source: IPA dataBANK

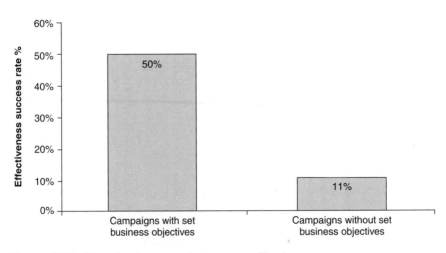

Figure 17.2 Clear business goals improve effectiveness success rates
Source: IPA dataBANK

enable the brand to raise its prices without suffering crippling sales declines (ie to reduce the price sensitivity of the brand), then the resulting communications are likely to be rather different from those arising from a campaign objective of building volume for the brand through trial. Thus the lack of clear business objectives can compromise the entire strategic development process and in this way reduce the effectiveness of the resulting campaign.

So the first rule of brand longevity is to define clear and achievable business objectives for all marketing activity. But some further clarification is needed here, because it's evident when one looks at the case studies that a lot of campaigns *do* have objectives – it's just that they are the *wrong type*. Objectives can be broadly divided into three types: business objectives (such as have already been discussed), behavioural objectives (such as penetration and loyalty) and intermediate objectives (such as brand awareness, brand image and so on). It is fairly common practice these days merely to set 'intermediate' consumer objectives for marketing activity. These are categorized and explained in the dataBANK under the headings shown in Figure 17.3.

The frequency with which each of these objectives is used is shown in Figure 17.4.

Clearly, these are often regarded as business objectives, and given all the importance implied by that; but the dataBANK has shown that this is a dangerous delusion. A clear priority is shown by the dataBANK: business objectives should dominate behavioural objectives, which should dominate intermediate objectives. Campaigns that observe this hierarchy with appropriately prioritized objectives are twice as effective as those that don't. It is, of course, perfectly sensible to set and monitor *secondary* intermediate objectives, especially if one can be confident that they are directionally consistent with the desired business outcomes. For example, creating awareness of a new or little-known brand is likely to help drive trial and hence share. But the important *primary* objectives in this case are first *share* and then *trial*, while there will be many other secondary intermediate factors that will contribute to success

Objective	Definition
Awareness	Building brand awareness/knowledge
Image	Creating brand values or user imagery that strengthens the brand's relationship with consumers
Direct*	Directly influencing behaviour such as trial or direct response or overcoming barriers to purchase
Differentiation	Differentiation or vitality, setting the brand apart
Fame	Building the 'fame' of the brand or perceptions of its strength or authority, ie the brand defines the category
Quality	Building a belief in the esteem and perceived quality of the brand
Commitment	Building commitment to the brand, a feeling of loyalty, brand relevance
Trust	Building a sense of trust or security in the brand

* 'Direct' includes, but is not limited to, direct-response campaigns with a specific response step such as a phone number or transactional website. Direct influence includes promotional offers and other short-term sales messages

Figure 17.3 Types of intermediate objectives and their meaning
Source: IPA dataBANK

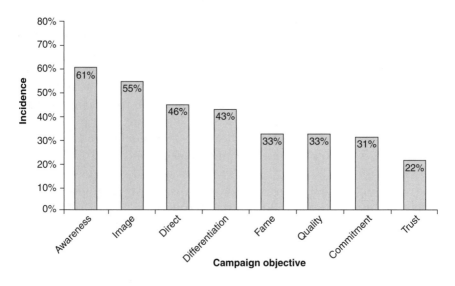

Figure 17.4 Incidence of intermediate objectives
Source: IPA dataBANK

(such as emotional affinity with the brand and perceptions of differentiation and quality). One of the most important general findings of the dataBANK is that the pursuit of single intermediate objectives generally reduces effectiveness – marketing needs to target broad shifts across many intermediate factors to improve its chances of success (Figure 17.5).

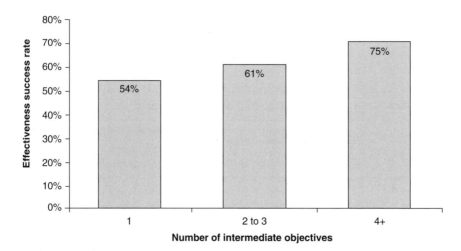

Figure 17.5 Effectiveness increases with the number of intermediate objectives
Source: IPA dataBANK

The corollary of this is that the most effective campaigns of the dataBANK (in terms of business effects) tend to have very wide-ranging intermediate effects (Figure 17.6).

However, evaluation of progress against 'soft' intermediate objectives is very useful to establish causality rather than effect, ie that it was the campaign that led to the observed effects, not other market factors.

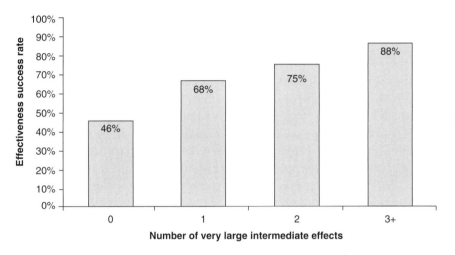

Figure 17.6 The more wide-ranging the effects, the more effective the campaign
Source: IPA dataBANK

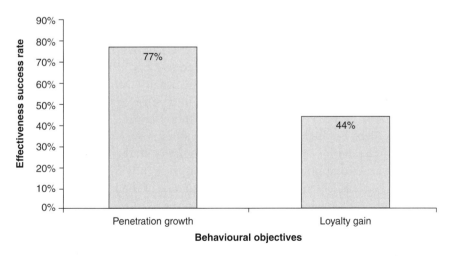

Figure 17.7 Penetration is a more effective objective than loyalty
Source: IPA dataBANK

Turning to behavioural objectives, Figure 17.7 reveals that penetration growth is a rather profitable campaign objective – a finding of the dataBANK that might seem rather uncontroversial until you consider its implications. In most situations, at the consumer buying level there are really only two ways in which marketing might affect volume sales: more consumers might buy the brand (penetration growth) or the existing buyers might buy the brand more often (loyalty growth). If penetration growth is a more profitable objective for brands, then, by implication, loyalty growth must be less profitable; and so it turns out. In fact the dataBANK gives loyalty a very hard time.

Despite being a very common communications objective, pursuing loyalty is considerably less profitable than pursuing penetration. Not only that, but where campaigns that ostensibly target loyalty are highly profitable, they are much more likely to have achieved this through *penetration growth* than loyalty! The dataBANK is clearly trying to tell us something here. The underlying finding is that marketing communications do not appear to be able to influence loyalty significantly, whereas they can make a big impact on penetration. This is, of course, exactly what Professor Ehrenberg and his team have been telling us for years; yet marketers and their agencies continue to pursue loyalty relentlessly.

The roots of this obsession with loyalty appear to go back to a famous pronouncement by management consultants Bain & Co, sometime in the 1980s, that a 5 per cent improvement in customer retention can cause an increase in profitability of between 25 and 85 per cent (depending on the cost structures of the business). Suddenly the customer relationship management (CRM) movement was born and marketing went loyalty mad. The problem with the pronouncement was that it was merely a 'thought experiment': a 'what if' idea worked through theoretically to its logical conclusion on profits. It was based on the observation that a brand's most profitable customers were always its most loyal ones. Turn less loyal customers into more loyal ones and bingo – in flow the extra profits. At the time no one had actually observed a business successfully turn its back on (expensive) new customer recruitment marketing and prosper through (relatively inexpensive) customer loyalty communications. Few have observed it since either. Because, as Ehrenberg has proven to us, behavioural brand loyalty simply doesn't vary much from brand to brand – it is pretty much fixed within a category (with the partial exception that we saw earlier that brand leaders always enjoy slightly higher loyalty than challengers, but this is a mathematical consequence of their greater penetration, not an effect that can be influenced by marketing). On a theoretical level the thought experiment is perfectly valid, just as was the thought experiment that spurred on the mediaeval alchemists to try to turn lead into gold. It's just that in practice, like alchemy, life isn't that simple.

But this unhappy observation doesn't mean that brands should turn their back on keeping their existing customers happy. Clearly, an unhappy customer will become someone else's customer and so penetration will ultimately be lost. Paradoxically, the loss of unhappy customers may have the effect of making the remaining customers appear on average to be happier – and herein lies a danger in measuring the *attitudinal* loyalty of one's customers (as many brand commitment or 'conversion' models do). But the real value in creating happy customers is that they help you recruit new ones. That is to say, they help drive penetration. This has been validated in recent years by Bain & Co's development of the net promoter score (NPS) – a measure of a customers' preparedness to recommend the brand to their friends. They have shown that a high NPS correlates well with long-term profit growth.

Thus many of the dataBANK campaigns that targeted loyalty by publicly demonstrating how well they treat their customers in fact ended up recruiting many new ones. Telling non-customers that your existing customers are well treated is, not surprisingly, a good way to attract them. This is illustrated by the 2006 Gold award-winning IPA case study for O_2.

> Then there's the O_2 loyalty rewarded campaign, which was very much about turning the tables completely on how the market had trained itself to fight for each other's customers. The acquisition cost was so high that it just wasn't a tenable ongoing business. We asked ourselves, 'What are we going to do about it? Right, let's stop and let's look at existing customers and let's stop doing these acquisitions.' It was a massively brave move for the market at that time, because everybody else was bribing new customers. We thought if we turn our attention to the 16 million customers that we had at the time, will it be that everybody else stops coming? Or will it be that they think, 'Oh, that's quite nice, I'll go and join them'? (Sophie Maunder-Allan, Planning Partner, VCCP)

In fact the O_2 *loyalty* strategy turned out to be a hugely effective *recruitment* one: two-thirds of the very considerable growth that ensued came from new customers, with the remainder from reduced churn.

And the same observation applies to the pinnacle of UK loyalty schemes – the Tesco Clubcard. There are clearly many benefits of building a database of 11 million customers, but a major part of the payback of this scheme – which costs Tesco almost £100m *per quarter* – is the effect it has had on the acquisition of customers and on the ability of Tesco to persuade them to extend their purchasing beyond the original core grocery categories. Both these benefits are in reality market penetration:

> Well, the payback initially was the fact that when we introduced it, more shoppers shopped with us, they then stayed with us, they then were happy to extend their brand portfolio. (Richard Brasher, Commercial and Trading Director, Tesco)

Clearly, in the case of Tesco (as with O₂) the benefits go beyond increasing the pool of customers, and Tesco is careful to monitor loyalty as a general sign of competitive health:

> There are two sides to loyalty. There's obviously physical loyalty in terms of what proportion of their income they spend with us on the products that we provide. And the other one is emotional loyalty, in terms of when you interview them and talk to them about whether the fund of benevolence is full versus empty. And by combining those two things we get quite a good read on consumers and we monitor our performance against competing stores. (Richard Brasher, Commercial and Trading Director, Tesco)

So the true value of the customer commitment studies and research models that have proliferated in recent years lies less in any indication they may provide of *behavioural* loyalty than in the indication they provide of likely *penetration* growth or decline in future. As leading indicators of the latter they may be very valuable.

Turning to business objectives, it becomes clear that even when campaigns do have clear business goals, not all of these are equally likely to lead to business success (Figure 17.8).

Some of the differences are fairly predictable (though that hasn't prevented widespread adoption of the weaker objectives): for example, it is better to target market share gain rather than sales gain, and within this, value share is better than volume share. Predictable though they may be, it is worth dwelling on these differences because there is more to them than first meets the eye.

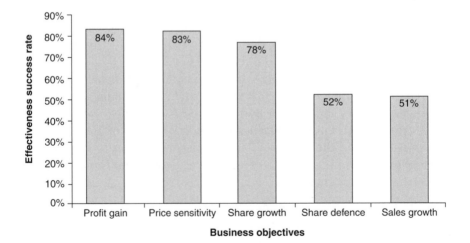

Figure 17.8 Not all business objectives are equally effective
Source: IPA dataMINE #2 (tables 11, 12, 14)

It is entirely obvious that pursuing sales growth in a *growing* category should be relatively straightforward: so long as the brand is pulling its weight in marketing terms, it should be able to take growth as a given. In such a situation, a sales growth objective (unless very aggressive) is unlikely to be particularly challenging and therefore unlikely to encourage the finest thinking from marketers and their agencies. A *share* growth target clearly strips out the 'given' category growth and places a requirement on marketing to beat this. But the finding applies across all category growth states, so it clearly runs deeper than this. There is another benefit of targeting market share growth – and that is the effect it has on strategy. The requirement to increase share focuses the minds of the team on where that share is going to come from: which brands or segments are most vulnerable and how they can best be stolen from. The sharpening effect this has on marketing and communications strategy brings observable improvements to effectiveness.

It is also fairly obvious that targeting value share gain is more likely to result in increased revenue than targeting volume share gain: if a brand cuts its price it is likely to sell greater volume, but not necessarily greater value. This is especially the case with temporary promotional price cuts once 'brought forward' sales are taken into account. More importantly, the effect on profit return of cutting prices may well more than negate the marginal contribution of the extra product sold. How do we know this? It has been a long-established finding of PIMS analysis of over 3,000 business units that company profitability strongly correlates with its market share position in the category it operates in (Figure 17.9).

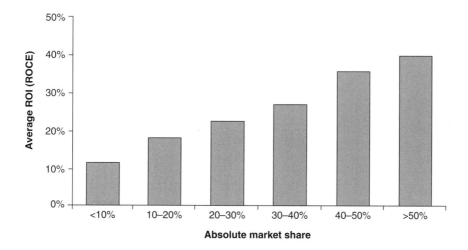

Figure 17.9 PIMS analysis of company profitability v market share
Source: PIMS

However, a study published in the *International Journal of Business* in 2007 by Armstrong and Green (from Wharton and Monash, respectively) showed that companies that had set pricing to increase market share to the exclusion of all else were consistently less profitable than those that had set pricing to ensure high profitability. The implication is clear: buying market share through aggressive pricing is not generally a good way to keep the CFO happy. For maximum profitability, market share growth must be achieved by creating consumer *desire* for the brand (through emotional affinity, perceptions of quality and so on). Although PIMS has long warned against 'buying your way into' categories, it seems that not everyone read that footnote to its charts.

So pursuing value rather than volume share is better because it includes, to a degree, an inbuilt safeguard against profit erosion. But also, once again, the objective has beneficial effects on strategy. The best way to build value share is likely to be a combination of reducing price sensitivity (and so enabling firmer pricing) and increasing penetration – Figures 17.7 and 17.8 demonstrate these to be two of the most profitable objectives according to the dataBANK. Reducing price sensitivity is a surprisingly rare objective given its potential contribution to profitability, but this may have more to do with the complexity of measurement than disdain for the objective. This hypothesis is supported by the scarcity of cases reporting price elasticity (only 20 per cent of cases).

Reducing price sensitivity in turn requires communications to increase the perceived relative quality of the brand. This has long been known

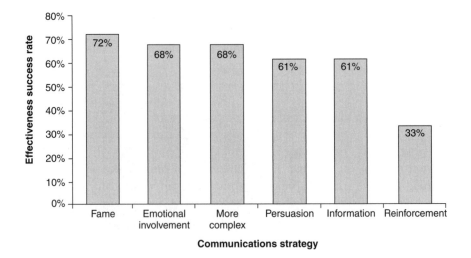

Figure 17.10 Not all communications strategies are equally effective
Source: IPA dataBANK

Strategy	Emotional or rational	Definition	Incidence
Fame	Emotional	Got the brand talked about/made it famous	9%
Emotional involvement	Emotional	Simply because of the emotions or feeling the campaign touched/how likeable it was	23%
Persuasion	Rational	Initially gained interest with information, then added emotional appeal	29%
Information	Rational	Simply because of the information the campaign provided	10%
Reinforcement	Variable	Reinforced existing behaviour rather than changed behaviour (the weak theory)	3%
More complex	Both	A more complex combination of these or other factors	25%

Figure 17.11 Communications strategies: their meaning and incidence
Source: IPA dataBANK

(again thanks to PIMS) to be a key driver of brand and company profitability. Increasing penetration will most likely require raising the profile of the brand's *raison d'être* among non-users and lapsed users of the brand. The combination of these two strategic requirements tends to produce particularly effective campaigns: this is evidenced in the dataBANK by the exceptional effectiveness of what are referred to as 'fame' campaigns. Each of the different types of campaign and their incidence is described in Figure 17.11.

Although characterized above, 'fame' campaigns need careful definition: they are not about simply creating brand awareness – most campaigns would hope to do this! Fame is about getting talked about and being seen to be the brand that is making waves in the category. This gives it a sense of authority in the category out of proportion to its size and provides valuable reassurance to consumers that the brand is widely esteemed. The Honda campaign by agency Wieden & Kennedy in the UK was a prime example of this (Figure 17.12):

> Honda was sensible and dull. It was no longer dull after our campaigns, so, in a very short period of time, we removed the prejudice. I used to say to people that my simple, first-step dream (which was achieved, actually) was that, when you are in public and someone says, 'What car do you drive?', they will say, 'A Honda'; they won't say, 'A Honda because…'. My first dream was to remove the 'because'; very simple. People stopped laughing at Honda drivers because they realized that the corporation wasn't sensible and dull. They started to understand that it had a heart. (Simon Thompson, Chief Marketing Officer, Lastminute.com, formerly Motorola and Honda)

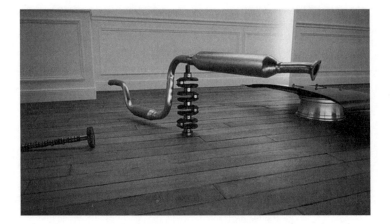

HONDA

The Power of Dreams

Figure 17.12 Honda Cogs TV advertisement, Wieden & Kennedy London
Reproduced by kind permission of Honda

Nor should fame campaigns be confused with 'celebrity campaigns' – they may well make use of celebrities, as does the highly successful Marks & Spencer campaign (IPA Effectiveness Awards Grand Prix winner, 2006 – Figure 17.13), but will do so selectively and strategically to create an appropriate talking point for the brand rather than just relying on 'borrowed interest' (as many celebrity campaigns do).

Fame campaigns have a unique ability to raise the quality perceptions of brands while also creating widespread depth of appreciation of them. Sadly, they are not nearly as widely used as their effectiveness would suggest. They are a shining example of campaigns that primarily use emotions to create the effects they seek. The dataBANK demonstrates what most seasoned marketers have discovered for themselves: that emotional campaigns are generally more effective than ones that rely on rational persuasion and the use of information for their effect (Figure 17.14).

The reasons for this are complex and the subject of much claim and counter-claim, as we saw earlier. But recent neuroscience is helping to clarify

Figure 17.13 (top) RKCR/Y&R's Grand Prix winning campaign for M&S and (bottom) Chairman Stuart Rose introduces model Lily Cole as the store's newest face
(top) Reproduced by kind permission of RKCR/Y&R and Marks & Spencer, (bottom) Reproduced by kind permission of Marks & Spencer

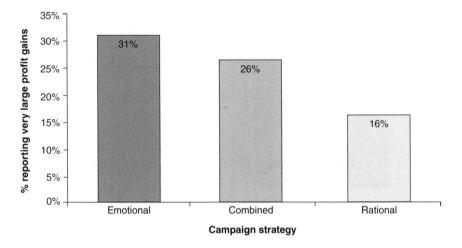

Figure 17.14 Emotional campaigns are more profitable
Source: IPA dataBANK

the picture. It has been widely understood, since USC professor of neuro-science Antonio Damasio published his seminal book *Descartes' Error*, that decision-making is heavily dependent on the primitive emotional centres of the brain. Patients who have suffered damage to these areas (illustrated most famously by the fascinating case of Phineas P Gage) are fully capable of rational thought and analysis but are incapable of making decisions. We may like to think of ourselves as reasoning beings, but in actual fact we make decisions emotionally. We have all at some time been confronted with facts about which we have felt uneasy and therefore disregarded because we simply could not accept them emotionally. It is therefore entirely sensible that brands that successfully engage us *emotionally* are likely to influence our purchase decision-making more powerfully than those that merely seek to inform or reason with us. Information has to be filtered through the cognitive areas of our brain and analysed before we can maybe begin to feel good about the brand and buy it. Engaging emotional brand associations, on the other hand, needs no cognitive processing and can get to work on our purchase choices without our thinking about them. As we saw earlier, Robert Heath's theory of low attention processing suggests we may not even be aware of what is influencing us.

But the power of harnessing emotions to brands does not end there – because neuroscience teaches us that emotional stimuli are more powerfully recorded in our memories than facts. Teachers, of course, have known this for many years: the best way to get a student to remember what you are trying to teach them is to make it fun – ie to engage their emotions. So not only do emotionally-charged brands influence our purchase decision-making more powerfully but also they do so more enduringly. This is a commercial double whammy of emotion-based marketing that would no doubt long since have consigned rational-based approaches to the dustbin of business practice were it not for two (not insubstantial) problems.

The first of these problems is that it is not easy to engage the emotions of consumers successfully. A 'killer fact' is a relatively easy idea to communicate to consumers (assuming the brand has one at its disposal), but an inspiring emotional concept is another matter, as any Hollywood film director will testify. It requires skill and commitment to create emotional brands – consumers will reject any hint of bogus posturing or slick advertising 'spin'. And brands need to 'walk the walk' as well as 'talk the talk' – an emotional promise broken can be very destructive.

There are many examples of brands that damage themselves, sometimes fatally, by failing to align their behaviour with their communications. London's Thames Water company made considerable profits for RWE Group, its former German parent, and therefore paid its directors rather too handsomely. These so-called 'fat cat' salaries were awarded while the company was being criticized for failing to invest adequately or quickly enough in repairing its leaking Victorian infrastructure. Meanwhile, the company sold off reservoirs for property development and imposed hosepipe bans during summer droughts, while running ads telling customers how to save water. Media and public outrage ensued.

So it is more important than ever that emotional branding is hard-wired into the fabric of the brand, not merely some veneer applied through communications. This naturally raises the stakes – a brand has to commit more than its communications budget to the task – and it needs to be founded on a reliable insight into consumer motivation that the brand can exploit credibly.

For brand leaders this may mean appropriating the key emotional drivers of the category such as Nike has done with the inspiring power of success in sport. This leaves smaller brands with a potential problem: if the emotional highground has been taken, where will they find sufficiently fertile emotional territory to survive? Here some canny challenger brands such as Ben & Jerry's and Jones Soda have been able to turn the tables on their bigger competitors by exploiting inherent limitations of their territory, using consumer segmentation. Segmentation as a recognized marketing tool has been around since at least the 1950s and has evolved greatly since then. But rarely is it used to best effect. The principle of segmentation is straightforward: identify clusters of consumers who share some need, attribute or outlook and create a targeted offering for them that is more powerfully appealing by virtue of its bespoke nature.

In the 1990s the late Professor Peter Doyle of Warwick University bequeathed us a useful checklist for assessing the viability of a segmentation proposal. The five criteria in Doyle's checklist are actually questions to be asked in the interrogation of an idea for a segment – is it:

1. Effective?
2. Identifiable?
3. Profitable?
4. Accessible?
5. Actionable?

First, in terms of effectiveness, are the needs of the people within the defined segment sufficiently homogeneous to make a market and also sufficiently different from the needs of people outside it to ensure that it's distinctive? Second, is this segment identifiable? Is it actually possible for the customers in this segment to be isolated and measured? Third, is the proposed segment likely to be profitable? Will there be enough potential customers in it for the company to achieve any kind of economy of scale and thus competitive pricing in serving it? Or alternatively, might customers be persuaded to pay an attractive premium to ensure profitability? So often it turns out that there may be a gap in the market, but no market in the gap! Fourth, is this new market segment accessible in media terms? Can it be sufficiently precisely defined and targeted so there is not too much wastage in communication terms? How big is the likely overlap with other target markets already being served by the company's current brands or its main competitors? Fifth and last, does the company have the resources to segment its product or service offer in the first place? What will be the implications for its existing brands if it is to divert time, money and talent into pursuing this new segment?

Despite the evolution of brands into values-based entities, segmentation often still operates at the functional needs and attributes level. It is very difficult for a brand to own such territories, and the brand leader can easily steal your ground by simply launching a product variant or perhaps a line extension. Segmentation's true value lies in unlocking new emotional brand strategies based on consumer attitudes and outlook. Conscious of its need to maintain maximum *breadth* of appeal, a brand leader is inhibited in its ability to counter the *depth* of appeal to a segment that a smaller brand can create. But inherent within pursuing such a strategy is the necessity for the brand to turn its back on other segments with different outlooks. This is what separates the men from the boys: it takes confidence and guts to do so and many chicken out, often fatally watering down their ideas to try to broaden their appeal. In doing so they lose the all-important depth of appeal that was the purpose in the first place.

One thing is certain: the risk of failure is much higher when attempting to establish a completely new category than segmenting an existing one. For example, a premium segment is being carved out within the massive £11 billion UK burger restaurant market dominated by McDonald's and Burger King with 1,800 outlets. The Gourmet Burger Kitchen, Hamburger Union, the Fine Burger Company, Ultimate Burger and the Natural Burger Co have only 50 restaurants between them, but their selling prices and their margins are as healthy as their imagery.

Sometimes brand leaders get lured into a self-destructive struggle to counter segmentation by their competitors by playing the same game and creating offerings (typically sub-brands) for each of the segments. In doing so they throw away much of their advantage in the category in terms of dominant saliency and economies of scale. But equally destructive is the complexity this introduces into the job of marketing: it's tough enough as it is without added complications.

The second of the problems with pursuing emotion-based marketing is the relative difficulty of *measuring* the emotional standing of a brand versus knowledge of it (awareness, functional benefits etc). This issue was discussed earlier and it need only be reiterated here that asking people to report their emotional response to a brand or its communications is fraught with methodological difficulties (to the extent that the dataBANK suggests that pre-testing communications can actually *reduce* their effectiveness). Only the fast-developing field of neuroscience offers us a direct way out of this problem, but for the time being £1 million MRI brain scanners the size of cars are not viable field research devices. However, analysis of the dataBANK has already hinted at a cunning way round the problem that we will return to in the next chapter: the pursuit of *multiple* shifts across a wide range of measures of brand standing with consumers.

So marketers pursuing emotional branding generally tend to have weaker evidence of the immediate effects of their marketing than those pursuing rational approaches. This matters ever more as the importance of accountability grows: managements are simply not prepared to trust that marketing is working until the sales results come in. They want immediate feedback and few will realize the impact this may have on true effectiveness by promoting the use of inefficient rational brand-building approaches.

So rational, predominantly functional, brands persist, despite the evidence of the dataBANK that this is a less effective model, and will no doubt continue to do so. Rational persuasion is, after all, not ineffective – it is merely less effective. If one cannot 'cut it' in the world of emotional persuasion, then rational persuasion is a workable second best.

There are many other brand behaviours that have lesser beneficial effects on brand health (see the report 'Marketing in the era of accountability' for details), but there is one remaining major area that has not yet been discussed: the choice of communications channels. Here the dataBANK teaches us that the mix of channels and the choice of lead channel can have a dramatic effect on the efficiency of marketing communications budgets. The greater effectiveness of emotional communications over rational has already been demonstrated, so it is not surprising that the communications channel that has the greatest emotive power also turns out to be the most effective: TV. In these days of prolific hype concerning the rapid growth of new digital communications channels, it has become fashionable to write off TV as yesterday's medium. Yet the reverse is true: the dataBANK reveals that not only does the use of TV as lead medium dramatically improve the efficiency of every £1 spent (Figure 17.15)... but also that the effectiveness of TV-led campaigns has grown over the last 25 years or so, not declined (Figure 17.16). As the number of 'screens' increases (TVs, PCs, games consoles, mobiles, laptops, PDAs, digital posters and so on), so will the proportion of audio-visual commercial communications – 'TV' is far from dead.

So any brand seeking immortality should put TV at the top of its communications channel shopping list. But what of other channels? Again the dataBANK can provide some useful general pointers here. The most non-contentious guidance relates to the development of integrated multi-channel campaigns, which are over twice as efficient (in terms of share gain per unit of excess share of voice) as traditional advertising-only campaigns. What is more, the effectiveness of such campaigns rises considerably with the number of non-advertising channels (in the traditional sense) that are added. Thus campaigns including four or more non-traditional advertising channels (such as programme sponsorship or search marketing) are 45 per cent more effective than those that include only one. There appears to be no sensible upper limit on the use of such channels – because brands use them to perform different tasks or to enrich the brand in ways that media advertising cannot (such as experiential marketing). So their effects are additive to advertising's rather than replicative – this is key to their efficiency.

However, the same is not true of the use of advertising media as is promoted by the current vogue for 'surround-sound' advertising. Brands seeking the greatest 'bang for their buck' should not spread their money across too many advertising media – three or four (depending on budget) appear to be optimal for most brands, with diminishing returns kicking in above this level.

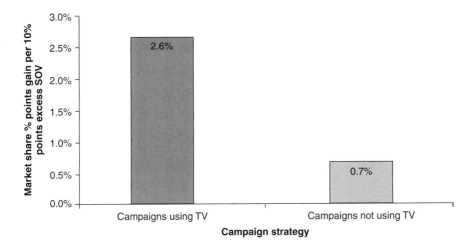

Figure 17.15 TV enhances campaign efficiency
Source: IPA dataBANK

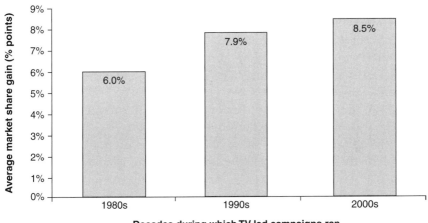

Figure 17.16 TV is getting more effective
Source: IPA dataBANK

18 Choosing the right KPIs

These are the key points from this chapter:

- The context for all consideration of KPIs is the fundamental ratio between share of voice and share of market.
- If a brand wishes to live long and prosper it should set hard business KPIs such as price sensitivity, value share, profitability and target market penetration.
- However, these are *lagging* indicators that take time to measure and thus can't be used for short-term decision-making.
- *Leading* indicators such as image and awareness cannot reliably predict success on their own, but used in combination they can be useful.

So which key performance indicators (KPIs) should a brand monitor if it wishes to live long and prosper? Clearly, the answer to this question will be tempered by the brand strategy as well as the life stage of the category it operates in – which the subsequent chapters will revisit in detail. But some general observations can be made at this point.

The first thing to bear in mind is the need to set all KPIs in the context of where the brand lies on the SOV – SOM scale. If SOV is less than SOM, then even the most inspired marketing will have its work cut out to shift KPIs in the right direction. On the other hand, if SOV is significantly greater than SOM, then KPIs damn well ought to be moving in the right direction! This fundamental relationship is very often overlooked in evaluation.

The unhelpful answer to the question of which KPIs to use is, in general, 'hard' business and behavioural measures such as price sensitivity, value share (rather than volume), profitability and target market penetration (rather than customer loyalty). Each of these measures can be a reliable indicator of business success and taken together as a scorecard of metrics can be even more so. Unhelpful because they are all *lagging* indicators, which by definition take some time to measure. This means they are unlikely to help management reach a quick opinion about the efficacy of its marketing.

So what about the *leading* indicators of brand health that are currently in use by companies – such as brand awareness and image? The general finding of the dataBANK is that none of these common intermediate consumer brand metrics is a reliable leading indicator of future business success. Some are more indicative than others; for example, brand consideration scores (a purchase intention measure) are more reliable than brand awareness measures. And measures of perceived quality, brand differentiation and level of emotional engagement will feed into the all-important price sensitivity of the brand and so are worth watching closely. So too are claimed usage and intended trial, as these are likely to relate to actual subsequent penetration. But the dataBANK suggests that advocacy measures such as the net promoter score ought to be more reliable, and, best of all, 'buzz' metrics. Buzz metrics essentially measure *fame* – in an important sense they go beyond the net promoter score by not merely recording whether people *would* recommend a brand to others but also by gauging the extent to which a brand has successfully mobilized the passions of consumers to become ambassadors and *actively proselytize* for the brand. This is hugely more valuable than a willingness to recommend, but is clearly linked – so to a degree the net promoter score may provide a crude proxy measure for it. Another useful measure of brand fame is to measure the perceived authority of the brand compared to its peers in the category: is it a 'thought leader' (to use Adam Morgan's terminology), or merely a journeyman of a brand? If the brand is a brand leader, it should be ahead on such a score – if not, then watch out for the one that is.

But *individually* even the best leading indicators don't seem to be able to predict success reliably. However, here the dataBANK can start to be a little more helpful, because it reveals, as we have seen, that although *individually* leading indicators may be unreliable, *in combination* they can be used as KPIs with much more confidence. The more leading indicators that shift for a brand, the more reliable the indication of impending business success will be (please refer back to Figure 17.6). This is true whether marketing is emotional or rational in nature, and so offers a way round the difficulties in measuring the progress of emotional marketing. So when it comes to leading indicators, a 'balanced scorecard' approach is not just desirable, but essential if they are to be reliable. Although a number of major companies monitor multiple leading indicators, Simon Thompson, former marketing director at Honda UK, had a particularly elegant way of reducing the complexity of multiple metrics:

I only ever had one metric and that was called the Unified Brand Metric. All it was was a score. And all it said is that Honda's 100, Volkswagen at the time was 150, and we needed to get to 150. That was it. It was developed over a cup of tea with the research agency, and I basically said to them, 'Look, I've got awareness and consideration and all those things coming out of my ears. I want to get to 150, and we're currently at 100, so make our research numbers equal 100 and make that company [ie VW] 150 and then we'll just step towards it.' (Simon Thompson, Chief Marketing Officer, Lastminute.com, formerly Motorola and Honda)

This is as far as we can go in identifying life-prolonging brand behaviours without considering the hugely influential factor of category life stage. So this will now be addressed in the subsequent chapters.

PART 6

How the rules for longevity vary with category life-stages

19 New categories

These are the key points from this chapter:

- Successful brands in new markets aim to define and 'own' the category. They are focused on creating awareness and generating trial.
- Their advertising doesn't only define the product or service's functionality, but also creates emotional engagement with the brand.
- Pioneer brands chase sales and share growth aggressively through new customer acquisition.
- The Number's 118 118 is an outstanding case study on how to do this.

As we will see, category life stage has a profound effect on brands and their optimum strategies. Clearly, if a brand is to be launched into a new category, then this consideration is impossible to avoid but is often overlooked in other categories, those that are growing, maturing or declining.

A key feature of new categories is their scarcity: genuinely new ones simply don't come along very often, so there's little documented experience to be guided by. This relative paucity is reflected in the entries for the IPA Effectiveness Awards: in fact only 24 cases out of the 880 are in new categories, so the analysis is inevitably limited. Despite this, there are vital lessons to be learnt which can not only help ensure a successful brand birth and childhood, but lay the foundations for a happy, healthy and potentially everlasting life.

New categories have the inbuilt attractions of virgin territory: space to grow, little or no competition and freedom. So share growth is at its easiest (if it ever *is* easy), as evidenced by two factors recorded in the IPA data.

First, the gradient of the share growth versus excess share of voice line is at its steepest. As market categories age, the gradient flattens progressively, meaning 'less bang for your buck', at least in share of voice terms. The dataBANK suggests that brands in new categories generate 7 per cent more share growth (in proportional terms) per point of excess share of voice (SOV – SOM) than in the average one. Clearly, if the brand is pioneering the new category, literally going where no brand has gone before, then share will be 100 per cent by definition and growth is limited only by the speed with which it can entice consumers into the new category by encouraging trial. This is also a function of marketing expenditure, but there will never be a better time to invest, so wise marketers spend ahead of growth at this stage, effectively 'land-grabbing' territory before slower brands arrive to stake their own claims. Once brand loyalties have been established it is difficult to disrupt them, so later entrants will largely be fishing in the diminishing pool of consumers experimenting with the category for the first time.

> You have to have investors with big balls, when you need an extra million or two. Whereas France Telecom had to go to their full board to make that decision, or Telegate had to go to the investors and say, 'we need a bit more', I make a phone call and say, 'look, we need to turn the heat up a bit' and so for the last two weeks we decided we needed a 40 per cent mindshare. (Chris Moss, Chairman of The Number 118 118)

Second, the success rate of brands in generating any very large business effects in new categories is almost 30 per cent greater than in the average category. Brands in new categories are more responsive to marketing. So launching into a new category may be a high-risk venture, but it is also a potentially high-reward one (Figure 19.1).

By definition, the brands in new categories are new launches (70 per cent of the new category cases in the dataBANK), repositionings or re-launches of existing brands (25 per cent), with just a few line extensions to make up the total. The relative lack of successful line extensions into new categories is indicative of the challenge facing would-be pioneers of categories: it's difficult to do it on the cheap. The available data suggest that the likelihood of success is much improved by a dedicated brand targeting the category opportunity. Further, it's almost certainly a false economy to line-extend into a genuinely new category. So most successful brands in new categories are, or behave like, 'pioneer brands' – new brands designed for new categories – and these have an important set of attributes that can not only help ensure survival by the protagonist brand but also make life much more difficult for those challengers who follow in its wake (Figure 19.2).

So what are the characteristics of successful pioneer brands? First of all, they aim to define and 'own' the category. These are brands with something to prove, and maintaining a disciplined focus on their key objectives is a fundamental part of their strength. They are focused on creating awareness in the category and on directly generating trial. There can be nothing more

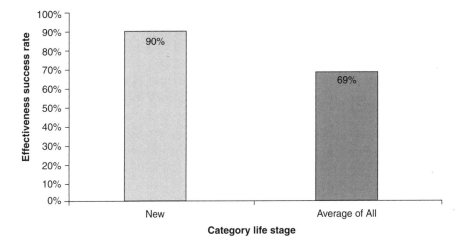

Figure 19.1 Effectiveness is greatest in new categories
Source: IPA dataBANK

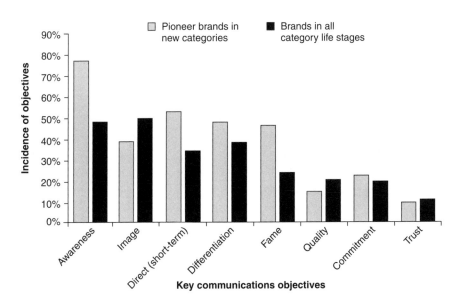

Figure 19.2 The attributes of pioneer brands
Source: IPA dataBANK

important than these objectives at this stage in the evolution of a category, given the inevitable corollary of Ehrenberg's analysis, that ultimate market share will be strongly influenced by the level of trial generated. It is worth noting that although it was observed earlier that, in general, awareness was a relatively unprofitable objective, but this is *not* the case among new categories: awareness as an objective leads to significantly greater business success in new categories than in the 'average' category. The launch of the telephone directory enquiries brand 118 118 into the newly deregulated UK market was a good example of this: they were focused on share of mind because they knew that this would drive usage:

> It is not just making people feel good about the brand, it's actually about awareness with action... a behaviour. It wasn't self-evident that 118 118 would be the winning number – it was a risky decision in some ways, because elsewhere in Germany and in Ireland, where this deregulation had occurred, the winning numbers had all been doubles, double this, double that, double the other. And 118 118 wasn't a doubling number, so it wasn't self-evident that that was going to be the winner, though it looked pretty good. Our judgement was that it's easier to remember one number, 118, twice. So we then had to work out, how do we get this number into everybody's brain? We came up with these characters – the twins (Figure 19.3). At the time we had done a lot of work on how the brain works, and we knew that brains are wired up to remember faces: if you do research showing faces, it's 10,000 faces before you make a mistake answering the question, 'Have you seen this face before?' (Robin Wight, President, WCRS Ltd)

Figure 19.3 118 118 runners, WCRS
Reproduced by kind permission of The Number 118 118

But 118 118 took ownership of the category a step further by assuming a role abdicated by the regulator, namely the responsibility for telling consumers that the old state monopoly BT's directory enquiries number was being shut down. This helped to create an air of authority around the brand that proved very valuable, while filling an urgent tactical need to get consumers to realize the importance of learning a new enquiries number. Brands launching into new categories would do well to learn from this: what actions could *you* take to create a sense of ownership and authority in the category?

So pioneer brands are much less distracted than brands in more mature categories by the complications of competitor activity, customer information overload and other category dynamics: they have the power of relative simplicity of purpose.

Second, we can observe that their advertising doesn't only seek to define the product or service's functionality, but also creates emotional engagement with the brand (Figure 19.4). While there is widespread use of the product demonstration technique, it is deployed in emotionally engaging ways. This is critical to their long-term success, because functionality will be copied by emerging competitors, but the emotional bonds forged now will endure into the future. Celebrity 'endorsement' is also at its peak among brands at this stage in the life cycle, as they seek instant reassurance and respect by associating themselves with famous people the public admires.

Third, pioneer brands chase sales and share growth aggressively through new customer acquisition. They aim to generate trial by new users and are out to change attitudes to drive that trial. Given what we have already observed

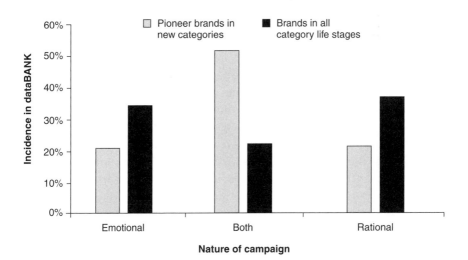

Figure 19.4 Pioneer brands build emotional engagement as well as establish functionality
Source: IPA dataBANK

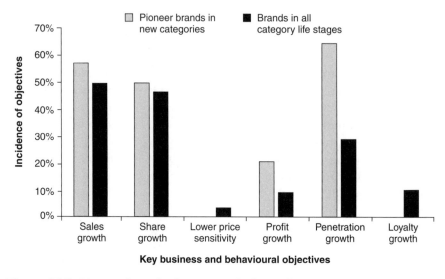

Figure 19.5 Pioneer brands chase growth through penetration
Source: IPA dataBANK

about the superior effectiveness of pursuing penetration versus loyalty, the fact that pioneer brands are seldom tempted to waste their communications on loyalty is also a source of their strength (Figure 19.5). Price sensitivity is not an issue for pioneer brands (although wise ones will be building the quality foundations that will underpin strong pricing later). At this early stage, brands are still finding their price levels, and consumers have little scope to exercise their right of choice, because there are often no other options. Instead, during this formative period, pioneer brand owners are strongly focused on cost control and achieving profitability (perhaps break-even), as they are likely to be investing heavily ahead of sales and hence return little or nothing to the bottom line. But once their target pricing level has been established, profits follow with volume growth and if volume growth is healthy, return on investment soon ceases to be a major issue at this stage in the life of the category.

Pioneer brands are driven by the need to achieve the customer perception of being the authoritative and defining brand in the category – 'fame', in the terminology of the dataBANK. These winning brands are much less interested in image and other soft objectives, as they are out to instil an absolute sense of worth and importance in the new category. They are the most prolific users of media and other communications channels, with a strong focus on TV as their lead medium, and as such are likely to have succeeded in achieving large increases in awareness and fame. Pioneer brands not only are more likely to run multi-channel campaigns but also are more able to demonstrate that they are getting the benefit of multiplier effects across them. Spending ahead of sales clearly focuses the mind on value for money and on squeezing every ounce of effect out of the budget. They also tend to be successful at using the media to spread the fame/buzz of the brand, demonstrating once again that necessity is the mother of invention. As Ernest Rutherford, Director of the Cavendish Laboratory at Cambridge University, said when his team complained of a lack of resources, 'We haven't got the money, so we've got to think!' Pioneers' entrepreneurial flair is informed with considerable use of research – these are *learning* brands – not so much pre-testing of advertising as in-market research. They are brands in a hurry and learn by *doing* rather than *deliberation*. But they are nevertheless very focused on measuring the results of their marketing – and profiting from them.

There is much that brands in established categories could learn from the pioneering spirit of successful brands in new categories. In particular, the determined focus on attracting new customers – the driving belief that 'if we don't recruit them now, somebody else will' – creates a sense of unique purpose and presence for brands that is often lost amid the dominant focus on competitors that is characteristic of established categories.

So, for brands pioneering in new categories, what does the IPA dataBANK suggest should be the key metrics for success?

Consumer metrics check-list for brands in new categories

Leading indicators:
1. Brand awareness
2. Brand 'fame' – the extent to which the brand gets talked about and is assumed to be an authoritative player in the new category
3. Level of emotional engagement with the brand
4. Trial/purchase intentions

Lagging indicators:
1. Trial levels
2. Penetration of usage
3. Value market share

CASE STUDY: The Number 118 118 – They Came, They Saw, They Conquered

Cameron Saunders and Yusuf Chuku, Gold, IPA Effectiveness Awards, 2004

The Number's 118 118 campaign shows how advertising can create a phenomenon in the dull world of directory enquiries, which in a matter of months enabled a relative upstart to take on and ultimately destroy BT's monopoly market dominance.

Ofcom, the UK telecoms regulator, announced the deregulation of the directory enquiries market in 2001, with the long-standing '192' number due to be switched off in August 2003, and replaced with a range of competing services all beginning with '118'. At the beginning of 2003, there were over 80 companies and 300 '118' numbers launched into this new market to contest the race to take over the provision of this service. Experience from other countries suggested that only two would survive the incumbent provider (BT) and be profitable. The key business issue facing The Number was how to launch and grow a new brand that successfully captured the public imagination and drove usage ahead of up to 20 competitors with similar numbers, without the ability to undercut or over-invest. A fundamentally important decision was spending £2 million of the advertising budget on buying the 118 118 number sequence. This enabled The Number to own the market generic '118'.

The strategy was simple and audacious: to act and behave as the new market leader, and advertise early, on the principle that first to mind would be first in market. It was a brave decision, particularly to advertise several months ahead of the switch-off of BT 192, but one that paid off. In order to capture public imagination in a low-interest category, a powerful brand personality was needed to register the number. This was achieved with the brand's iconic 1970s runners, twins, like the twin 118 118 number. Their catchphrase 'Got Your Number' was slipped neatly into the public consciousness. The runners first appeared, as part of the pre-launch campaign, on their own dedicated website in February 2002. This contained photos, videos and interviews with the pair of 'powerful, powerfully moustachioed men who quite literally refused to stop'. Links to the site were seeded in key internet locations and weblogs, and in a matter of days the site had generated hundreds of thousands of hits.

The next phase of the campaign was to create mass awareness of the 118 118 runners. An integrated multimedia campaign was launched across TV, outdoor and radio. At this stage The Number's 118 118 and Conduit's 11 88 88 were leading the competition. The gloves were now off, and it was time for 118 118 to play its trump card, owning the market generic and the memorability of its number. The runners were cleverly placed at key events such as Wimbledon and tens of thousands of vests were placed in Cancer Research shop windows; both generated awareness and became the fancy dress of choice at that summer's cricket Test Match series between England and South Africa. By August 2003 the runners had become a national icon and the brand had developed significant status among opinion formers, particularly in media and marketing circles. This provided a crucial point of leverage among journalists in the run-up to switch-off, to the extent that 80 per cent of the articles about it featured the 118 118 runners. This highly original communication idea had been transformed into a cult-like phenomenon by equally inventive media thinking.

To consumers, 118 118 was now the only brand and by the August 2003 'switch-off', the 118 118 runners had already clocked up 17 million calls.

Post switch-off, 118 118 dominated the deregulated market while charging people a premium for it. At the time of this paper's submission, 118 118 had 44 per cent of the directory enquiries market. Next with 34 per cent was the incumbent BT, which had the luxury of a 47-year relationship with the British public. By focusing on the period when consumers still had a choice of calling 192 or the new 118 number, this paper provides a straightforward advertising effect: £11.5m communications spend (plus the campaign cost, of buying the number, of £2 million) delivered £45m in revenue. Robin Wright, President of WCRS Ltd, the agency which developed the campaign explains:

We wanted to be the new 192, and so the consumer brain had to be rewired up as a default option: you know, 999 is for emergencies, 118 118 is for directories and that's basically what our goal was. This whole deregulation was unpopular, though: 'Why do I need to remember any more? I've got enough numbers in my head. There's my bank code number, my phone numbers' – people have a lot of numbers in their head, so there's a limit to how many they want to have to handle.

BT had 118 500 and we had to establish our number and that's why we went for 118 118 – we saw the twin numbers could be more memorable. Our 'Twin Runners' campaign idea and spending ahead of switch-off achieved that, but some consumers stored BT's number as well as 118 118 as a reserve. So basically, lots of people's brains were equipped with 118 118, and 118 500.

When the service didn't work properly at first (118 118 had enough resources to deal with 30–40 per cent of the market, not the 60 per cent it got on switch-over day), there was an extraordinary phenomenon. Normally, when services don't work, the consumers abandon them and they use something else, especially when such a high-profile service was getting a hammering in the media. But in this case, lots of consumers simply could not physically remember another number; they could not remember anything apart from 118 118, so the business held up despite everything.

Now 118 118 did a great crash course to deal with its under-capacity. It bought in new call centres, but it took between three and six months for the service to get up to scratch. Along the way, people were complaining that 'it didn't work very well, it cost more than the old 192'. The mobile sector is the most robust for us, as when consumers are at home or in the office they can search online or they can still use hard-copy phone directories for enquiries.

So what also happened in that first year was that the overall market size went down by 30 per cent to 40 per cent, as people became aware of the increased costs. Even though the market size had gone down, which happens in all these deregulations, 118 118 has approximately 45 per cent of the market, while BT had about 30 per cent. So 118 118 has kept its initial dominance – we did 'rewire' pretty effectively. (Robin Wight, Chairman, WCRS Ltd)

Figure 19.6 The Number 118 118's *Rocky* inspired TV ad by WCRS
Reproduced by kind permission of The Number 118 118/WRCS

20 Growth categories

These are the key points from this chapter:

- Increasing the level of profitability should be a major objective for brands in growing markets.
- Brands in growing markets should also continue to target new customers; to increase trial and recruitment.
- Success in creating differentiation within a growth market is getting harder to achieve, but remains essential to the enduring health of the brand.
- Orange, British Airways and O_2 are excellent case studies on how to succeed in dynamic growth markets.

In contrast to new categories, there are many more examples in the IPA dataBANK of brand campaign successes in growing categories. Growth attracts new entrants like bees round a honey pot. And rightly so: the risks facing the category pioneers have largely passed, the opportunity is proven and the key features of the category are now becoming clear. Margin levels are likely to be good, and have stabilized, and so be reasonably predictable. Growth still comes easy for all and probably will continue to do so for a number of years, with genuinely new mass markets often taking a decade or more to mature. Even smaller brands in the category are enjoying success, and vicious retaliation against growing competitors is less common and appears less necessary. So the gradient of the share growth versus excess share of voice line has not yet begun to flatten. On average the successful brands in growth markets documented in the IPA dataBANK still achieved around one percentage point of market share growth for every seven percentage points by which their share of voice exceeded their share of market. But this is not the whole story: competitive pressures are starting to grow. The cost of achieving an excess point of share of voice is increasing as more entrants 'up the ante'. And other drivers of profitability are coming under pressure too: pricing is not so easily maintained as additional market entrants, often brands seeking to undercut the pioneers, increase price sensitivity in the category. With more competing brands, retailers and other intermediaries are able to demand better terms by playing one off against another. And so on. The net result of all this is that effectiveness success rates have started to fall from their astral heights in new categories. In proportional terms, effectiveness success rates in growth categories have fallen by 17 per cent, but are still almost 10 per cent greater than the average across all life stages (Figure 20.1).

Thus brands in growth markets still have a great opportunity to generate attractive returns on marketing investment and, if managed professionally, to create long-term shareholder value. But in fact many brands begin to develop bad habits at this stage of market growth, as we can discern from the dataBANK (Figure 20.2).

We start seeing the first signs of defensive behaviour emerge as, like gamblers with some winnings behind them, players start to worry about losing what they have won. The trouble with defensive objectives is that they are less successful than offensive ones. And actually these are the formative times: the brands that push to the front aggressively are the ones that are likely to stay there as the category grows and matures. This is no time to get defensive. By now profitability levels should be a major objective for brands as volumes rise and the potential for good returns on investment grows, yet profitability is still rare as a

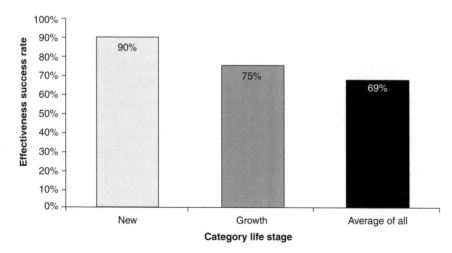

Figure 20.1 Effectiveness is still strong in growth categories
Source: IPA dataBANK

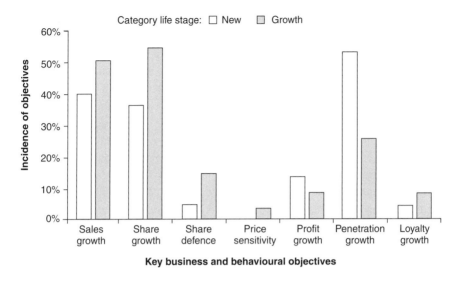

Figure 20.2 Not all developing habits in growth categories are good
Source: IPA dataBANK

primary objective in the IPA cases and has in fact *fallen* compared to new categories. Moreover, price sensitivity has *just* crept onto the radar of brands, but only for the tiny minority. No doubt pricing pressures have yet to become painful, but in anticipation of approaching category maturity, brands would do well to ensure that they are building strong, price-resistant foundations.

We also see a dramatic decline in the proportion of campaigns targeting new customers and a growth in those trying to build the loyalty of their existing customers. We saw earlier in Chapter 17 what a recipe for underperformance this is. Clearly, while it was widely understood in a new category that brands should seek new customers, in growth markets this no longer appears to be so: already brands are being misled into wasting their communications budgets on less productive attempts to build loyalty. Very large increases in customer trial and recruitment are a defining feature of successful brands and their communications at this key stage of market growth.

Although less prevalent than in new categories, the most common communications objective is still brand awareness – which, as we saw in Chapter 17, is in general not the most productive objective, but it does still yield *slightly* higher effectiveness success rates in growth categories versus the average. So *perhaps* a focus on awareness-building is still justified at this stage in the development of the category: there are, after all, many re-launches, repositionings and new launches all competing for attention. In addition, budgets are growing along with the brands they support and some brands are advertising for the first time. But brands should definitely be wary of a solitary focus on achieving awareness. All around them competitors are trying new creative approaches or media channels. Everywhere there is evidence of the dynamic cycle of experimentation and learning. Other brands jostle for position in the growing mêlée of the category, and tighten up their grip on the territories they've staked out. It will take more than awareness to secure a profitable position in the category. And while there is a healthy growth in the proportion of brands seeking to establish their quality credentials, this is nowhere near as widespread as it should be for maximum effect. Wise marketers bear in mind the PIMS analyses that show the link between perceived quality and profitability, and they invest heavily in creating these key quality perceptions.

Quality, of course, can mean a thousand different things. For UK mobile brand O_2 it was as much about the way it communicated its service offer as the details of the offers themselves.

> We decided in a sea of shouting, we wanted to be the antithesis of that: a calm brand, very much taking a step back. We've never had an ad where somebody's walking along with a phone in their hand, because we're not that obvious or blatant. (Sophie Maunder-Allan, Planning Partner, VCCP)

Ill-advisedly, there is also a jump in the proportion of brands focused on 'image', which is shown by the dataBANK analysis to be unproductive in two senses: it is less successful in driving business success than other intermediate objectives, and seldom changes a brand's image meaningfully anyway – so it is a good recipe for frustration, but little else. 'Fame' unfortunately remains a minority objective despite its proven efficacy as a profit driver, and is even less widespread than for the pioneer brands when the category was new (Figure 20.3).

But, encouragingly, there is an increasing focus on market share growth. The successful brands are the ones that do not allow themselves to be seduced by the sales growth that comes easily in a rising market, but focus on their relative performance and pursue share growth aggressively. It's important not to miss the fact that a growth market offers brands the most critical opportunity for *share growth* of any market life stage, since new consumers are coming into the category all the time and loyalties have not yet been fully established: 40 per cent of the brands in growth categories in the IPA dataBANK achieved very large share growth. This proportion falls as markets mature; it will never be as high again – so 'go for share growth' in a growth category is the clear message from the dataBANK.

Looking at other dimensions, we can see that intermediate objectives have broadened compared to new markets. This is healthy – the broader the effects the more likely business success will follow. And brand differentiation has sensibly jumped up the priority list. In a growth sector the battle is on for the hearts and minds of consumers in the long term. Success in creating

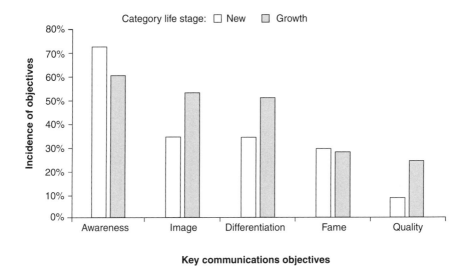

Figure 20.3 Key developments in communications objectives
Source: IPA dataBANK

differentiation is getting harder to achieve but remains essential to the enduring health of the brand. Wise brand owners know that impressions created at this stage, while consumers are forming their opinions (consciously and unconsciously) about the category, will endure.

Consistent with this is an increase in the proportion of brands using emotions in their advertising, as the need grows to develop a *defensible* differentiated presence in the category amid growing and increasingly similar competition in a functional sense (Figure 20.4).

The challenge to seduce consumers grows and the level of news in the category starts to reduce, making low attention processing of communications more important to their effectiveness. The use of humour as a creative vehicle for emotional engagement with brands jumps to its most dominant level among any category life stage (around 45 per cent). Meanwhile, purely informational advertising falls away in usage, though another form of rational advertising – 'rational persuasion' – grows to take up some of the slack. Immortality is often forged at this stage as winning brands reinforce their emotional territories, while it is still possible or affordable to do so.

Once again O$_2$ provides a fine example of best practice here.

So one of the things that we are doing is making sure that you do all of the basics, but how you differentiate is more on emotional things rather than so many rational things: become the most loved brand, not just in mobiles but in communications. (Ian Priest, Founding Partner, VCCP)

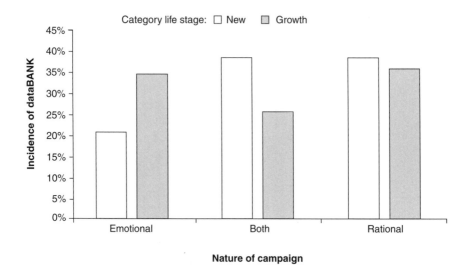

Figure 20.4 The growing use of emotional communications
Source: IPA dataBANK

But the O_2 team wisely recognize that an emotional play will not work if the service does not deliver at an appropriately high level – something many brands overlook:

> You've got to have the foundation, so whatever emotion you're trying to conjure up, it's lost if it doesn't have some substance to it. It will soon be seen as fake and you'll end up discredited like Tony Blair. (Charles Vallance, Founding Partner, VCCP)

But what of communications channel usage in growth categories? As their financial resources grow, do brands wisely invest in greater numbers of non-advertising channels, as the dataBANK findings suggest they should? Sadly, despite growing budgets there is little if any increase in the use of different media and communications channels in growth markets compared to new ones. Much marketing appears to follow an atomistic channel-by-channel assessment of which channels demonstrated greatest returns in isolation, rather than a holistic analysis that accounts for multiplier effects across channels. If more sophisticated analyses of multi-channel effects were the norm, then channel usage would undoubtedly grow as categories (and therefore budgets) grew.

Sensibly, based on the precedents in the dataBANK, TV still dominates as the lead medium for successful brands (in over 80 per cent of cases), typically taking around 50 per cent of the budget. But in the digital era the internet has become a very important secondary communications channel, used by around

60 per cent of dataBANK brands in growth categories and typically taking over 5 per cent of the budget. As internet speeds increase, high-quality video content becomes more commonplace and increasing numbers of people watch 'TV' on their computers, we might expect this trend to continue. And since press typically accounts for around 15 per cent of budgets and posters 6 per cent at this stage in the life of a category, the internet still has plenty of scope for growth.

Dependence on pre-testing of advertising declines as confidence in category knowledge and judgement grows and, wisely, this is balanced by a strengthening in the focus on measuring the real effects of marketing. The sheer likeability of a brand's communications is of greater significance in the intensifying battle for customer hearts and minds, and the collateral effects of advertising are becoming more important too – especially the effect on investors and employees.

Growth markets are usually self-evident, hence their attractiveness. But sometimes – just occasionally – they are not. The UK rail travel category in the 1990s would probably have been described at best as 'mature' and probably 'declining'. Why then would a company like the Virgin Group, which generally enters growing categories, choose to acquire two major rail franchises in 1997? This was never going to be a quick-fix, quick-buck opportunity: the trains and routes Virgin acquired were in a mess and needed massive long-term investment to put right. But Virgin forecast that rail travel would enjoy a renaissance as environmental concerns about air and car travel and Britain's overcrowded roads made rail travel seem a better option in future. Virgin's belief that the railways would be a growth category in the 21st century seems to be coming true: in one year alone (2004–05), Virgin's passenger numbers on the London to Manchester route grew by 96 per cent, raising its market share vis-à-vis air travel from 40 to 58 per cent. Were it not for all the media negativity surrounding rail travel, this would surely be fêted as one of the most exciting business areas. As any Briton will testify, it was not a smooth path – it took longer than Virgin anticipated to iron out the problems and the government insisted that from day one the service was Virgin branded. So the brand took a lot of flak that it inherited from the moribund days of British Rail. But Virgin's belief in the business and its strategic importance to the Group was strong:

> Now, the philosophy – why we went into the business – was to do with our view of the future of what was going to happen to transportation and aviation. There is no other company in the world that operates an airline and a railway company: we're the only one. So we've learnt an enormous amount from that. We've also learnt an enormous amount about how railways work, because our view for a long time was that short-haul aviation is going to come under increasing pressure in the first part of the 21st century. Short-haul aviation is extremely environmentally unfriendly, compared to long-haul aviation, because the big things in using fuel are taking off and landing. So short-haul aviation is going to be

where the pressure starts and also where national government is going to have to regulate. We knew in the late 1990s, we could design a train which would be more energy efficient than any other train built in history, which it is: the Pendolino Train (Figure 20.5). So if you board an easyJet 737 from Glasgow to London, you're putting nine times as much CO_2 into the atmosphere as a passenger, as you are in a Pendolino train from Glasgow to London – the reason being that we built the trains using aircraft aluminium manufacturing techniques, so they're incredibly light, we put regenerative braking into them which puts 17 per cent of all the electricity back into the overhead catenaries, and on top of that we designed the trains with an electromagnetic tilt system, which is very, very energy efficient. It allows them not to have to slow down to go round the corners. Those three things combined means they use half as much energy as the trains on the east coast mainline, which are 1989 technology. Now, for us, that meant that we could, in the long term, have a sustainable business in ground transportation. (Will Whitehorn, President, Virgin Galactic and former Group Corporate Affairs and Brand Development Director, Virgin Group)

Virgin Trains' next stop will be in the United States, and given the changing of sentiment towards environmental issues there, their arrival might well be timely.

The Virgin case reminds us that even in growth categories it can be tough to build a business – all sorts of pressures, beyond mere growing competition, are building. But arguably, not all of the decline in effectiveness success rates in growth categories can be put down to unavoidable unwelcome developments in the marketplace. In part it is a reflection of the changing nature of brand activity in growth markets.

Figure 20.5 Virgin Pendolino train
Reproduced by kind permission of Virgin

First, the number of brand launch campaigns in the dataBANK that are brand launches is smaller, whereas re-launches and repositionings have begun to increase from a low base (so too have copy changes – ie new campaigns) (Figure 20.6).

In part this is inevitable as earlier launches switch to new strategies, but there is a consequence. Launches (if they are successful) are inevitably more likely (by about a third) to generate very large business effects than re-launches, repositionings or new campaigns: they start from a lower base. So a decline in the proportion of launches in growth markets is likely to mean a decline in the average scale of business effects (ie the effectiveness success rate).

So the re-launch of BT Cellnet as O_2 in the still-growing UK mobile telephone category of 2001 was a relative rarity. Brands seldom need a *complete* re-launch so early in their lives. Indeed, this is a double rarity, because brands are hardly ever voluntarily killed off so early in their lives. So why was BT Cellnet, after many millions of pounds had been invested in its development, brought to such a premature death? In part it was forced on the brand by its divestment from British Telecom: so the BT part of the branding would have to be dropped. This made a review inevitable, but the brand could easily have been re-launched as Cellnet and retained its brand equity investment. But there was too much negativity remaining from when the brand was part of a duopoly with Vodafone, and in the meantime Orange had come along and rewritten the rules of mobile telephone branding and customer service. New CEO Peter Erskine realized it was time for a radical rethink and briefed agencies to reinvent his brand, including identity specialist Lambie-Nairn:

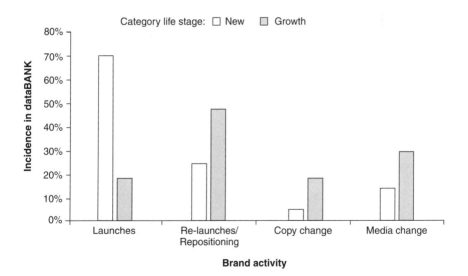

Figure 20.6 The changing nature of brand activity in growth markets
Source: IPA dataBANK

In 2001, the UK mobile market was going crazy, but BT Cellnet wasn't responding and keeping up with growth in the market. Worse than that, it was in decline, BT had big debts and BT Cellnet was a failing brand. So the decision was made to re-launch it. Originally they weren't going to change the name, the brand identity was just going to be refreshed, but it was still going to be called BT Cellnet. Peter Erskine, who was chief executive of the company, and still is chief executive actually, is an extremely good marketer and very, very interested in the brand. How the brand looks and behaves is really important to him. He said, 'If I'm going to run this business we're going to change the name, we're going to change everything.' (Nick Hough, former Chief Executive, Lambie-Nairn)

What Peter Erskine sensed, and Lambie-Nairn quickly realized, was that there was a much more powerful branding route that would signal the kind of sea-change in outlook and customer service that the company needed so badly:

Lambie-Nairn did a piece of research in which somebody said, 'My mobile phone's as essential to me as my house keys and my wallet, I wouldn't leave home without it'. That was an interesting insight in 2001, because it made us realize, 'Blimey, people's mobile phones are really important to them'. And that led us to the brand positioning. The key thought we came up with was that we were going to make this new brand 'essential for life'. So we asked ourselves, OK, so what is essential for life? Food, water, oxygen? In fact there wasn't much debate about it: oxygen was very quickly settled upon as the name, which Lambie-Nairn then turned into the logotype of O_2, illustrated with blue and bubbles. (Nick Hough, former Chief Executive, Lambie-Nairn)

The next hurdle was to create a clear sense of distance in design terms from Orange, because inevitably the new brand would be judged against the category revolutionary (Figures 20.7 and 20.8):

The context was that Orange could do no wrong. At the time, as far as telecoms were concerned, Orange was the most famous brand in the market. Our challenge was to do something better, which meant being very different. So we knew right from the start that to have any impact on the already crowded marketplace, we had to create something extraordinary. But not extraordinary in the sense of weird, funny and quirky, but by devising an identity that would contain a common visual language, which would be consistently applied to absolutely every expression of the brand. We judged that a bold, clean and modern solution, consistently applied, would give O_2 maximum visibility, set them apart from the competition and give them the flexibility to appeal to the breadth of its audiences, from teenagers to mature business. (Martin Lambie-Nairn, Founder, Lambie-Nairn)

And so the iconic blue oxygen bubble brand identity was born. O_2 is a powerful demonstration of the value of courage in the face of adversity. Most marketers would have re-launched in an evolutionary way as 'Cellnet', to play safe – and missed out on the massive commercial benefits of re-branding. This step did involve the death of a brand, but whereas BT Cellnet was floated off

Figure 20.7 Orange logo, Wolff Olins
Reproduced by kind permission of Orange

Figure 20.8 O₂ logo, Lambie-Nairn
Source: Photograph by Jonathan Knowles. Reproduced by kind permission of
VCCP and O₂

at a market value of £6 billion, just four years later O₂ was bought by Spain's
Telefónica for £18 billion.

So for brands jostling for position in growth categories, what does the IPA
dataBANK suggest should be the key metrics for success?

Consumer metrics check-list for brands in growth categories
Leading indicators:

1.   Brand 'fame'
2.   Perceived quality (however it may be defined in the category)
3.   Brand differentiation

4.   Level of emotional engagement
5.   Claimed usage
6.   Trial/purchase intentions
7.   SOV – SOM

Lagging indicators:

1.   Penetration of usage
2.   Trial levels
3.   Value market share
4.   Price sensitivity
5.   Profitability

Orange is a good example of a new brand launching successfully into what was then a growth market.

CASE HISTORY: Orange: Orange Just Talk: The Campaign That Made the Competition Go 'Ouch!'

Steve White, Gold, IPA Effectiveness Awards, 2000

This is the story of the most successful single campaign Orange has ever run. It took Orange from fourth in the pre-pay mobile phone market to first. This case shows how a single campaign cut through the cacophony of Christmas advertising to make Orange the most 'top of mind' brand and the brand most considered when buying a mobile phone. It shows how this increased purchase consideration is a direct response to the advertising campaign and that it managed to do this by building on brand values rather than trading off them.

Pre-pay phones were launched in 1997, by Vodafone, and the mobile phone market was democratized. Initially, Orange had taken a cautious approach to the pre-pay market, mindful of protecting its contract business and not wishing to encourage switching to pre-pay. To test the waters, a pre-pay product called 'Just Talk' was launched in quarter 4 of 1998. However, the bulk of marketing spend (75 per cent) remained behind contract products. The attractiveness of pre-pay was massively underestimated. Contract customers continued to be the most profitable, but the sheer number of people subscribing to pre-pay made the sector impossible to ignore. By June 1999, pre-pay accounted for 80 per cent of new subscribers, and yet Orange's share of this growing market was in decline.

The success of Orange was founded on the fact it was a challenger brand. Had Orange mimicked the long-established Vodafone and Cellnet when it launched in 1994, it would undoubtedly have been a failure. Instead it changed the status quo, championing fairness in a market where customers expected to be exploited. Orange became perceived as the market innovator and the people's champion. So the task was to apply these principles to challenge the conventions of the pre-pay market. The objective of this campaign was to raise Orange's share of pre-pay from 11.2 per cent to 19.5 per cent, increasing sales by 70 per cent, in the last quarter of 1999.

The communication solution sidestepped confusion and cynicism and set the brand apart. It was unusual in that instead of talking up the product features, it was decided to talk about the absence of negatives, encapsulated in the line 'There's no ouch in our voucher' (referring to the removal of expiry dates for vouchers).

There is little doubt that much of the success of Orange 'Just Talk' over the Christmas period was due to the product, not least the removal of expiry dates for vouchers. However, once advertising began, a week later, sales rose a massive 119 per cent to 63,000. Advertising awareness for Orange was high prior to the campaign, hovering between 80 and 90 per cent. The upward shift seen in November/December is not in itself remarkable. What is notable is that, despite equal or heavier spends over the same period, advertising awareness for the other three major networks declined over the same period. Only Orange appears to have been unaffected by Virgin Mobile's entry into the market. By the end of 1999, Orange became the most 'top of mind' telecoms brand, including the mighty British Telecom. The value of being the bestselling brand is not quantifiable, but we do know it breeds valuable word of mouth. This may explain why Orange continued to be the best-selling brand throughout the first quarter of 2000, despite competitors matching the product and outspending Orange in advertising.

Return on investment (if calculated as growth of pre-pay subscribers over growth in the market) works out at a lifetime value of £1.95 billion. A more rigid calculation is an increase in purchase consideration equivalent to £394 million return on an adspend of £9.6 million.

> The name Orange was a random thought and funnily enough I found the book that inspired me yesterday, a book called *Colour*, given to me as a present while I was at Virgin. Colour in brands is really important; as soon as I say that, I see Cadbury's Dairy Milk, there's a purple there that appears so strongly. I thought, 'Well OK, here's a chance, we've got a blank space, we're going to create a new colour right at the top, the colour or the lack of it as well'.
>
> Digital had come in, and GSM. We had a new product, a smaller, lighter phone with a SIM card in and then technology was supposed to make it all clear, so one of the thoughts was 'Why don't we call it Clear as a name?'. It's a clearer signal and clearer transparent tariff. We fiddled around with some more names, as Clear was not quite right. Early on we had Red. Red, because it's a very strong quite aggressive word, but of course Vodafone owned red.

The other idea was Orange. It was one of those things that felt quite interesting. I went to this book that I had got and Orange was described as a very powerful colour and suddenly, there was a name that was quite interesting. (Chris Moss, Chairman of The Number 118 118, formerly Orange and Virgin)

BA is a good example of a brand maintaining or strengthening its position within a growth market.

CASE HISTORY: British Airways – Climbing above the Turbulence. How British Airways Countered the Budget Airline Threat

Richard Storey, Rob Day and Andy Edwards, Silver, IPA Effectiveness Awards, 2004

This case study tells the story of how BA faced up to new competition using communications to drive through a fundamentally restructured business model.

BA was facing huge threats from low-cost airlines that were jeopardizing its long-term position in Europe. The airline had dropped out of the FTSE 100, but rather than bail out of Europe, BA believed it had to battle to survive. If it turned its back on its short-haul service, the company figured its premium long-haul operation would be next to suffer.

BA took on the budget airlines at their own game by competing on price, but also using its strong service heritage to its advantage. Research showed that consumers wanted 'services that matter' such as centrally located airports and allocated seating, as long as the price wasn't out of their reach. BA launched its communication strategy, exposing the false promise of 'no frills' and creating awareness of BA's lower prices. At the core of BA's communications strategy was the element of surprise. It bought typically un-BA media such as street projections and ATM machines to supplement its commercials.

This campaign re-set the value agenda and began to reframe the competition. In doing so, it has played a crucial role in safeguarding BA's standing among the public, its staff and the City. BA posted increased profits of £230m for year ending March 2004 and has re-established itself as a FTSE 100 company. Its European position looks secure.

O_2 is a good example of a brand re-launching within a growth market.

CASE HISTORY: It Only Works if It All Works: How Troubled BT Cellnet Transformed into Thriving O$_2$

Andrew Cox, Alex Harris, Sophie Maunder, Louise Cook and Joanna Bamford, Grand Prix, IPA Effectiveness Awards 2004

O$_2$ is the story of a corporate transformation. In April, BT Cellnet was a troubled business, losing ground consistently to competitors. A month later it was reborn as O$_2$: a vibrant, modern brand that has generated a turnaround that would have been inconceivable only weeks before.

In November 2001, mmO$_2$ Plc (formerly BT wireless) was de-merged from BT Plc in a one-for-one share offer, creating a wholly independent holding company. The UK brand, BT Cellnet, was re-launched as O$_2$ in April 2002. The new brand faced significant challenges that BT Cellnet had manifestly failed to tackle. The market had matured, making revenue growth increasingly hard to come by, and competition for that growth was intensifying. This mature market presented new challenges. Success could no longer be guaranteed by a growing market. Instead, revenue growth had to be found either by enticing customers away from competitors and/or increasing average revenue per user (ARPU) primarily by stimulating the usage of non-voice services. Growth was further hampered by the difficulty of securing technical advantage. In essence, all brands were working with the same technical raw material. Real advantage had to be fought for on the marketing battlefield. The new brand also had to take on extremely well-established and well-supported competitors, as well as facing the launch of two new brands, 3 and T-Mobile. BT Cellnet had been heading in the wrong direction. It was struggling on all the key metrics: new connections, total subscriber base, non-voice transactions, ARPU and revenue. To prove its cynics wrong, O$_2$ needed to build a strong brand, one that would be capable of turning around business performance.

O$_2$ was not a new enterprise, but it was a new brand, the attractiveness of which would be fundamental to the future fortunes of the company. Two principles that have driven O$_2$'s approach are custom-building the brand for its times and ensuring full integration, to build rapid brand awareness, revenue-driving products and tariffs for short-term revenue growth and a strong, attractive brand for the future. This has all resulted in O$_2$ becoming an entirely different animal from its predecessor. It is a vibrant, healthy brand that drives consideration and growth: performance against every one of the key business metrics has been reversed.

One of O$_2$'s most impressive achievements is how quickly it established itself in the market. O$_2$ is also now the most salient brand on the market, with an awareness level of 28 per cent. The consumer-led positioning of O$_2$'s products has led them to be more compelling than they would have been under BT Cellnet's 'manufacturer-led' approach. It has also ensured that, simultaneously, O_2's products have a broader impact on positive impressions of the brand. As salience and brand image have been transformed, there has been a parallel turnaround in consideration, which has grown consistently since its launch. Staff morale has also improved: as BT Cellnet was hindered by low morale, O_2 is aided by the enthusiasm of the staff for the new brand and its consumer orientation.

O_2's investment in communications will pay for itself more than 60 times over, generating at least £4,799 million incremental margin over the long term. The ultimate payback is expected to be 62 : 1. The mmO_2 share price has also outperformed the FTSE 100, Vodafone, Orange and BT, with many experts agreeing that the success of the O_2 brand has been fundamental to this.

Perhaps the final word goes to Hans Snook, the founder of Orange: 'They have done a superb job. They have done a superb job on branding' (*The Times*, February 2004).

21 Mature categories

These are the key points from this chapter:

- Many successful brands in mature categories still achieve profit growth by remaining focused on share growth through customer acquisition. They are likely to deploy defensive strategies only in parallel.
- If more brands focused on profit growth as an objective and recognized the huge contribution that reduced price sensitivity can make to brands, then category maturity would pose much less of a threat.
- At this mature market stage, brands need to be innovating in every sense; however, many are characterized by conservatism and risk aversion.
- Cravendale Milk, Honda and Skoda cars, and Branston Baked Beans are excellent case studies on how to succeed in difficult mature markets.

Of the four market life stages examined in this book, 'mature' is the most common environment in which winning brands in the IPA dataBANK find themselves. This isn't surprising as categories spend more time in the mature phase than any other, but it is certainly not because brands find it easier to succeed in mature categories. Quite the reverse. The analysis shows that in mature categories winning brands score just one percentage point of share growth for every eight percentage points that their share of voice is ahead of their share of market, whereas in growth categories the ratio was 1 : 7.

Partly caused by this toughening relationship, but also by many other competitive pressures, the scale of business effects brands can hope for has fallen across the board since the heady days of underlying market category growth. Major share increase happens in only three-quarters as many cases as in new categories, while major customer growth happens in only two-thirds as many cases. This is a dog-eat-dog environment.

But what of building customer loyalty? It is at precisely this stage in the development of categories that the evangelical cries of customer relationship management become most seductive: 'it is difficult to steal customers from competitors so better make sure we increase the loyalty of our existing customers', runs the logic. Sadly, many brands are seduced by this 'logic', and the proportion of campaigns aiming to build loyalty almost doubles from the levels seen in growth categories. Sadly too, the already very low success rates in building customer loyalty seen in new categories have also fallen to three-quarters of that level in mature categories. The net result of all these declining factors is that the overall measure of business effects – the effectiveness success rate – has fallen 9 per cent in proportional terms from new to mature categories (Figure 21.1). It is now slightly below the average of all categories. There's no easy way out: life can be tough in a mature market as the key brands firm up on their territories and harden up their defences. And yet brands do succeed against these mounting odds, as the dataBANK testifies: the proportion of brands achieving major profit growth has held steady at around 1 in 5.

Once again we see a continuation of the pattern of changing activity that was observed with growth categories. Successful launches have become rarer as the attractiveness of the category declines, while re-launches and repositionings have become more commonly employed tactics. As the psychology of brand teams becomes more risk-averse, defensive action has become almost as commonplace as offensive action, inevitably yielding lesser results. Copy

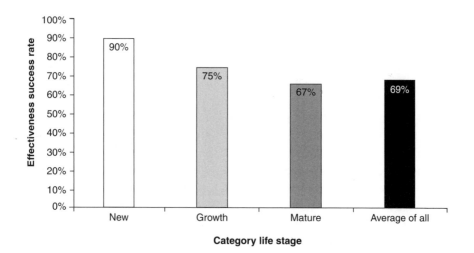

Figure 21.1 Effectiveness has weakened in mature categories
Source: IPA dataBANK

experimentation continues for successful brands, but media experimentation has declined markedly. Small wonder that achieving significant business effects has become rarer in this mature category environment, and major share growth in particular has declined (Figure 21.2). Significant changes in the relative positions of brands are becoming more unusual, so how have the successful brands managed to maintain profit growth?

Many winners in mature categories still do achieve profit growth by remaining focused on share growth through customer acquisition. They are likely to deploy defensive strategies only in parallel to resist competitor recruitment of their customers; share growth is their chosen profit driver.

It is worth pausing here to review the astonishing success story that is the renaissance of retailer Marks & Spencer in the UK. Not just because their success was built on winning back lost customers, which epitomizes the customer acquisition mindset that we have already demonstrated to be such an important driver of profit growth. But also because the predicament that the previous management of M&S had precipitated was, in many ways, a *mise en abîme* of brands in mature categories.

> I think M&S was producing far too much information, which meant people were spending an awful lot of time looking at information and failing to be traders. After all, when you cut to the credits, this is a simple business. When I got here we had 14 sub-brands in lingerie. Well, I don't know about you, but I don't think there are 14 different reasons to wear a bra. There might be four or five, but having segmented 14 different ways... in pseudo-brands? (Steven Sharp, Executive Director, Marketing, Marks & Spencer)

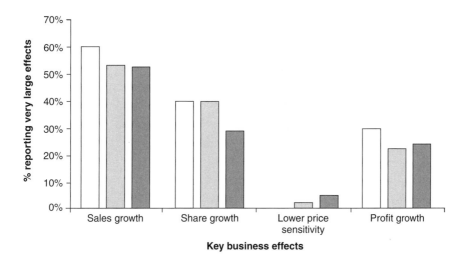

Figure 21.2 Share growth is becoming tougher as categories mature
Source: IPA dataBANK

The temptation to over-complicate brands, in a desperate attempt to create growth in categories where there is little to be found, can be very destructive. In the case of M&S this drove bewildered and unimpressed customers out of the stores. Certainly there were many other elements in the brand's predicament, such as lack of investment in the retail environment, deteriorating customer service, problems with fashion styles and so on. But in a sense many of these are symptoms of a more fundamental malaise: the management had become overwhelmed by what it saw as the complexity of the business.

So a large part of what the new CEO, Stuart Rose, and his rescue team had to do was to simplify and focus the company and the brand on the key issues:

> The whole thing had got very complicated, so it was back to basics, and the basics of this business were about quality, innovation, trust and value. So let's make sure that those are the guiding principles to everything that we do. And as with any business success story, it's never one thing that does it, it's a whole series of things that come together that actually make it work. So, what ingredients are there? Well, there's the merchandise, which was clearly wrong in lots of instances. We were heavily overstocked and had to liquidate stock, clean the business and get some better product in. Secondly, the stores had begun to decay. They were under-invested in, they were dowdy, they were old-fashioned, and so the environment needed changing. Now, that takes time. So far, we have spent around £2.5 billion, and we still haven't finished. (Steven Sharp, Executive Director, Marketing, Marks and Spencer)

Clearly, these priorities for action were somewhat different from the previous team's, and benefited from a clarity of purpose that had eluded them. The outstanding results suggest he was right. But, as Sharp confirms, the benefits of clarity were greater than simply sorting out the basics of good retailing:

> The new clarity and authority we brought to our messages were also key. We had been guilty of promoting too many messages in store, across too many sub-brands, which inevitably led to a confusing story for the customer. The introduction of 'Your M&S' provided the focal point for one brand message. And combined with strong, iconic photography, a clear focus on the product and simple, clean graphics, the store messages became simpler and more readily understood by the customer.

The famous celebrity clothing campaign was born, featuring several famous models, but in particular 1960s icon Twiggy, who, as a 'national treasure', was herself as revitalized by the campaign as M&S. This, along with food advertising that was so appetizing and indulgent it is referred to by some as 'food porn' (Figure 21.3), induced customers to come back to 'their' M&S, and they liked what they found.

In large part, then, the M&S renaissance was a result of pursuing customer (re-) acquisition as an objective, and it is through the resultant share growth that the business has prospered.

Your New Autumn Collection
Autograph corsage cardigan £55
Roll neck jumper £15
Kickflare trousers £32
Tassel boots £65

WHAT'S YOUR
M&S

www.marksandspencer.com

Figure 21.3 Twiggy/M&S poster advertisement, RKCR/Y&R
Reproduced by kind permission of RKCR/Y&R and Marks & Spencer

But there is one other rarely measured success factor that has started to increase in importance in mature categories and is undoubtedly a major driving force for brands that achieve profit growth at this stage: *price sensitivity*. Despite the difficulty in measuring price sensitivity and against a backdrop of otherwise declining business effects, price sensitivity stands out conspicuously as a growing success factor for brands in maturing categories. It may only have been recorded in 4 per cent of mature market cases, but this reflects the fact that only around 4 per cent of cases set out to achieve it and were therefore measuring it: its importance in reality is much, much greater than this. It is likely to have become at least as important to profit growth as share growth now is. So if more brands were focused on profit growth as an objective (instead of the meagre 10 per cent that are at this stage), and the huge contribution that reduced price sensitivity can make to brands was therefore more widely appreciated, then category maturity would pose much less of a threat to brand immortality.

Sometimes it helps to have the sword of Damocles above your head to help a brand come to terms with the financial fundamentals. The renaissance of Honda was founded on the need to increase the amount people were prepared to pay for its cars:

> They said the issue is fundamentally people don't want to buy our products, so until people want to buy the products, you can't charge enough, and if you don't charge enough, you don't make any money. So that's really how it started, real basic business reality. Bearing in mind that Swindon had cost £1.2 billion without any form of UK government handout, and there's three and a half thousand people working there, it probably made sense that we started selling some products and making some money. (Simon Thompson, Chief Marketing Officer, Lastminute.com, formerly Motorola and Honda)

Unusually, Honda had done exactly the kind of price elasticity research that is so rare among brands in mature categories, as Thompson reports:

> We did lots of surveys where you take the badge off the car and ask people how much they'd pay for it, and they'd say X. And you stuck the badges on and it ended it up being X minus.

But crucially Thompson also realized that the problem did not lie with the cars, but with the brand. And that in particular 'It wasn't that the brand was bad, it's just that it lacked any sense of emotion'. His solution was to communicate the philosophy of the company through a campaign of highly engaging commercials that never showed a car. This is heresy to most car marketers, for whom, in Thompson's words, 'A car ad is a winding road, squealing noises and you get the job, get laid, or get to a great destination'. But committing this heresy certainly worked for Honda:

> On the day I started in that particular role, a Honda Civic was a £9,000 price-cut special edition and it ranked number four in the retail market. And on the day I left, the Honda Civic's average sales price was £16,500 and it was number one in the retail market. (Simon Thompson, Chief Marketing Officer, Lastminute.com, formerly Motorola and Honda)

Evidence once again of the immense benefit of having your fundamental business objectives clearly understood, before embarking on any marketing activity.

Although awareness is no longer the dominant communications objective among most brands at this mature category life stage (which should be good for business), building brand image takes over and there is a general tightening of focus on fewer objectives (which will be bad for business). Here we need to draw a clear distinction between the *benefits* of focus when it comes to customer perceptions of the brand and the *drawbacks* of focus when it comes to the objectives and metrics of the brand. We saw how simplifying the consumer proposition was a huge benefit for Marks & Spencer. But it would be a mistake to assume that the logical corollary of that is that brands should measure little and have very few objectives. It is not true of M&S and it is certainly not true of another retail success story:

Tesco. Tesco is perhaps the ultimate mass-market brand. It has set out to appeal to all sections of the population and to do so deeply. This cannot be achieved with limited metrics.

> This is not a brand run purely on instinct, this is a brand run on quite a large number of things that we look at. And we look at them regularly, and we look at them in a fair amount of detail. So I have 'customer insight', which is less to do with pure market research focus groups, but it embodies all of our studies in terms of consumer dynamics from data, which we get through Clubcard. It involves all the feedback we get via our customer question times in stores, where we get customers to come in. Every store will run at least one a year where we just get feedback from the people who shop in those particular stores and from our call centres in Dundee. But we obviously measure trade, and trade's a great indicator of how healthy your brand is. There's no point in you pretending that everybody thinks your brand is in really good health if actually your trade's not good. So trade tends to be a very good early indicator. But we will also segment customers: because we want to service a broad church, you can't look at it as an amorphous mass. You have to break it down and say, well, actually, what do people think if they're less affluent? What do people think if they've got families? What do people think if they're old versus they're young? The north versus the south? The urban versus rural? So we have quite a comprehensive segmentation, so that we can then monitor whether people are happy with our quality, or happy with our prices, or happy with our service, or happy with our availability, and those would be core things that we would end up looking at on a weekly, monthly basis. And then once a year we do a brand review, which would go into more depth on particular issues. So, in the current climate some people are confident, some people are less confident, some people are challenged, some people have different priorities, and therefore you get in underneath people's ambitions or insecurities in life. Our role in life, our role in society are important, given that we touch quite a large proportion of the population. Those would be things that, on either a six-monthly or annual basis, would be an MOT, a health check of the brand to see whether there were any emerging issues that you couldn't see if you just looked at the top line. It's a sort of MRI scan – there's no obvious signs of ill health but you better give it a full thorough check, because by the time you can see a problem it might already be a bigger problem than you've imagined. So we tend to view prevention as important as cure. (Richard Brasher, Commercial and Trading Director, Tesco)

Much has been written about how Tesco is a business driven by data and clearly the Clubcard has been a major provider of those data. Indeed, it is apparent that the major business benefit of the Clubcard lies in the information it provides to Tesco to help it run the business in a more customer-focused way, rather than as a loyalty scheme. The trick that Tesco has mastered so well is in managing and using the data: it puts the customer in the driving seat and keeps the business humble. Humility is not a quality of Tesco that the media like to talk about, but it is very apparent at HQ (and in particular in its architecture and interior decor):

I can tell you that if I drop the ball, customers notice, and they go somewhere else. I can monitor that if the quality of my produce isn't right, they punish me. If my availability is not good enough, they punish me. And we very much view the consumer as being in charge. Not this idea of 'well now, we're big, we can pull the drawbridge up and we can just dictate terms'. Anyone who thinks that is in a completely alternative universe. (Richard Brasher, Commercial and Trading Director, Tesco)

So one of the many lessons from Tesco is that multiple objectives and multiple metrics are key to profitable growth, especially in a mature category where growth can be hard to find. The IPA dataBANK analyses showed that this was true for brands in general – it is not merely a consequence of being a world-class retailer.

Differentiation in mature categories remains an important objective but has unwisely fallen back in prevalence among all brands. At this time more than any other, brands need to be innovating in every sense: in their products and services, in the way they are brought to market and in the way they represent themselves. Mature categories are sometimes described as 'low interest' ones, because consumers are very familiar with them and difficult to inspire. Brands in mature categories sometimes hide behind this, using it as an excuse not to seek to create surprise. It may be a cliché that 'there is no such thing as a low interest category, only low interest brands', but like all clichés it is built on a truth, which brands would do well to remember as their category matures.

For most brands at this stage, not only has differentiation fallen back as an objective, but so too has building quality perceptions, albeit slightly (Figure 21.4). This is most unwise: in almost 50 per cent of cases in mature categories where there was a major shift in quality perceptions, so too was there major profit growth. Only major shifts in brand fame can match this and, as we saw earlier, fame is generally the best objective to have. Unfortunately, fame too has diminished as an objective amid the generally tighter focus on fewer objectives.

There can be few brands that needed to raise quality perceptions as greatly as Skoda did in 2000 (or that used 'fame' with such success to do so). Despite launching a brand new car – the Octavia – in 1998, under VW stewardship, design and quality controls, the marque languished as a source of 'bad car' jokes in the UK. There were many of these, but perhaps the most illustrative of the problem facing the brand was this one:

Q: How do you double the value of a Skoda?
A: Fill the tank!

Despite a £10 million launch campaign only two and a half thousand Octavias were sold in 1998. Not a ROMI (return on marketing investment) most CMOs or indeed CFOs would wish to be associated with. The Skoda marketing

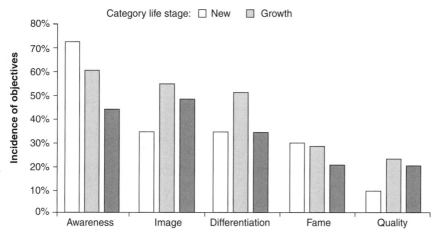

Figure 21.4 Brands start to aim low in mature categories
Source: IPA dataBANK

director expressed the scale of the problem in a succinct and stimulating way to the agencies pitching to re-launch his brand:

> Chris Hawken just said, 'Look, the nub of the problem is this. We've had children crying in our showrooms… when they've realized that dad is serious about getting a Skoda'. (Laurence Green, Chairman, Fallon London)

Wisely, the team at Fallon decided to take the widespread *emotional* rejection of the brand head-on, rather than trying to *persuade* people that it was time to re-evaluate the brand with facts about the product:

> Any sort of persuasion strategy still leads you to 'yes, but it's still a Skoda'. And every time we began to explore it, every time we talked about it, you were always left going, 'but it's still a Skoda'. So however great the campaign and line, it would still have been flawed. (Laurence Green, Chairman, Fallon London)

Instead the agency developed a highly successful campaign that acknowledged the fact that the brand was a joke, but humorously revealed the joke to be blind prejudice. In so doing the campaign made the brand's detractors appear out of touch:

> What the commercials very quickly did was make them [the detractors] look stupid and so you kind of reposition everybody, because the people in those commercials who hold the anti-Skoda prejudice are actually the nation. So I think when people saw them in their living rooms, they realized they were being as prejudiced and dopey as the stooges in the advertising. Very quickly, they don't want to hold that position. (Laurence Green, Chairman, Fallon London)

The new Fabia.
It's a Skoda. Honest.

Figure 21.5 The Fallon London campaign that revivified perceptions of Skoda
Reproduced by kind permission of Skoda

The advertising was enriched with some clever direct mail: 10,000 Skoda badges were mailed to prospects in a little box emblazoned with the words 'Live with it for a little while and see how you feel' (Figure 21.6 opposite).

Although the campaign was intended to launch a new model – the Fabia (which it did extremely effectively) – it was in fact the re-launch of the whole marque. Sales of the previously undesirable Octavia also flourished. But looking back at success tends to minimize the bravery of the decision by the marketing team to run a campaign that gives airtime to those prejudices. It was the right thing to do in the circumstances of the brand and the category, but the marketing director had to lay his career on the line to sell the campaign to a sceptical general management who did not see this as a good way of raising quality perceptions.

What Skoda provides is an elegant example of the power of emotional marketing to alter quality perceptions of a brand and they have continued in that vein (Figure 21.5). But brands in mature categories are in general far too little concerned about improving quality perceptions.

To cap it all, there is less use of emotions in advertising in mature categories, as some marketers, feeling the growing pressure to be able to demonstrate that they are making some progress, unwisely reach for rational persuasion. Rational marketing messages may be easy to measure in the marketplace, but they are inefficient sales engines, as we saw in Chapter 17.

Figure 21.6 Badge DM, Archibald Ingall Stretton
Reproduced by kind permission of Skoda

Delivering these rational messages, celebrity and testimonial advertising grow in prevalence despite the fact that these creative approaches are the least effective of those examined in the dataBANK (see the report 'Marketing in the era of accountability'. This is a time of uncertainty and unclear thinking.

The launch of Cravendale Milk provides a rare opportunity to compare the results of rational and emotional advertising in a mature category. The brand launched, initially following the model that had worked in Canada, with rational advertising stressing the fresher-tasting and longer-lasting benefits of this filtered milk over normal milk. It soon became apparent that the launch was not going to meet its business targets, and for a number of reasons directly connected with the rational approach:

> The advertising went largely unnoticed in the beginning, but among those people who *did* notice, we found we had prompted a rational response. As a result, we opened the door to a whole host of questions. For example, people were saying, 'Well OK, it lasts longer. But just what exactly have you done to good, standard milk that we've been happy with for hundreds of years, to make it last longer?' Confronting people with a host of rational benefits was asking for trouble, because people were fundamentally happy with milk and didn't see anything wrong with the existing product. Engaging rational thought processes had simply invited people to question how we'd 'meddled' with their milk. (Elisa Edmonds, Strategy Director, DDB London)

So in addition to the general finding of the dataBANK that rational communications are less effective, Cravendale encountered an unforeseen downside to the application of product-benefit advertising to a natural product. The solution came out of the dual recognition that a more impactful approach was necessary that could jerk consumers out of their existing purchasing and that an *emotional* dramatization of the superior taste could unlock the true potential of the brand:

> Just asserting great taste is never a great way to communicate taste. I can't think of a single campaign for food that just asserts great taste successfully; it must in some way bring great taste to life in a surprising manner. (Elisa Edmonds, Strategy Director, DDB London)

The subsequent, much more successful advertising got right back to basics with an amusing campaign featuring a bunch of cows who wanted their milk back, because it tasted too good to give to humans.

And once again the benefit of a strong brand idea is that it helps the development of strong integrated communications: an engaging door drop was created consisting of a ransom note from 'The Cows'.

Brand awareness leapt and so did sales – a characteristic emotional 'double whammy' of greater impact and stronger persuasiveness. Sadly, in mature categories relatively few brands avail themselves of this opportunity.

Consistent with the reduction in use of emotional marketing in mature categories, likeability of advertising falls back in perceived importance while rational 'persuasion scores' grow in prevalence as an evaluation measure of advertising. Neither is a good development for effectiveness.

Media and channel diversity hit an all-time low as conservatism and risk avoidance grow. Partly mitigating the damaging effects of this, TV's dominance strengthens to the point where it typically consumes almost 60 per cent of the budget. Even the internet's role in mature markets weakens to around 3 per cent of a typical budget. Apart from TV, only the press medium makes it into double figures in terms of share of budget. This is not a time of radical change for most brands: they are largely sticking to their knitting and hanging on in there.

Pre-testing of advertising remains commonplace but there is a decline in quantitative pre-testing at this stage of a category's life and a growth in qualitative pre-testing. Perhaps marketers are hoping that insights gleaned in qualitative research will sprinkle magic dust over their campaign, though the evidence of the dataBANK is that it rarely happens. Quantitative measurement of advertising effects remains widespread as the pressure for accountability is intensified, with no easy growth coming through to calm nerves. But with costs generally being pared back, there is slightly less focus on learning than before and even campaign tracking falls back slightly in prevalence.

Collateral effects of advertising appear to become less important to brands, with the exception of employee satisfaction and productivity, such is the focus on cost and efficiency at this stage in the life of the category.

In many ways these mature years are the dark ages for brands: the crucible of market decline has yet to forge the bold imaginative plays that will ensure brand immortality. The era is characterized by relative conservatism and risk-aversion.

So for brands grinding it out in mature categories, what does the IPA dataBANK suggest should be the key metrics for success?

Consumer metrics check-list for brands in mature categories

Leading indicators:

1. Brand fame – perceived brand momentum is invaluable in a sluggish category
2. Perceived quality (however it may be defined in the category)
3. Emotional brand differentiation and engagement
4. Perceived innovativeness (not just product news, but in a rounded sense)
5. SOV – SOM

Lagging indicators:

1. Price sensitivity
2. Value market share
3. Penetration of usage/conquest users
4. Innovations' share of sales
5. Profitability

Cravendale is a good example of a new brand launching successfully into a mature market.

CASE HISTORY: Cravendale. Cash from Cows: How Integrated Communication Built a Premium Milk Brand

Elisa Edmonds, Sara Donoghugh, Justin Notley, Les Binet and Sarah Carter, Gold, IPA Effectiveness Awards 2004

How can you better milk? How can you break extraordinarily entrenched buying behaviour? How can you persuade people to pay more for a version of something they feel perfectly happy with? This is a story of how Arla built a new premium milk brand worth £41m from a standing start.

PurFilter, a process whereby milk is passed through a fine ceramic filter, and therefore contains fewer bacteria than standard milk, had been a success in Canada. Nevertheless, Arla recognized that the British market would be tough to crack. The main points of difficulty were that the market was unbranded; people were not used to making choices or paying a premium for milk; the product was undifferentiated; milk was a low-interest commodity category; the basic quality of the product was high; and milk stands for natural goodness, so the notion of improved milk raised suspicions of tampering. If that weren't enough, Cravendale was an unknown brand with no heritage or equity to leverage and yet needed to command a substantial price premium.

Arla's long-term objective was to establish Cravendale as a top 30 grocery brand by 2008, ie growing brand value to £60–65 million – in the same league as Whiskas and Nescafé Gold Blend. The scale of the task was such that Arla decided to take a 'test and learn' approach by rolling out Cravendale regionally, in four waves.

The first campaign centred around 'Mr Hinchcliffe', an enthusiastic Cravendale spokesman who keeps trying to prove that Cravendale PurFilter stays fresh longer, but is constantly foiled by people who can't resist their craving to drink the milk. However, although sales grew, the performance wasn't strong. Why? The research showed that the advertising lacked impact, the message and targeting lacked focus and the campaign lacked appeal. Cravendale had to perform or it would be withdrawn.

It was decided to focus on families, focus on taste and make Cravendale stand out in stores. The new creative idea was simple but perfect: cows are experts on great-tasting milk, and because it tastes so great they want it back.

The cows idea was far more powerful, engaging, impactful and efficient than Mr Hinchcliffe. Brand awareness jumped. Cravendale is now a big brand, worth £41 million. This puts Cravendale well on its way to making the Grocery Top 30 list. At current growth rates it should achieve its objective by the end of 2005, three years ahead of schedule. We can also prove from econometrics that the activity paid for itself: every £1 spent on BTL activity delivered an additional £1.10 profit. Advertising's payback was even higher: every £1 spent on TV delivered £1.30 extra profit.

There were three fundamental factors that explain Cravendale's success. 'The Cows Want It Back' is an excellent example of a strong, focused idea that was able to work across channels in a highly efficient manner. The ultimate value of this idea is reflected in the incremental profit it generated. The value of a robust channel strategy and creative consistency had huge impact on the success of the campaign. Finally, continuous evaluation also helped Cravendale learn along the way. Without that, Cravendale wouldn't be around today.

When Arla set out to shake up the milk market in 1998, everything was stacked against them. There was no British precedent for what they planned to do. Cravendale successfully overcame the hurdles and Arla is now in the happy position of needing to invest again – £20 million on a new factory to produce more Cravendale:

> In a market that is about habitual purchase and low involvement, confronting someone with a boring rational message as to why you should buy an alternative product to what you were already perfectly happy with is not a great way to break people out of their current behaviour. I think you need to go beyond that; you need to engage with their emotions. Our failure to do so was basically the problem. There were other issues as well, such as lack of single-minded focus on a message, but I actually think that it was the rational approach that just didn't work for people. It simply didn't engage their emotions.
>
> What's relevant to children is great-tasting milk. We discovered that lots of children don't like the taste of milk. Of course, mums want to get milk into children and children consume milk in situations where the taste of it is far more noticeable, that is, on cereal and drunk neat (as opposed to in tea as with adults). So that helped to focus the benefit on great taste as well.
>
> Obviously the whole rational campaign with Mr Hinchcliffe was just not working. So this new brief was written, focused around taste, with a strong pointer to the creatives on tonality. We identified we'd need to do something radically different, to move away from the conventions of the category in order to break people out of their current behaviour, to make them sit up and take notice and think differently about milk. The result, I'm happy to say, was the 'Cows Want It Back' idea. (Elisa Edmonds, Strategy Director, DDB London)

Honda is a good example of a brand strengthening its position successfully in a mature market.

CASE HISTORY: Honda – What Happened when Honda Started Asking Questions?

Stuart Smith, Gold, IPA Effectiveness Awards, 2004

Honda had been selling cars in the UK for 29 years. Not many knew. Or cared. Even Honda owners felt compelled to justify their choice, with 'I drive a Honda because...' instead of the proudly simpler 'I drive a Honda'. They were buying them for the perfectly rational reason that the cars were excellent. Trouble is, 'rational' is in the same neighbourhood as 'sensible', which is only a few doors away from 'dull'. The business goal was simple but challenging: to grow annual sales to 100,000 units by the end of 2005. In March 2002 the figure stood at less than 67,000.

In a market littered with launches and product news, Honda decided to inspire people about their belief in 'The Power of Dreams'. This vision came directly from, and celebrated the values of, the company's creator, Soichiro Honda. The Book of Dreams merged creative strategy with execution. The integration of 'what we say' and 'how we say it' early in the process was fundamental to its value. It was fashioned around Honda reality and defined a unique voice for the brand. It illuminated Honda's philosophy and way of behaving, while creating a distinctive look, feel and even vocabulary.

People went out of their way to engage with this campaign; Cog was downloaded 2.3m times from Honda.co.uk. People knew more about Honda, knew the right things about Honda, which increased desire to own one.

Communications generated £388 million revenue for Honda, sales have increased by 28 per cent and the campaign generated, at a conservative estimate, £84 million of extra profit for Honda. The paper shows that the idea became more powerful when people were exposed to it both above and below the line. The campaign changed the way people felt about Honda, prompting more people to consider and actually purchase a Honda vehicle. Beyond incremental sales of more than 22,000 new cars, there is the positive impact the campaign has had on dealers, staff turnover, current owners and even used cars.

The most commonly used word in the world is 'OK'. A word which means all right. Satisfactory. Not bad. Not everybody believes that OK is OK. Honda certainly doesn't.

Skoda is a good example of a brand repositioning successfully in a mature market.

CASE HISTORY: Skoda – 'It's a Skoda. Honest.': The Profitable Return on Brave Communication

Laurence Green and Felicity Morgan, Best New Agency prize, IPA Effectiveness Awards, 2002

This paper relates to the turnaround of a brand so maligned that until very recently the very notion of an IPA submission on its behalf would have had a marketing audience bracing themselves for the inevitable Skoda joke. In brief, the ridiculed brand and ailing business stumbled on a decent car and radical advertising, which enabled the VW Group's ugly duckling to be reborn a swan.

In the late 1980s a partnership with Volkswagen bore fruit in the form of the Felicia, a car impressive enough to win seven consecutive *What Car?* magazine's 'Budget Car of the Year' Awards. Though Skoda was ridiculed as a brand, its UK sales grew through the mid-1990s and extraordinary levels of loyalty were achieved.

However, no one could argue that the Skoda brand was ill-defined or its franchise particularly open to competitive incursion. But nor could it be argued that Skoda was making genuine inroads against the broader consumer base; rejection figures for the new brand remained stubbornly fixed at around 60 per cent over the period. As the brand's future product reality became more obvious, it was apparent that Skoda's image deficiencies would soon become a critical commercial limitation. Higher-quality, more expensively priced cars would be rolling off the production line (as VW moved to a shared platform production strategy), so Skodas would have to compete for different consumers and against a new competitive set. Skoda's brand rehabilitation in the UK was not just a matter of pride, but a commercial imperative.

The launch of the Octavia in 1998, despite the car being praised by *What Car?*, was a failure. This was because of strategy; the Octavia's marketing had been model-specific and product-centric, targeting the small band of brand considerers. Skoda was behaving like a brand without a problem rather than facing the truth and addressing the stigma.

There were two key strategic building blocks in the Fabia launch:

- a new role for advertising: use the Fabia to confront the biggest barrier to buying a Skoda, ie the irrational prejudice against the brand;
- a new target audience: create a general shift in attitudes so that potential buyers feel confident they can choose a Skoda without being laughed at.

The advertising objectives and strategy were well understood, but the consumer, of course, sees neither. The creative response to the brief, summarized in the line 'It's a Skoda. Honest', turned ambitions into tangible reality. Skoda would make advertising featuring people who still thought Skoda's cars were poor. Gently ridiculing these people would lead the consumer to conclude that he or she wasn't 'one of them'. The creative work didn't so much reposition the brand as reposition the consumer's attitude to the brand.

The first evidence of in-market effectiveness came from an unlikely source, the campaign being voted top of *Campaign*'s 'People's Jury'. Some plaudit for a much maligned brand, but no use if the campaign was failing to win minds as well as hearts. Given the ambition to publicly reshape the brand's reputation, a truer measure of effectiveness was the apparent sea-change in attitudes towards the brand in the national press, which coincided with the advertising and PR efforts.

Since the Fabia launch, volume growth has easily outstripped the market, winning record share for the brand. In the years 2000 and 2001 there was an incremental revenue uplift of £185m and a profit uplift of £18.5m. The total marketing spend over the period was £15.4m.

The Octavia was re-launched in 2001, with a smaller budget than for the launch. This was a complete success, with a long-term profit of £8.9m against a budget of £5.2m. So without taking into account the value of considerers who have not purchased yet, the Octavia's halo effect on overall brand consideration, dealer profits or profits from parts and maintenance, the Octavia marketing still pays back handsomely:

> I think this brand was so broken there was not an incremental way back. I don't think modern timescales allow it, but even if they did, I don't think you can do it partially; I think you do have to do it profoundly.
>
> We backed the brief up to something like 'Skodas are better than you think', which actually was the right start point because it was something evidence-based that acknowledged what people thought about it. And the truth is, everything we did in those first couple of years drew all of its power from acknowledging what people thought, rather than anything else. Rather than product shots, end lines, you know, it was all a pure sort of communication power of 'We know what you think; think again'.
>
> For the last couple of years we've been in a 'How do you build business quickly on a relatively small budget and occupy distinctive advertising territory and cut through all that on a small budget? kind of thing. We've found some niche requirements that are particularly well served by Skoda's models, so you might have seen a fat gymnast dancing across the gym hall, and the end line to that is 'Big and agile? You don't see that very often!' They are not leaders in anything, because they're a small brand, but the speech was 'Be the leader in the big and agile category'. We'll create niches that you're the leader in because otherwise you're the 14th biggest brand in the medium sector. (Laurence Green, Chairman, Fallon London)

Branston Baked Beans is a good example of a brand stretching and launching successfully into a mature market (Figure 21.7).

Figure 21.7 Branston beans, The Big Kick
Reproduced by kind permission of DLKW and Branston

CASE HISTORY: Branston Baked Beans — How Going Head to Head with the Brand Leader Created a World where Beanz Also Meanz Branston in Just Three Months

Lisa Conway, Steven Gregory, Steve Marinker, Rhona Hurcombe and Barbara Holgate, Silver, IPA Effectiveness Awards, 2006

Premier Foods had just three months to make a success of the Branston Baked Beans launch or face an annual revenue shortfall of £15m. To rocket-launch the brand we had to change entrenched consumer behaviour overnight. There was only one way to achieve this: taking the brand leader head-on. This paper will prove how bravery in battle reaps rewards. In just three months we had created a new baked bean brand worth in excess of £14 million, and on course to be worth £30 million by the end of the year.

There are three main reasons why this is such a difficult sector in which to launch a new brand.

- There is a dominant brand leader. Beanz Meanz Heinz.
- Own label accounts for 25 per cent of the market and quality has improved significantly, while cost compared to Heinz has decreased.
- There are ingrained consumer habits.

The strategy decided upon was straightforward: develop a product that was better than Heinz, with the strongest brand name available. Premier developed a new baked bean with a richer, thicker tomato sauce. Meanwhile, a brand from Premier Foods' stable, with a reputation for big taste and big personality, was chosen to support it: Branston. In the orange corner, at 41p, was Branston. In the turquoise corner, also at 41p, was Heinz.

From initial taste tests we knew that the way to convert people to Branston was simply by getting them to try our beans versus Heinz. But we couldn't afford to sample the whole nation. The Great British Bean Poll was born. This was a real-life poll, inviting Britain to decide on the nation's best baked beans. All they had to do was to try Branston Beans versus their regular choice and vote for their favourite. The conditions were ripe for the Bean Poll. Britain loves beans. Britain loves voting (the more trivial the subject the better). And Britain certainly loves an underdog. The idea captured the fun of baked beans, and if Branston was prepared to let people decide for themselves which product was better, and publicly risk its reputation, then it must have an amazing product.

Ultimately, 76 per cent of those who voted chose Branston. All commercial targets were exceeded by an average of 70 per cent. In three months, Branston had become the number two brand and gained widespread respect. The campaign is also estimated to have produced a payback of £12.75 million on a £3.5 million investment.

22 Declining categories

These are the key points from this chapter:

- The only brands that generally prosper in declining categories are the leaders, or strong challengers.
- Survival for smaller brands in a declining category depends on finding pastures new.
- Reducing price sensitivity and the use of emotions in communications is more prevalent and more essential in this category life stage.
- Success for the large brands in a declining category is more dependent than ever on radical change through re-launches or repositionings.
- Olivio/Bertolli, Marmite and Hovis are inspiring case studies on how to survive and prosper in declining markets.

At the beginning of the book we pointed out that many of the most prevalent business school and management consultancy tools, in particular the Boston Matrix, regard businesses in declining markets as 'Dogs' to be disposed of. So if ever there was to be a challenge to the thesis that brands can be immortal, this market life stage presents it. If a brand can survive and thrive in such an intractable context, and not necessarily by skipping frog-like over the lily pads to another, sunnier place in the pond, then surely the case is made?

In fact there are slightly more IPA case studies proving success in declining markets than there are in new ones. The difference may not be large but it demonstrates two important points: categories rarely decline in growing economies and *all is not lost* when they do. So, as with new markets, while our sample size for analysis is limited, there are still lessons to be learnt from these few gems.

Although categories may be in decline for many years before they are quietly laid to rest, their attractiveness to brand investment is likely to die long before the category does. And not without reason. Growth is now very difficult: the gradient of the share growth versus excess share of voice line has flattened considerably. Successful brands can only hope to achieve 1 percentage point of share growth for every 12 percentage points that their share of voice is ahead of their share of market, whereas in mature markets the ratio was 1 : 8.

It is also immediately clear from the data that the only brands that generally prosper in declining categories are the big brands: around 80 per cent of the IPA case studies at this category life stage are for leader brands or strong challenger brands – ie brands with a strong but not a leadership position (Figure 22.1). This is in marked contrast with growth categories, where they only account for around 36 per cent of case studies of success. Even in mature categories, leader and strong challenger brands only accounted for around 60 per cent of case studies, so a significant lengthening of the odds of success has occurred. If ever the saying 'get big, or get out' were true, it is in declining markets.

The effectiveness success rate – the success rate of brands in generating any very large business effects – has fallen by almost a quarter in proportional terms since the already low level seen in mature categories (Figure 22.2). It now stands at a little over half the level it was in new categories and is, not surprisingly, at an all-time low of any category life stage.

It is to a degree inevitable that as a category shrinks, the economies of scale make life especially tough for smaller brands and few will have the resources to mount a significant marketing putsch. Survival for these brands will depend

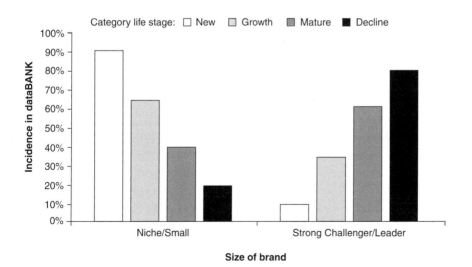

Figure 22.1 The odds strongly favour big brands in declining categories
Source: IPA dataBANK

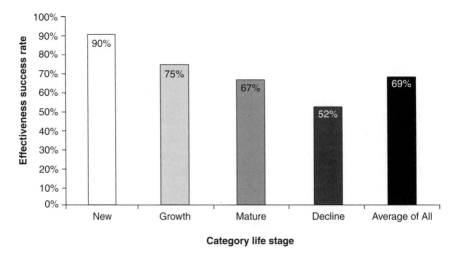

Figure 22.2 Effectiveness is difficult in declining categories
Source: IPA dataBANK

on finding new pastures to graze. And clearly many, but not all, do. Brands do die needlessly at this stage, be they packaged holiday companies faced with the explosion of low-cost airlines, music retailers faced with MP3 downloads, or ale brands faced with the onslaught of lagers (and now cider). Happily, there are many examples of brands that found pastures new: like Imperial Leather, which was reborn as a shower gel range exploiting its luxury heritage when faced with the decline of traditional soaps – though for many, this is more about survival than growth. Nevertheless, there is evidence of this cycle of brand rebirth among the success stories of the dataBANK: of the 40 or so brands that re-launched or repositioned in new or growth categories, more than half came from categories or segments that were at best low-growth. This is undoubtedly the most common, and ultimately most certain, route to immortality for brands faced with the decline of their category. But not all brands turn and run in this situation: some refuse to accept the death of the category and fight on to restore life with the defibrillator of marketing innovation. The remainder of this chapter is about these fighters.

Activity in declining categories is more important than ever: there may be very few successful brand launches (after all, who would want to launch a brand?) but success for brands is more dependent than ever on being re-launched or repositioned (Figure 22.3). Radical change is called for.

Copy experimentation continues and there is renewed interest in media experimentation, but the dataBANK demonstrates that it will take more than tinkering with an existing campaign to turn a brand around amid the enveloping decline. It is as if the challenge of decline has re-energized the successful brands that remain and given them a new determination and willingness to take risks.

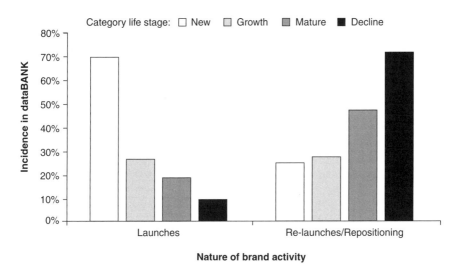

Figure 22.3 The odds strongly favour re-launches and repositionings in declining categories
Source: IPA dataBANK

There can be few better examples of this than Marmite. Who would have rated the chances of turning around a salty residue of the brewing industry, traditionally targeted at infants, at a time of heightened concern about dietary salt? Other brands (such as Bovril and Australia's Vegemite) appear to have long since given up, content to eke out a dwindling presence in the diets of their residual, ageing users. The 2003 Vegemite campaign certainly has a faint whiff of managed decline about it (Figure 22.4).

Figure 22.4 Vegemite advertisement,
JWT Melbourne
Reproduced by kind permission of
Vegemite/Kraft Foods Australia

By contrast, the Marmite team decided to take the bull by the horns and shake consumers out of their growing indifference to the brand:

> We felt the market was turning against us, I think the breakfast market has been in decline now for years and years, and the spreads market has been in decline for years. I would say it was radical what we did with Marmite. What they were doing with it beforehand wasn't. It was pretty radical because it was a different target audience: it was young adults. It was a different message because we weren't talking about the growing-up spread, we weren't talking about it being good for you, we were talking about the taste. And it was designed to be quite disruptive, and to make people look again, so it was actively designed to say, 'it's not the cosy safe thing you thought it was'. You need something provocative that you're going to get people either to disagree or agree with, if you're going to give people something to belong to. (Lucy Jameson, Executive Strategy Director, DDB London)

But crucially the team realized that there is a huge potential trap in trying to reinvent a brand:

> If you're a brand with a load of heritage, you kind of owe it to yourself and to everyone else to use that wisely. I think you run the danger of being fake if you don't have some truth to it at the core. There are so many brands that try and reinvent themselves and just look really naff. You can look really bad when you try and reinvent yourself without some truth to it. (Lucy Jameson, Executive Strategy Director, DDB London)

And so the love/hate campaign was born out of the *truth* of the polarizing nature of the taste of Marmite (Figure 22.5). The team found that the huge value of this insight lay in its ability to motivate lapsed users as well as reinforce existing users, both of which loved the idea.

We mentioned the sale of Birds Eye earlier on, but it deserves a more detailed examination here. Permira's decision to buy the brand from Unilever demonstrated a belief that the brand could be given a new relevance to consumers and that the cause of frozen foods was not lost in the face of the relentless march of chilled foods. The Birds Eye team at Unilever shared this belief too and had identified that they needed to change the consumer view of the category. To do this would take the brand outside of the Unilever comfort zone:

> It became very clear that the pro-freezing messages we wanted to get across to people were, when understood, very powerful, and made them think differently about their attitude to frozen *and* chilled foods. The ideas undermined their confidence in chilled, and increased their confidence in frozen because these messages were disturbing, both to consumers and to others with vested interests. One ad about artificial colourants had salmon farms up in arms, but was adjudged by the ASA to be quite accurate and fair; Unilever felt that this was overly aggressive as an approach. Only once the sale was announced did

Figure 22.5 Marmite Hate/Mate jars
Reproduced by kind permission of Unilever

we get the freedom to take the gloves off and do what was really needed. We had an idea that said, 'Would you cook a meal and then put it in the fridge for two weeks before you ate it? No! But that's what you do with chilled food.' Though again the facts were accurate, both Unilever and regulators stymied that thought. (Jerry Wright, former Marketing and Innovation Director, Birds Eye UK)

Despite these concerns, Jerry Wright's new Birds Eye team came out fighting, with a stream of innovation that grew revenue by 15 per cent and the 'Truth' campaign that challenged consumers' views about frozen versus chilled foods (see Figure 7.2 on page 49).

Despite this promising start, Unilever decided to sell the business to Permira:

One of the reasons Birds Eye was sold was that it isn't operating in a market that by its very nature can be managed as a global business. The new Unilever business and organizational model works when you manage things across boundaries, where consumer habits are broadly the same, where the competitive framework is broadly the same and where you need to take a few big bets on the R&D programme. Take washing powder as a good example. If P&G pops up with a new product in France, it will also appear in Argentina as well. It's pretty much the case that if you go to Italy you find people do their washing in largely the same way as they do in the UK, using the same sorts of products on similar sorts of clothes in similar machines. Scale is critical to success, particularly with heavy R&D investments, and finding a new product idea or technology that works in a lot of different markets is both possible and necessary.

However, if you're in the frozen food business, you are in a market where national cultural differences across countries are significant and in which the core of the national cuisine is diverse. If you look at the frozen food portfolio in Italy, Germany and the UK, they're very, very different. They have fish fingers in common, but little else; the biggest-selling vegetable in the UK is peas, by a country mile, and in Germany it's spinach. Cod and haddock are Britain's favourite frozen fish, but they are not popular in Italy, and so on across all the various market sectors.

To run frozen food successfully you need to be quite agile and more like a retailer, fleet of foot. You put things into the range, see if they work, take them out if they don't, and 'churn' recipes and variants. By contrast, the Unilever system is more about 'Let's decide on what the two or three big hits are that we launch everywhere and stick to them', and so frozen foods didn't really fit that business model.

I think another factor in the Birds Eye sale was that frozen food wasn't a global business for Unilever, it's only a European one, and it wasn't even everywhere in Europe.

It was also true that, historically, business growth targets hadn't been reached in a market that was declining, but I think the jury's still out on whether the future will reflect that past downward trend. Chilled food has done well, but it doesn't have to be that way. Increasingly a number of people believe that frozen has the ability to grow again, as the superiority of freezing as a preservation system over chilling becomes clearer to consumers. And there are already signs in 2007 that the frozen food market *is* starting to grow again. (Jerry Wright, former Marketing and Innovation Director, Birds Eye UK)

Innovation and the creation of news is a common element in the success of many brands in declining categories – whether Marmite's heart-shaped single-serve packs, love/hate jars, and squeezable dispenser (Figure 22.6), Birds Eye's frozen soya beans, PG Tips pyramid teabags, or Hovis's radical repackaging of its traditional loaf (and of course its extension into more buoyant bakery segments).

Of course, the business case for investment in a major initiative in a contracting market will be weak, so much of the activity in declining categories tends to be relatively low cost and thus seldom enough to revitalize the category, but it can help a brand eke out a few extra years of profitability. As we have seen, achieving major business results in general has become extremely difficult and simply hanging on to volume in the face of adversity is as much as some brands aspire to. Defensive objectives are almost *de rigueur* in declining categories and by a considerable margin the most common objective (Figure 22.7).

Brands become focused on what they are trying to avoid happening rather than on what might be. While understandable, this is not a helpful frame of mind: the big success stories (like Marmite) are hardly defensive actions – they are bold and determined.

Les Binet, Chief Econometrician at DDB Matrix, sees another, more insidious threat from this introspective defensive mindset:

Figure 22.6 Marmite squeezy
Reproduced by kind permission of Unilever

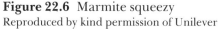
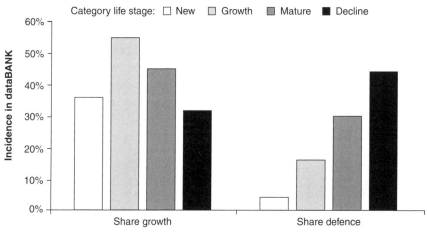

Figure 22.7 Defensive objectives become common in declining categories
Source: IPA dataBANK

> Supposedly, if you put a frog into cold water and then slowly heat the water up, you can actually boil it alive because it never jumps out. So the real problem is that if you are in a slowly declining category, then from year to year there seems no point in doing something as major as redefining the category. Brands tend to focus on whether a competitor is stealing share. (Les Binet, European Director, DDB Matrix)

Although big share movements are rare, with competition falling away under these market pressures, profit growth is not impossible for the determined marketer and the better-resourced larger brands: they are no less likely to achieve this than in mature categories. As competition declines, those that fight on may find fewer rewards, but also fewer obstacles.

So what is the secret of profit success within a declining category?

We have already seen that innovation is likely to be necessary, but it is unlikely to be sufficient. Loyalty effects continue to dwindle in importance – only 8 per cent of dataBANK brands have anything major to report here. Even new customer acquisition has become a less dominant driver of growth, though in some IPA Effectiveness cases brands do enjoy modest success in recruiting customers: presumably from failing or defeatist brands in the category.

But there are a number of clear developments in the patterns of success among brands in declining categories that we *can* learn from. Curiously, they do not stem from the objectives that brands set out with, as these rarely reflect what they actually achieve amid the uncertainty of declining categories. The first and perhaps most important development is a marked rise in the incidence of major reductions in price sensitivity. Figure 22.8 shows that this has risen to 12 per cent of cases, but given the difficulty of measuring price sensitivity it is likely to be a much more important factor in value and profit growth than is implied by this number. In part this will be driven by a decline in competition as weaker brands fall by the wayside, but evidently not entirely. Brand differentiation, fame and perceived quality have all suddenly leapt in incidence among successful brands at this category life stage: they are clearly contributory factors in the reduction of price sensitivity. They all improve *value* perceptions of the brand without the need to cut prices, an unaffordable option at this stage (Figure 22.9).

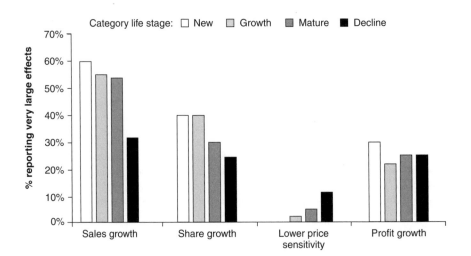

Figure 22.8 Share growth is tough but profit growth is still possible in declining categories
Source: IPA dataBANK

Another significant development is the sudden dramatic decline in the use of primarily rational communications in this final chapter of the category (from 41 per cent of cases in mature categories to 12 per cent of cases now) (Figure 22.10). Marketers, perhaps freed from some of the shackles of 'accountability' that unconstructively tied their hands in more closely scrutinized life stages, are now able to unleash the lethal force of emotions to revitalize brands.

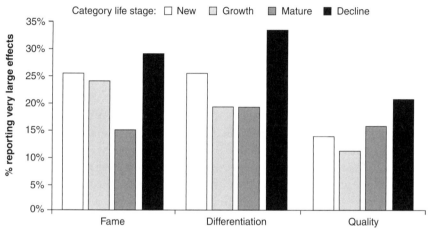

Figure 22.9 The drivers of brand profitability in declining categories
Source: IPA dataBANK

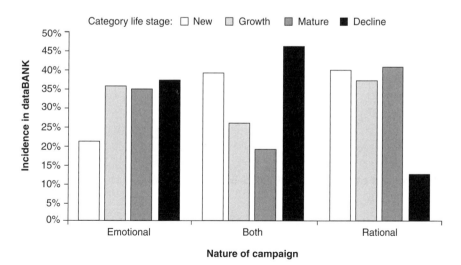

Figure 22.10 The use of rational communications plummets in declining categories
Source: IPA dataBANK

There is a suggestion that some brands discover the power of emotional advertising only at this stage in the category life cycle, when rational models are increasingly unable to deliver a return on investment. News-based advertising and other forms of rational persuasion are simply not up to the job at these demanding times, in part because the *major* product or service innovations upon which their efficacy is largely based are no longer viable. But also over 90 per cent of declining categories in the dataBANK have become 'high feel' ones where emotions are very important in brand choice. Product demonstration campaigns therefore become much less prevalent, in favour of more engaging creative approaches.

Media and channel experimentation resumes in earnest as brands seek ways to make limited budgets stretch further: these are among the most diverse channel users. TV's domination strengthens and is now the lead medium in 96 per cent of dataBANK case studies, typically accounting for around 60 per cent of budget, but the remaining 40 per cent is spread widely among the other channels available. Use of the internet as a communications channel widens to almost 60 per cent of brands. And usage of most communications channels except cinema also widens to levels seen among growth categories: in many ways category decline has brought on a new golden age of inventiveness in media deployment.

The use of all forms of pre-testing falls to their lowest levels in this era of constructive risk-taking, though quantitative evaluation remains strong. Qualitative research is now more in favour as a general learning tool, as brands seek to ride the emotional currents of the category and need techniques sensitive enough to help them to do so. In the complex system of a declining category, econometric modelling becomes more important as a means of determining the effect of marketing.

Collateral effects assume a much greater level of importance for these resource-poor brands. Media coverage, staff enthusiasm and multiplier effects in particular strengthen in importance, as brands seek to squeeze every last ounce of benefit from their budgets.

So, for brands fighting for life in declining categories, what does the IPA dataBANK suggest should be the key metrics for success?

Consumer metrics check-list for brands in declining categories

Leading indicators:

1. Emotional brand differentiation and engagement
2. Perceived quality (however it may be defined in the category)
3. Claimed usage
4. Brand fame – perceived brand authority will determine who survives
5. Perceived relevance (fuelled by innovation)
6. Staff enthusiasm for the brand
7. SOV – SOM

Lagging indicators:

1. Price sensitivity
2. Value market share
3. Penetration of usage/conquest users
4. Profitability

Olivio is a good example of a brand launching successfully into a declining market.

CASE HISTORY: Olivio Bertolli – 'Divided We Dine, United We Dream': How the UK Campaign for Olivio Spread across Borders against All Odds

Mike Holmes, Patricia McDonald and Helen Firth, Best International, IPA Effectiveness Awards, 2002

Food is one of the most difficult categories to internationalize. Different eating habits make developing international food advertising challenging, if not impossible. One man's meat is another man's poison. This paper demonstrates how Olivio spread and its continental equivalent, Bertolli, have developed successful international advertising in this most parochial of categories. By expressing a higher-order benefit, an idea about the way people want to live, rather than the way they want to eat, Olivio/Bertolli has created a powerful emotional resonance across markets. This campaign is a solution to one of the pressing business issues of the 21st century – how to sell the same brand in the same way to people who use it, buy it and understand it differently. Olivio/Bertolli's answer is to focus not on the realities that divide, but fantasies that unite. In the 1997–2001 international campaign for Olivio spread, the successful UK campaign was rolled out by Olivio (Unilever Bestfoods) and Bertolli into four key markets – the UK, Belgium, Germany and Holland. Food is thought to be especially susceptible to local and cultural influences; this paper shows that one campaign can work in many countries, if rooted in relevant emotional associations.

Olivio, the first spread to contain olive oil, was created in the UK by Unilever Bestfoods with a view to possible roll-out in other markets. After several years of steady growth in the UK, there was a clear conceptual model for how the advertising worked in the UK, borne out by statistical analysis. The campaign drove awareness and built engagement with the brand benefit. This drove trial, and the depth of the emotional connection would prompt triallists to talk about the brand, recruiting friends and family to Olivio. In this way, advertising drove a series of consistent steps upwards in growth. Building genuine emotional engagement was the single most important factor in driving success. At roll-out, we were initially unsure whether we could make the same emotional connection in other countries with very different attitudes to food.

In Belgium, yellow fats divide the nation. Butter dominates the French region, margarine the Flemish. The butter and margarine market is fragmented, with butter bought from local farms leading to a profusion of tiny local 'brands'. In Holland, margarine is used extensively for cooking, and shallow-frying liquid margarines are enjoying a new-found popularity. The Germans' preference for natural foods favours butter, while the margarine sector is less sophisticated and segmented than that in the UK. Curd cheese is also a popular alternative to spreads in Germany.

The key to a successful international roll-out lay in the breakthrough thinking behind the UK strategy. This was rooted in extensive analysis among opinion formers which unearthed a new trend – 'positive health'. The Mediterranean was seen as the cradle of 'positive health', conjuring images of happy, relaxed individuals enjoying life. More importantly for Olivio, olive oil was seen as the epitome of this Mediterranean lifestyle.

The original Olivio launch ads ran a rational longevity message, but this generic built the category, not the brand. At re-launch, olive oil became a symbol of the whole Mediterranean approach to life. Rather than selling generic long life, Olivio created a whole brand world based on the Mediterranean idyll of enjoying a longer, fuller life. Olivio's focus on higher-order benefits offered the key to extending the brand into other markets. Just as the Mediterranean dream could bypass everyday attitudes to food in the UK, it appeared to unite consumers across countries.

By end 2001, the brand had built critical mass in all four countries, and become Unilever Bestfoods' fastest-growing food brand in Europe. Growth came both from penetration and average weight of purchase. Econometric modelling shows that ad effects were a significant component of sales volume in all four markets, taking account of distribution, promotions and DM. The sales in each country were between 47.5 and 83.6 per cent higher than they would have been without advertising, and the ways the advertising should work were confirmed and achieved; it raised awareness, brand benefit was communicated, trial increased, and the brand was talked about. The international campaign also saved the company some £3 million in local executions.

The Olivio/Bertolli model offers an unconventional way of thinking about global advertising, as it did not start out as an international campaign. There was an eye to the long-term roll-out, but the immediate focus was to make it work in the UK.

Marmite is a good example of a brand strengthening its position in a declining category.

***

CASE HISTORY: Marmite – 'Please Don't Spread It Thinly'

Laurence Parkes and Les Binet, Silver, IPA Effectiveness Awards, 2002

It is commonly believed that getting a foothold in the public's attention requires a presence across a greater number of communication channels. This paper, however, shows how quite the opposite can also be true. It shows how a brave and focused new strategy, concentrating firepower (both creatively and in media terms), elevated an already strong brand to new heights.

Marmite has a heritage as strong as its taste. It has been popular as a healthy food-stuff since this useless leftover of the brewing industry was first made edible and sold to the British public 100 years ago. Full of B vitamins, the brand established itself as a healthy spread for children through promotion in traditional 'village hall' clinics. However, in the 1970s these clinics were replaced with welfare centres where retail sales were forbidden. To compensate for this, the owners of Marmite began to use consumer marketing more heavily.

At first, heavier investment in consumer marketing appeared to work; sales growth had been strong during the 1980s. But by the early 1990s growth had slowed. The reasons for this were that the consumption of bread, Marmite's traditional companion, had moved into decline; breakfast, where Marmite was usually eaten, was also a declining meal occasion since 1990; and finally the number of under-four-year-olds in the population, an important group for driving sales, was also in decline.

In 1996, following a period of expensive restructuring and a period of aggressive acquisition, CPC (then owner of Marmite) was keen to squeeze out more profit to pay off its debts. This meant, despite recently stalling sales and no increase in marketing budget, that Marmite's sales target was set at an ambitious 5 per cent growth per annum. This target appeared even more ambitious when the strength of the brand was assessed. When looking at specific brand measures, important brand image attributes had been eroded. Consumers were emotionally detached from the brand and awareness was low. Marmite's marketing was also complicated by the 'Marmite life cycle'. Marmite's unique taste means that people usually acquire a liking for it when young. Nowadays, rather than being recommended in village hall clinics, the habit for Marmite is passed on from generation to generation when parents, who have acquired the taste as children, feed it to their children as a healthy spread. Within this life cycle there are two junctures where Marmite usage can lapse; as older children they may favour sweeter spreads and will not return to Marmite until they are parents, and once their children have grown up, older people also often lapse out of the brand.

It was acknowledged that in order to achieve the ambitious sales target, there had to be brutal focus in the thinking. Marketing were advised to focus on adult lapsed users. This was a large group of people who had already acquired the taste for Marmite. By focusing on lapsed users the required volume growth could be achieved. Calculations showed that if one in ten lapsed users became a light user, the sales target would be achieved.

The 'Hate/Mate' creative idea was groundbreaking in its honesty. It appealed to the cynical target audience and also generated publicity. The idea also allowed both users and non-users to get involved with the campaign, useful for bringing it into public consciousness and jolting the brand back into lapsed users' minds.

The new campaign was a tremendous success. After five years of stagnation, sales saw an immediate increase and have been increasing ever since. As a result, the marketing objective of 5 per cent growth per annum has been achieved. The advertising became more front-of-mind for the tightly defined target audience but also a topic of conversation for the general population.

Advertising, and the PR amplification, combined to get Marmite back into the public's consciousness. Far from making the brand more modern to the detriment of the traditional attributes, all aspects of the brand were strengthened. The appeal of the brand overall increased, along with brand awareness and image. Marmite had become a national icon. The week this paper was published, Marmite was chosen (by 20- to 30-year-olds) as one of the top five brands that would ideally represent Britain in the future in research by Corporate Edge.

Hovis is a good example of a brand re-launching successfully in a declining market.

CASE HISTORY: Hovis – Repackaging Goodness

Andrew Deykin and Vicki Holgate, Silver, IPA Effectiveness Awards, 2002

This case demonstrates how the re-launch of Hovis resulted in massively increased profits.

Back in the spring of 2001, British Bakeries was about to celebrate Hovis's 115th birthday. On the surface, things were looking good. Hovis's sales were rising. This was made more impressive by the fact that the market as a whole was in decline.

Hovis's market share had almost doubled in the last two years. However, under the surface, all was not well. British Bakeries was selling more and more bread, but it was making less and less money out of it. Since May 1999, profits had been in decline, despite the increase in volume.

The objective was simple: to increase Hovis's profits significantly by the end of 2001. In doing this, British Bakeries wanted to build value back into the bread category to try to reverse the devaluation. Unfortunately, Hovis's brand equity was also declining along with price. Spontaneous brand awareness of Hovis was in long-term decline, whereas its rival Kingsmill's awareness was on the rise. Hovis was seen as old-fashioned and was becoming increasingly distant from bread buyers.

In order to improve the underlying demand for the Hovis brand and break out of the vicious circle of falling prices and falling advertising investment, it was decided that nothing short of a total re-launch would suffice. The budget was £4.2 million, double the spend of the previous year, and the re-launch was timed in conjunction with planned price rises.

The re-launch included radical new advertising and packaging based on the core brand value of 'everyday goodness', a consistent, differentiating and motivating quality. It drove demand to such an extent that Hovis was able to increase volume at the same time as increasing price – totally counterintuitive. Hovis was the fastest-growing non-alcoholic grocery brand over the last year (+26 per cent), achieving its business objectives. Both the advertising and packaging more than paid for themselves.

Figure 22.11 Innovative Hovis packaging by Williams Murray Hamm
Reproduced by kind permission of Williams Murray Hamm/Hovis

PART 7

New threats to brand immortality

23 Future threats and opportunities for brands

These are the key points from this concluding chapter:

- The Future Foundation and the IPA have identified 12 key trends that will impact on marketing and advertising over the next decade.
- Technological trends feature the most heavily owing to their implications on media reach and consumer use of media.
- Social trends such as the 24-hour society and economic and political trends such as increasing longevity and government legislation will also have a significant impact.
- Environmental issues and globalization will also be very important.
- The rate of innovation will quicken and brands will have to keep pace with rapidly evolving market categories and new ones too.
- The fundamental rules of brand immortality as set out in this book will persist and intensify. Professionally managed brands will live long and prosper.

We have looked at some of the basic workings of the human brain and the impact on marketing and communications of phenomena such as 'selective perception', 'cognitive dissonance', the 'herd instinct', 'double jeopardy', 'customer commitment', low attention processing and the implication of ageing populations in Westernized economies. Drawing from the IPA Effectiveness Awards dataBANK and using the learning from dataMINE analyses, we have seen how marketers and their agencies have successfully managed brands in new, growth, mature and declining market contexts. But what of the future? What new challenges might be expected over the next few years, and what sorts of issues will these raise for brand managers?

The networked society	100%
New bandwidths galore	98%
Navigating choice and complexity	92%
Legislation creep	88%
Desperately seeking innovation	88%
24-hour society	87%
Wireless worlds	85%
Global mobility growth	83%
East ascendant	81%
UK economic prospects	81%
The entertainment aesthetic	81%
Longevity and the decline of youth	81%

Figure 23.1 Top 12 trends selected
Source: Future of Advertising Agencies, IPA (2007)

In 2006, the IPA commissioned the Future Foundation, a leading forecasting consultancy, to explore what lay in store over the next 10 years. It produced an economic model of the size of the UK advertising market for 2006–16 and developed a range of scenarios depending on certain key assumptions. These assumptions were themselves derived from analysis of the key drivers of the media market. The impacts of globalization and new technologies, coupled with profound changes in consumer behaviour, are being felt across all businesses, and advertising is no exception.

The Future Foundation identified the 12 key trends that would impact most significantly on the advertising business in the next decade. Of the 12, not surprisingly, technology trends featured most heavily, though largely because of their implications on media reach and consumer use of media.

In summary, the 12 key trends identified by the think tank were as shown in Figure 23.1.

These trends can be grouped into three main categories: technological, social and economic. While these top 12 trends were determined specifically in relation to the advertising market, they also have implications for the realm of brands. Thus it seems reasonable to look at these three categories and discuss their likely impact on the relationship between companies and their customers.

Technology trends

The relentless pace of technological change is largely predicated on what has come to be known as Moore's Law, originally described in his now-famous article 'Cramming more components onto integrated circuits'. In it Gordon E. Moore, then Director of the Research and Development Laboratories of

Fairchild Semiconductor, forecast that 'With unit cost falling as the number of components per circuit rises, by 1975 economics may dictate squeezing as many as 65,000 components on a single silicon chip.' The implications became known as Moore's Law, which states that the number of transistors on an integrated circuitry for minimum component cost doubles every 24 months, ie computing power does so too. Moore co-founded Intel and this company has capitalized on his insight and dominated the microprocessor market ever since (Figure 23.2).

One consequence of Moore's law and the massive increase in computing power is the introduction and speed of adoption of broadband, which is reshaping the landscape (Figure 23.3).

With the expansion of the data-carrying capacity of each successive wave of new technology (both fixed and mobile), new bandwidths allow richer content, and more of it, simultaneously. This, and the inherent interactivity of all these platforms, has huge implications for brands. It also enables much greater contact between customers and companies – multiplication of 'touch points' – and this means millions of 'moments of truth'. Each of these contacts can reinforce and keep the brand promise or undermine and break it. This presents huge challenges to companies and their leaders. It's vital that they develop a complete set of 'brand manners' so that the internal values of the company are aligned with their external ones. It's also crucial for them to

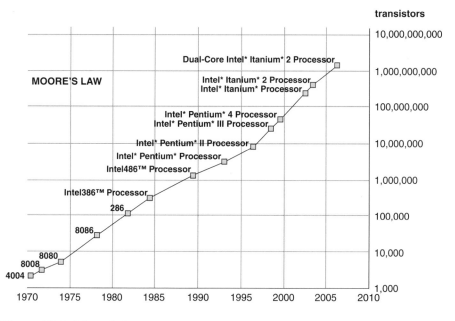

Figure 23.2 Moore's Law
Copyright © 2005 Intel Corporation

Number of households that subscribe to a broadband internet service at home – nVision forecast

2006-based projection

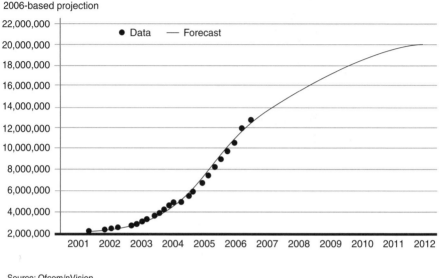

Source: Ofcom/nVision
Base: UK

Figure 23.3 The future of broadband access
Source: The Future of Advertising and Agencies, IPA (2007)

move from a 'command and control' management culture to one where the whole organization is sufficiently self-confident to act individually as ambassadors for the brand.

This huge increase in broadband availability puts more and more power into the hands of the customer and accelerates the potential for 'disintermediation' – the elimination of middlemen such as wholesalers and retailers. In April 2007, US bookstore giant Borders Inc announced a strategic review of its international operations. In 2006 this accounted for 16 per cent of total sales, of which 70 per cent were in the UK and Ireland. However, these operations had made a previous-year loss of £250,000 and as a result Borders decided to close down its UK operation. Borders, like other retailers, had suffered from the intense squeeze between supermarkets like Tesco cherry-picking and discounting the best-sellers, and Amazon disintermediating, out-stocking and under-pricing them (Figure 23.4).

Broadband also facilitates the price comparison websites and online transactions that enable people to do in minutes what would formerly have required many days or weeks. This represents a big threat to companies that fail to deliver good customer service, and especially those that underestimate the downsides of outsourcing key functions. Charlie Dawson of The Foundation

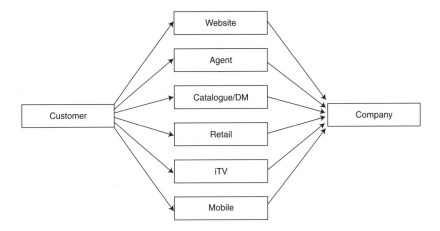

Figure 23.4 The squeeze on traditional retailing
Source: Stephen Fox, 'Home retailing: the death of home shopping?' *Market Leader*, Issue 32, Spring 2006

expressed this threat as follows: 'Companies value their customer's time at zero, but their own in hard currency.' Companies can estimate the lifetime value of customers, but what they don't do is calculate the time cost to customers of doing business with them. This missing factor in the total value equation is going to become increasingly important to the longevity of brands for two related reasons: 1) there will be more money-rich, time-poor people; and 2) there will be greater use of automated customer service systems.

Companies need to develop more sophisticated customer relationship management systems that can improve online customer service transactions. The nightmare of 'Helpline Hell' must be converted to 'Helpline Heaven'. Companies struggling with legacy systems or utility mentalities still have unacceptably slow and un-navigable systems. The challenge for them is to see new technology as a way of adding value to the customer experience, rather than of cutting costs at the expense of the customer's wasted time. In April 2007 HSBC announced it was diverting calls from its less affluent UK customers to foreign call centres, while more affluent clients would continue to be dealt with in the UK. This policy caused outrage in the popular press, but it's likely that the high net worth customers sighed with relief.

Online retailing is changing customers' shopping patterns, especially for higher-value purchases such as holidays and durables. Honda reports that the average number of test drives in the new car buying process has fallen from an average of five or six to one or two. Nowadays, many prospective purchasers do all their research online, narrow down to their preferred make and model and then go straight to the retailer. This puts a heavy reliance on the quality of service that the buyer encounters at the dealership.

This culling of the shortlist before a physical contact is ever made has intensified competition in the car market hugely, and is relegating expensive high street shops to the status of showrooms. This powerful trend led DSG (Dixons' Store Group), the UK's leading high street electrical retailer, to relocate its once-dominant high street brand Dixons to the internet, converting the physical stores to its other brand, Currys. As we saw earlier, Apple created its retail presence to serve existing owners as much as new buyers.

But it's not a one-way street. Dell, a veteran of online-only trading, has been forced to move into physical retailing in order to shore up its position. In May 2007, after 23 years in business, and having lost its number one position to Hewlett Packard, Michael Dell announced a radical departure from two fundamental tenets that had defined his brand. First, Dell would now sell standardized 'off the peg' computers made for a retailer, as opposed to 'tailor-made' ones specified by an individual user. Second, it would allow these computers to be sold in 3,000 Wal-Marts in the United States and Puerto Rico – just like any other PC brand, as opposed to direct to customers. Dell had had a retail presence – around 160 stores in the United States and Canada – but these had been product showcases as opposed to sales outlets. The decision to choose Wal-Mart was intended to appeal to the mass-market notebook customer as opposed to the business user of desktop machines where Dell had built its franchise. It remains to be seen whether this new strategy will damage the credibility of Dell in its quality heartland. Perhaps Dell should have migrated its brand at its peak of success to other related product categories where its core proposition of mass customization and value for money could also have been applied.

This online empowerment of the citizen consumer presents a particular challenge to companies that behave unethically or whose products and services perform poorly. The power of bloggers to mount negative campaigns was demonstrated after the launch of the Kryptonite Evolution 2000 U-Lock, which was 'hacked' using a Bic ballpoint pen! The lessons of crisis management are to grasp the nettle, own the problem and communicate relentlessly how the problem is being addressed. A warning from the 'Bloggers Code of Conduct' by Jimmy Wales, founder of Wikipedia, and co-author Tim O'Reilly, and originating from George Bernard Shaw, is worth remembering: 'Never wrestle with a pig. You both get dirty, but the pig likes it.'

Customers are also complaining more, helped by the effortlessness of online and the viral spread of negative PR. Even the traditional apathy of customers towards their current accounts may be ending; the UK's Financial Ombudsman Service reported complaints about bank charges up 47 per cent on 2006. No doubt this activism has been prompted by widespread publicity about banks making out-of-court settlements in the thousands of pounds for overcharging on unauthorized overdrafts. Growing pressures are also being felt by corporations over top executives' pay – so-called 'fat cat' salaries. The issue has already moved beyond the fringe malcontents into the arena of institutional shareholders and regulators.

During 2007, there was growing concern in the UK about the emerging class of private equity, hedge fund managers and non-domiciled entrepreneurs, whose enormous wealth but low taxation was feared to be a potential source of serious social unrest. The number of people earning more than £500,000 a year has increased by 60 per cent in four years. While there is clearly a 'trickle-down' effect of spending power from the super-rich to the economy at large, there are also drawbacks to this concentration of wealth – for example in the UK domestic property market, where the amount of money coming in at the top end makes housing unaffordable at the bottom. A key moment in the debate was reached when UK private equity boss Nicholas Ferguson admitted that 'people in my industry pay less tax than a cleaning lady' and in October 2007 the UK Chancellor of the Exchequer moved to get rid of the tax breaks that favour private equity and the non-domiciled. One of the unfortunate consequences of this 'fat-cattery' is that some outstanding business leaders, who have contributed enormously to increasing shareholder value, have been bracketed with others less deserving.

Unsurprisingly, the US Securities and Exchange Commission is seeking to improve the transparency with which executive compensation is reported – currently obfuscation is the name of the game in many major corporations' accounts. However, the mere title of the SEC's interim final rules does not augur well for more clarity: 17 CFR Parts 228 and 229 [Release Nos. 33-8765: 34-55009; File No s7-03-06] RIN 3235-AI80 Executive Compensation Disclosure. Perhaps it's more likely that a popular backlash against the corporate brands in question will curtail pay packets more effectively than regulatory intervention.

Such a backlash can come rather quickly, as Lord Browne of BP found to his cost. Oil spills in Alaska, environmental concerns about its pipeline in central Asia, and the death of 15 people as a result of an explosion in 2005 at its Texas oil refinery turned once-positive market sentiment against Browne. The subsequent enquiry led to harsh words about BP's commitment to profits rather than safety and severely tarnished the corporation's reputation. But the exultant and persistent tone of the media exposé was fuelled by his remuneration package – so huge that his 'early resignation' cost him £15 million in anticipated 'retirement' payments. As General Electric's former CEO Jack Welch used to say, 'Hierarchy defines an organization in which people have their face towards the CEO and their ass towards the customer.'

Social trends

Against the backdrop of Lord Browne's demise the new CEO of BP, Tony Hayward, is fighting back in the best way possible – by innovating in its business and responding to regulatory, governmental and social demands. The EU has declared that it wants to see at least 10 per cent of road fuel derived from plants by 2020 and US President George Bush recently announced a 15 per cent target for replacement of petrol by biofuels in vehicles. By the end of 2009, biofuel production in the United States will double to about 7 per cent of all petrol consumed. So, in 2007 BP made two major forward steps in developing these new environmentally friendly fuel technologies. The first of these was a joint venture with Associated British Foods and DuPont in a £200 million project to produce ethanol from wheat and carry out research into biobutanol, an advanced biofuel. The second was a joint venture with D1 Oils to create D1-BP Fuel Crops, with BP injecting working capital of £31.75 million and establishment of a 50 : 50 partnership to undertake global planting of 1 million hectares of jatropha trees over four years. Jatropha is an oilseed tree that grows in tropical and sub-tropical regions and produces high yields of inedible vegetable oil that can be used to produce high-quality biodiesel. It can grow on non-arable, marginal and waste land and thus does not compete with food crops for good agricultural land or result in the destruction of rainforest. It is an extremely promising biofuel crop and source of employment in developing nations. However, BP and other major energy companies are going to have to persuade governments and citizens that fears over the environmental impacts of biofuels are unfounded. If they succeed in this, their brands will have achieved a significant repositioning from the negatives of 'Big Oil' to the positives of 'Big Energy' (Figure 23.5).

Increasing numbers of companies are seeking to respond to the growing regulatory and social pressures to deliver on their 'triple bottom lines' (Figure 23.6). For example, in July 2007 McDonald's announced that it was converting its 155-vehicle UK transport fleet to be run on used chip fat. Used cooking oil will be mixed with pure rapeseed oil to create biodiesel, an eco-friendly alternative to diesel. McDonald's estimates an annual carbon saving of 1,675 tonnes – the same as removing the equivalent of 2,424 family cars from the roads.

It's possible to remove 10 million cars' emissions without removing 10 million cars.

If every driver filled up with ULTIMATE fuels in the 13 countries it's available, the reduced emissions would be equivalent to taking over 10 million cars off the road.

bp
beyond petroleum

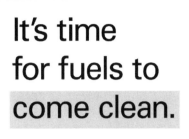

It's time for fuels to come clean.

Our ULTIMATE fuels help vehicles deliver more performance and less pollution, and are now available in 13 different countries. If all the drivers in these markets were to use ULTIMATE, the reduction in harmful emissions would be equivalent to taking more than 10 million cars off the road.

bp
beyond petroleum

It's time to think outside the barrel.

Emissions We were the first major energy company to acknowledge the need to take steps against global warming. One step uses recycled steam to supply power to one of our largest facilities. This process boosted the plant's performance by $20 million, while eliminating more than 50,000 tons of emissions.

Environment To provide heat, power and mobility for the U.S., new pipelines have to be built. In Louisiana, BP pioneered a new standard for pipeline construction. Working with environmental groups, community leaders, even local oystermen, we produced a solution that will help preserve wetlands.

Education BP's A+ for Energy program has awarded $4 million in grants and scholarships to 3,000 California teachers over the last two years. BP supports energy education throughout the country, from a traveling classroom that teaches alternative energy to the Solar Decathlon in Washington, D.C.

bp
beyond petroleum

Figure 23.5 BP advertisements, Ogilvy & Mather
Reproduced by kind permission of BP

Figure 23.6 Together.com advertisement, The Climate Group
Reproduced by kind permission of The Climate Group

Meanwhile, UK supermarkets are readdressing one of the fundamentals of their operation – plastic bags. Since their introduction in 1977, the number of plastic bags has grown enormously with the spread of supermarket shopping and a wealthier society. Nowadays UK consumers use an estimated 10 billion bags a year, ie an average of 167 bags per person, and each of these bags takes 500 years to degrade in landfill sites, according to social change organization 'We Are What We Do' (WAWWD).

Building on the success of their bestselling book *Change the World for a Fiver* (Figure 23.7), We Are What We Do's first nationwide campaign was 'Action 01: Decline Plastic Bags', for which they co-created the 'I'm Not a Plastic Bag' with Anya Hindmarch (Figure 23.8). Made of unbleached cotton and selling out within an hour of going on sale at £5, this inspired idea kick-started the campaign and built massive awareness. Both Ireland and Denmark have introduced a tax on plastic bags and, perhaps spurred by this and the WAWWD campaign, Sainsbury's has tested a 'No Bag Day' and Waitrose is introducing 'green tills' for people with their own shopping bags.

Figure 23.7 'We Are What We Do' front covers
Reproduced by kind permission of 'We Are What We Do'

Figure 23.8 Anya Hindmarch
Reproduced by kind permission of Anya
Hindmarch and Sainsbury's

The number of businesses open outside of regular business hours grew massively in the late 1990s in response to growing consumer demand for greater flexibility. The demand was led by more dual-income families, working longer hours, and increased affluence, creating greater economic activity. The demand is still strong in 2008, but now it is being driven by a desire for self-fulfilment, and the cramming of more leisure activities into the same amount of free time. If wireless technology means that there is no longer a need to be wired to technology devices in order to transmit and receive information, then digital communication in the new decade will be, literally, anytime and anywhere. With greater affluence, consumers are spending more time out and about, rather than in the home. The ability to make buying decisions through mobile devices means the new channels have opened up shopping to any time of the day or night. This presents companies with significant logistical challenges, including distribution, staffing and late-night security.

In an essentially individualistic society, where old-style institutions have less relevance, trust shifts to relationships. Networks become central to the functioning of social, workplace and even family groups. As technology develops, so a greater number of links are possible between consumers and companies.

Social networking websites allow consumers to bypass marketers and media owners. They create a new channel for brands, but with different rules. Facebook, originally called 'The Face Book' after the books that are distributed to new students to help them identify people on campus, was set up by Harvard students in February 2004. Facebook was originally restricted to members with a college or university e-mail address, but has since been made available to anyone. In May 2007 Facebook opened up its application programming interface to outside programmers and within a month some 40,000 new applications had been developed for the site. As of February 2007, the website had an estimated 28 million registered users worldwide, almost 10 per cent of them in the UK (Figure 23.9).

Marketers and agencies, previously secure in the belief that they were in control of the brand communications 'supply chain', now operate in a new world order; caught between consumers on the one hand, and media owners on the other. There is a growing consumer ability to pick and choose how much information to receive, and when to receive it, using blocking software on their computers and PVRs to schedule their TV viewing to avoid commercial breaks. So far, according to research by Thinkbox, in the UK the PVR does not appear to have undermined the impact of commercials on TV. This may be counterintuitive but it's because homes with technologies such as Sky+ actually watch more television, much of it live as opposed to recorded, and

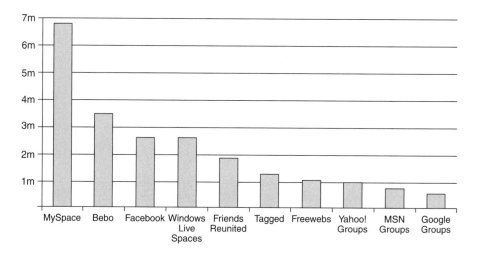

Figure 23.9 Top 10 UK social networking sites by visitors, April 2007
Source: Nielsen/NetRatings

thus they are exposed to more commercials than homes without PVRs. However, forward-thinking brand owners are working on the assumption of a transition from 'interruption' to 'engagement' and from 'push' to 'pull' as the core tenets of the future consumer communications model. Achieving this transition will require greater emphasis on gathering data and knowledge about consumers and interacting with them on a 'permission-only basis'. Brands will need to invest a growing proportion of their budgets on collecting information and securing that permission.

Economic trends

Traditionally, there has always been a strong correlation between GDP growth and growth in commercial advertising expenditure (Figure 23.10). There is a strong likelihood that this pattern is set to continue. If economic prospects are positive, then the same is more than likely to be true for commercial advertising.

Longevity is one of the most profound demographic shifts shaping society, now and into the future. Not only are we living longer, more affluent and healthy lives, we are also reproducing less. The 'Baby boomers', now in their

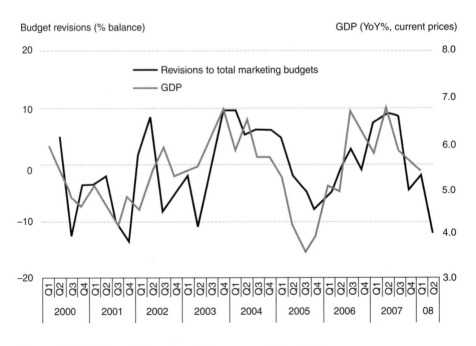

Figure 23.10 Growth in advertising v growth in GDP
Source: IPA Bellweather

late 40s and 50s, will account for an extra 5.2 million consumers in the 45–74 age group by 2016, representing disproportionate buying power in many markets. Youth segments will decline by over 1 million. Not generally known for their interest in the older consumer, or even the middle-aged worker, marketers are only now gearing up to this new challenge. In an earlier chapter we saw the differences between UK and US data on the potential for older customers to try new brands, and it's clear that companies will need to understand much better the attitudes and behaviours in their categories and geographies if they are to survive with an ageing population of buyers.

Governmental legislation and regulation's effect on the economy is a daunting threat to the longevity of brands – daunting because for politicians an attack on advertising is one of the easiest of all electoral gambits: it requires no research, just an opinion, and it's very low risk. Tobacco advertising has been banned, advertising for alcoholic drinks has become more controlled, and there are changes in the regulation around food advertising and advertising to children at both an EU and a UK level. The UK media regulator Ofcom has calculated that there will be a loss of £39m a year in broadcast revenues as a result of its ban on all advertisements for food and drink products that are high in fat, salt and sugar in and around all programmes appealing to under-16s. This is likely to result in a further disinvestment by commercial broadcasters in original UK programming for children, which has been in a seven-year decline owing to increasing pressures to reduce advertising to them. 'Legislative creep' is intensifying rather than abating, and advertisers and agencies need to respond with more responsible campaigns identifying consumer risks as well as consumer rewards.

Forecasts from the World Travel Organization suggest that the current level of international mobility – 15 trips for every 100 head of global population – will increase to 21 by 2020 (Figure 23.11). Clearly, the patterns of travel are disproportionately weighted to the affluent West, but we can expect greater movement from the Eastern economies to the West, both as tourists and as business people. This means that air travel brands will face radical change – not just airlines but airports too. And the threat of global terrorism has introduced new operational factors on a scale that could not have been anticipated 10 years ago. On top of this come growing environmental concerns and environmental taxation, which will work against otherwise buoyant forecasts for international travel.

The growth in global mobility, coupled with global internet connectivity, makes it harder and harder to protect brands against piracy, theft or unfair competition. The counterfeiting industry in countries like China is huge and there's hardly an Eastern European nation where tourists cannot find pretty good replicas of the major luxury brands. These purchases are damaging in more ways than just forgone profits – the much lower price points enable

Arrivals generated per 100 population per year...

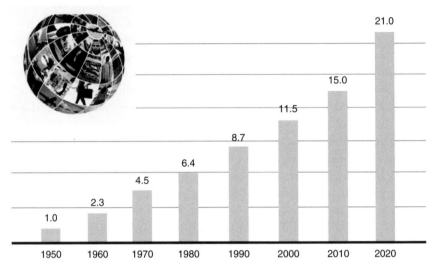

Figure 23.11 Global mobility growth
Source: The Future of Advertising and Agencies, IPA (2007)

people outside the normal target market to acquire these brands and then be seen with them on the ordinary high street back home. This undermines the prestige of these luxury goods, making them less attractive to their high net worth aficionados. Burberry actually temporarily 'retired' its signature check fabric as a way of tackling the problem and has taken tough action against its misuse.

In the same vein, brand owners increasingly need to protect their brand's intellectual property rights. To do this, Cadbury Schweppes is taking legal action in Australia against Darrell Lea, which it alleges is using a purple colour with a striking and obvious resemblance to its own distinctive 'Cadbury Purple' (Pantone 2685C), used on its flagship brand, Dairy Milk, and other lines. Cadbury adopted this colour in 1905 because of its regal associations and implications of a rich and indulgent eating experience. Pantone 2685C is cited in its Trade Mark/Patent Office registration. Cadbury lost the first trial but has appealed successfully and secured a re-trial on the grounds that the judge made mistakes over expert testimony. Legal actions such as these are very costly, but essential if a brand owner is to protect the intellectual property in its brand.

By the end of the next decade both China and India will have overtaken the UK in terms of size of economy (Figure 23.12). By 2050, forecasts indicate that China will be the world's number one economy, with today's developing markets, including India, Brazil and Russia, also in the world's top five. Global

US $ billions   --- China ····· India —— Russia —·— Japan — UK ······ US

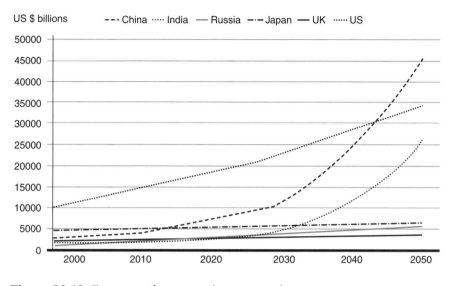

Figure 23.12 East ascendant: growing economic power
Source: The Future of Advertising and Agencies, IPA (2007)

financial institutions (eg the G8, IMF and WTO) will have to evolve and restructure in order to allow emerging nations to play a more significant role in managing the global economy.

Western brands are already recognizing the impact of India and China – not just as markets, but also as manufacturing centres: widespread outsourcing of manufacturing already takes place to emerging economies, and this will continue. The challenge for Western brand owners is to nurture and develop the skill sets required to strengthen their knowledge advantage. High-quality education and training, creative ideas and innovative solutions will all be key to this.

Meanwhile, the variable quality of Chinese-produced goods is giving forward-looking Western producers time to develop premium positions. In June 2007 the Consumer Product Safety Commission reported that imported goods from China were recalled by the United States twice as often as products made everywhere else in the world, including the United States (Figure 23.13). Of the 152 product recalls announced by the Commission since January, 104 had been for products made in China. But a single recall can result in tens of thousands of individual toys, electrical items or foodstuffs having to be withdrawn from distribution and returned by customers. The Chinese use of lead paint on children's toys has been a key problem: 1.5 million Thomas & Friends trains and rails sold by RC2 Corporation were found to have been coated with lead paint. The CPSC also noted that the US market is saturated with counterfeit circuit breakers, power strips, extension cords, batteries and holiday lights that are causing fires, explosions, shocks and electrocutions. The industrialization of China is causing other problems too, such as pollution and a massive contribution to global warming and its consequences (Figure 23.14).

No doubt China will get through these issues in time, but meanwhile these product recalls are tainting the 'Made in China' label and enhancing the trustworthiness of brands of US or European origin.

In one sense, developing economies have an advantage over developed ones, as they can use the latest technologies to leapfrog decades of evolution that more mature markets have had to go through. For example, there are 680 million people living in sub-Saharan Africa. There, the price of a home satellite TV system has fallen 60 per cent in five years, from rich expatriate pricing levels to a more mass-market price of $200. MTV Africa already has a potential audience of 50 million. Now there are more than 150 channels carried on the Intelsat satellite and increasing amounts of locally produced content such as by Nigeria's 'Nollywood'. Ten years ago just 1 per cent of Africans had a mobile phone; now it's estimated at 140 million people and forecast to rise to 280 million by 2010, or 40 per cent of the population. By 2007 over 33 million had an internet connection. How soon before Africa joins the 'BRIC' nations of Brazil, Russia, China and India?

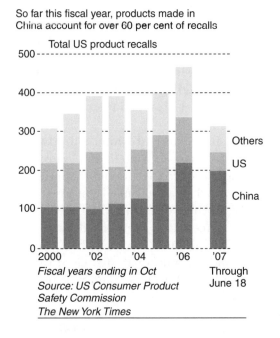

Figure 23.13 Faulty products

Figure 23.14 Dragon polluter
Reproduced by kind permission of Peter Kuper

As the economy globalizes, we can expect individual countries or regions to seek to protect their brands, just as the champagne region of France has always been very aggressive in defending its unique *appelation*, 'champagne'. In a similar move, the Federation of the Swiss watch industry, the manufacturer's trade association, voted in July 2007 to toughen up its criteria. Under its new definition, 80 per cent of the value of a mechanical movement has to be Swiss to retain the 'Swiss made' label. Further, for mechanical watches at least 80 per cent of production costs for the whole watch must be undertaken in Switzerland itself. It seems likely that this will be approved by the Swiss government, but then there is the question of how to enforce this on an international basis. The future of globalization is beginning to look uncertain as the United States, once its champion, is increasingly becoming protectionist in the face of declining global economic domination.

But just as globalization can create threats, or countervailing trends to localization, it can also present great opportunities for commercial cooperation. Boeing is one of the latest US manufacturers to stake its future on global outsourcing, with the Boeing 787 'Dreamliner'. A crucial element in its successful sales proposition has been the localized manufacturing of key components of the new aircraft, with Boeing's construction partners building plants in Italy, Japan and South Carolina to produce the aeroplane. This strategy has given national carriers and government decision-makers additional reasons to buy Boeing. However, this strategy has not been without its problems, and delivery has been postponed well beyond the original delivery date, with the third delay announced in October 2007.

Traditionally, a buyout by private equity or venture capitalist meant identifying a failing company, acquiring it at low price, stripping out as many costs as possible and then selling it on at a significant profit. In the process the marketing budget was often a casualty but, given the short cycle involved, the damage to the brand did not become apparent until later. Nowadays, the financial engineers have recognized the significance of intangible assets, and brands within them. This means private equity funds have become a lot more cautious about cutting marketing expenditure. Cost cutting in service businesses can be more risky. For example, owners Permira and CVC Capital have instigated 3,400 redundancies in the UK's Automobile Association (AA). They may be holding the top-line advertising budget at the pre-acquisition level, but time will tell whether the brand image will suffer as a result of adverse brand experience.

What does this all add up to for brands?

In this brief review of future trends, a picture has begun to emerge of the key factors that brands need to plan for:

- technological change in the shape of a faster and ever more functional internet that will increasingly put consumers in the driving seat not just of brand choice but also of brand reputation;
- social change in the shape of new ways of networking on a global level that, by altering the way consumers interact, will alter the ways in which brands can mediate that interaction to their own advantage;
- economic change in the shape of the rise of the developing economies and the new global brands they will bring to the world of marketing, as well as the effect they will have on existing brands and on an increasingly uncertain outlook for 'globalization' as we have come to know it.

So how will these factors change the fundamentals of brand success? It seems most likely that they will *intensify* the rules that have been outlined in this book.

Certainly emotional engagement will become an even more vital component of brands. It may well involve new 'angles' such as environmental good citizenship and ethical 'purity', and it may well benefit from new communications channels such as social networking, but engagement will remain king. Why? Because it creates permission for brands to enter the increasingly defensible world of the consumer. And because it strengthens the impact and retention of brand impressions in the conscious and subconscious brain – and until the human brain changes, this will remain so. Within this world of emotional engagement, there is every reason to believe that the 'fame' model of communications will grow in importance as the means by which brand buzz can be started and propagated, proliferate and become more widely and easily accessible.

The pace of innovation for brands in terms of both functionality and representation will almost certainly quicken. The old-fashioned model of the brand as the unchanging rock belting out the same message year after year will be laid to rest for good and replaced by an ever more elastic entity prepared to voice its point of view about an ever-widening range of issues that matter, and delivering the goods to match. Technology will enable many more consumers to be invited in to help participate in this innovation, rather than merely left to vote on the outcome with their wallets: the open source model will migrate from software to colonize other categories.

The fundamental economics of brand communications will not change: brands will still need to create consumer touch points and by definition these will always be subject to market forces. Share of voice may well become ever more difficult to measure as the diversity of potential touch points grows, but it will remain a governing force of growth – or decline.

It is likely that global brands will increasingly need to adopt global *branding* – free from cultural associations with any particular nation or region (unless this is intrinsic to their appeal). Symbolism will strengthen its domination over language in the way these brands identify themselves. And English may recede in importance. But we can expect a growing backlash of national brands playing to nationalistic sentiments as segments of populations seek to dissociate themselves from globalization.

So apart from some shifts of emphasis and some new issues to take on board in maintaining brand health, the fundamental rules of brand immortality will persist. Brands will endure because people want and need them and because *they work*. The very idea of a rationalist consumer future in which brands no longer have a role is too grim for humanity to contemplate and runs counter to the very nature of the human mind. True brands will live long and prosper.

Figure 23.15 Inspiration for brands seeking to defy death: *For the Love of God*.
© Damien Hirst. Courtesy Science Ltd (London)

Appendix:
How to access the IPA dataBANK

The IPA Effectiveness dataBANK represents the most rigorous and comprehensive examination of advertising and marketing communications working in the marketplace, in the world. Since the 1980 launch of the IPA Effectiveness Awards competition, the IPA has collected over 1,000 examples of best practice in advertising development and results across a wide spectrum of marketing sectors and expenditures. Each example contains up to 4,000 words of text and is illustrated in full by market, research, sales and profit data.

Access

The dataBANK is held in the IPA Information Centre for access by IPA members only. Simply contact the Centre by e-mailing info@ipa.co.uk. Simple or more sophisticated searches can be run, free of charge, by qualified, professional knowledge executives across a range of parameters including brand, advertiser, agency, target market (by age, sex, class, and so on), medium and length of activity, which can be specified by the user, and the results supplied by e-mail or other means as required.

Purchasing IPA case studies

Member agencies will be allowed a maximum of 25 case studies for download in any given calendar year, after which they will be charged at £17 each. Alternatively, members can sign up to WARC.com at a beneficial IPA rate and can then download case studies as part of that subscription.

From February 2009, we will be able to supply all IPA Effectiveness case studies directly from the IPA website. Members will have a free allocation of 12 case studies per year and will then be able to download individual studies, directly from the site, for £25.00 per copy. Non-members will be able to purchase for £40.00 and there will also be a special rate for students of £10.00.

Further information

For further information, please contact:

Information Centre
IPA
44 Belgrave Square
London SW1X 8QS
Tel: +44 (0)20 7235 7020
Fax: +44 (0)20 7245 9904
e-mail: info@ipa.co.uk
www.ipa.co.uk

The IPA case histories can also be accessed through the World Advertising Research Center (WARC). Reached by logging on to www.warc.com, the world's most comprehensive advertising database enables readers to search all the IPA case histories. The list of case histories follows below. WARC also offers thousands of 'how to' articles on all areas of communication activity from sources such as the *Journal of Advertising Research*, *Admap* and *Market Leader* magazines and the ESOMAR conference series.

IPA DataBANK – NEW ENTRIES 2007

List of papers (denotes a winner)*

2007   Aqua Optima*
2007   Army Cadet Force
2007   Brother*
2007   BT
2007   Carex*
2007   Churchill Square
2007   Coca-Cola Zero*
2007   Cornwall Enterprise
2007   Curanail
2007   Direct Payment (Department for Work and Pensions/COI)*

2007	E4 Skins*
2007	Erskine*
2007	First Scotrail
2007	Glasgow City
2007	Hastings Hotels Group
2007	Historic Scotland*
2007	Home Office and COI
2007	IRN-BRU 32
2007	Magners Irish Cider*
2007	Metropolitan Police (Trident)*
2007	National Trust
2007	Northern Bank
2007	Northern Ireland Fire and Rescue Service
2007	Original Source*
2007	P&O
2007	P&O Cruises
2007	Pilkington Activ*
2007	Police Community Support Officers
2007	Police Service of Northern Ireland
2007	Pomegreat
2007	Road Safety Authority (Republic of Ireland) and the Department of the Environment (Northern Ireland)
2007	Ryvita*
2007	Scottish Executive (anti-drugs)*
2007	Scottish Executive (organ donation)*
2007	Subway
2007	Tesco
2007	The Big Plus
2007	The Irish News
2007	Translink Metro
2007	Waitrose*
2007	Weetabix*

NEW ENTRIES 2006

2006	100.4 smooth fm
2006	Actimel*
2006	Anti Drug (Scottish Executive)
2006	Ariel
2006	Audi
2006	Axe
2006	Bakers Complete*
2006	Barclays Global Investors (iShares)
2006	Bendicks
2006	Bertolli
2006	Branston Baked Beans*
2006	British Heart Foundation* (Anti Smoking)
2006	Brother
2006	Bulldog
2006	Cathedral City*
2006	Daz*
2006	Dero*
2006	Disability Rights Commission
2006	Dogs Trust
2006	Eurostar
2006	Felix*
2006	Halifax Bank of Scotland
2006	HM Revenue & Customs (Self Assessment)*
2006	Homebase
2006	Horlicks
2006	ING Direct*
2006	Jamie's School Dinners*
2006	Johnnie Walker
2006	Kwik-Fit*
2006	Make Poverty History (Comic Relief)
2006	Manchester City*
2006	Marks & Spencer*
2006	Mastercard
2006	Monopoly Here & Now*
2006	More4*
2006	Naturella*
2006	Nicorette*
2006	NSPCC
2006	O_2*
2006	Petits Filous

2006   Privilege Insurance
2006   Road Safety – Anti-Drink Driving (DoE Northern Ireland)
2006   Road Safety – THINK! (Department of Transport)
2006   Ryvita Minis
2006   Sainsbury's
2006   Seeds of Change (Masterfoods)
2006   Sobieski (Vodka)
2006   Sony BRAVIA
2006   Sony DVD Handycam
2006   Sony Ericsson K750i/W800i*
2006   Sprite
2006   Teacher Recruitment*
2006   The Famous Grouse*
2006   Travelocity.co.uk*
2006   Tropicana Pure Premium*
2006   TV Licensing*
2006   Vehicle Crime Prevention (The Home Office)*
2006   Virgin Trains*
2006   Visit London
2006   Volkswagen Golf*
2006   Volkswagen Golf GTI Mk5*
2006   Wall's Sausages
2006   Women's Aid*

Numerical

2000   1001 Mousse*
2003   55 Degrees North

A

2004   AA Loans*
1982   Abbey Crunch
1990   Abbey National Building Society
1990   Abbey National Building Society (plc)
1980   Abbey National Building Society Open Bondshares
1990   Aberlour Malt Whisky*
2004   Ackermans (SA)
1996   Adult Literacy *
2002   Aerogard Mosquito Repellent (Australia)

1999	Agri Plan Finance
1986	AGS Home Improvements*
1988	AIDS
1994	AIDS*
1986	Air Call
1990	Alex Lawrie Factors
1980	All Clear Shampoo*
1992	Alliance & Leicester Building Society*
1990	Alliance & Leicester Building Society*
1988	Alliance & Leicester Building Society*
1984	Alliance Building Society
1990	Allied Dunbar
1984	Allinson's Bread
1984	Alpen
1990	Alton Towers
2003	Alton Towers 'Air'
1999	Alton Towers 'Oblivion'
1992	Amnesty International
1990	Amnesty International*
1990	Anchor Aerosol Cream
1994	Anchor Butter
1988	Anchor Butter
1992	Andrex
1994	Andrex Ultra
1986	Andrex*
1986	Anglia Building Society
1996	Anglian Water
2002	Anti-Drink Driving*
1997	Anti-Drink Driving (DoE Northern Ireland)
1990	Anti-NHS Reform Campaign (BMA)
1994	Anti-Smoking
2000	Archers*
2004	Army Recruitment*
1998	Army Recruitment*
2005	Arriva Buses*
1996	Arrol's 80
1994	Arthur's (cat food)
2005	ATS Euromaster*
1988	Audi
1990	Audi*
1998	Audi*
1982	Austin Metro*

1980   Austin Mini*
1990   Auto Express
1996   Automobile Association*

B

2004   B&Q
2002   B&Q
1988   Babycham
1988   Baby Fresh
1998   Bacardi Breezer
1996   Bacardi Breezer
2000   Bahlsen Biscuits
1992   Bailey's
2002   Bakers Complete*
2005   Bakers Complete*
2005   Bank of Ireland
1988   Barbican
1990   Barbican Health & Fitness Centre
1996   Barclaycard*
1992   Barclaycard
1998   Barclays Bank Current Account
2002   Barnardo's*
1994   Batchelors
1998   Batchelors Supernoodles*
2005   Baxters Soup
2004   Beck's Bier (Australia)
2001   Belfast Giants
1998   Bell's Whisky
2002   Benadryl*
2005   Belfast City
1986   Benylin*
1990   Billy Graham's Mission 89
1986   Birds Eye Alphabites*
1992   Birds Eye Country Club Cuisine
1994   Birds Eye Crispy Chicken
1982   Birds Eye Oven Crispy Cod Steaks in Batter*
1999   Birmingham, City of
1988   Birmingham Executive Airways
1990   Black Tower
1996   Blockbuster Video

2005	Blood Donation*
1982	Blue Riband
2000	Bluewater*
2005	bmi baby
1994	BMW*
2004	BMW Films – The Hire*
1994	Boddington's*
1990	Bodyform
2003	Bonjela
1994	Book Club Associates
1998	Boots Advantage Card
1988	Boots Brand Medicines
2004	Bounty (paper towels)*
1998	Boursin
1994	Boursin
1986	Bovril
2000	Bowmore
1990	Bradford & Bingley Building Society
1986	Bradford & Bingley Building Society*
2005	Broadband for Scotland*
1980	Braun Shavers
1982	Bread Advisory Council*
1982	Breville Toasted Sandwichmaker
2002	Britannia Building Society*
2004	British Airways*
1996	British Airways
1994	British Airways*
1984	British Airways Shuttle Service
1994	British Diabetic Association*
1980	British Film Institute*
1994	British Gas Central Heating
1988	British Gas Flotation*
1988	British Nuclear Fuels
1988	British Rail Young Person's Railcard
1982	British Sugar Corporation
1980	British Turkey Federation
1992	BT
2004	BT Broadband*
2005	BT Broadband (Consumer)
2000	BT Business
1996	BT Business*
1994	BT Business

1992   BT Call Waiting*
2002   BT Cellnet*
1986   BT Consumer*
2001   BT Internet (Northern Ireland)
1999   BT Northern Ireland
1986   BT Privatization*
2002   BT Retail*
1998   Bud Ice
2002   Budweiser*
1988   Budweiser
2004   BUPA*
2002   BUPA
2000   BUPA
1980   BUPA
1996   Butter Council

C

1996   Cable Television
1994   Cadbury's Boost*
1992   Cadbury's Caramel
1998   Cadbury's Creme Eggs
1988   Cadbury's Creme Eggs
1984   Cadbury's Creme Eggs
1992   Cadbury's Crunchie
1984   Cadbury's Curly Wurly*
1980   Cadbury's Dairy Box
2004   Cadbury's Dream (SA)
1982   Cadbury's Flake
1984   Cadbury's Fudge*
1994   Cadbury's Highlights
1999   Cadbury's Jestives
1990   Cadbury's Mini Eggs
1994   Cadbury's Roses*
1986   Cadbury's Wispa
1988   Café Hag
1996   Californian Raisins
1980   Campari*
1992   Campbell's Condensed Soup
1988   Campbell's Meatballs*
1994   Campbell's Soup

1996	Cancer Relief Macmillan Fund
1984	Canderel
1994	Car Crime Prevention
1992	Caramac
2003	Carex
1998	Carex
1997	Carex
1996	Carling Black Label
1994	Carling Black Label
1984	Carousel
1998	Carrick Jewellery
1986	Castlemaine XXXX*
1992	Cellnet Callback
1988	CenterParcs
2004	Central London Congestion Charge*
1992	Central Television Licence Renewal
2000	Channel 5
1990	Charlton Athletic Supporters Club*
1980	Cheese Information Service
1996	Cheltenham & Gloucester Building Society
1988	Chessington World of Adventures
2003	Chicago Town Pizza
2002	Chicago Town Pizza
1998	Chicago Town Pizza
1994	Chicken Tonight
2000	Chicken Tonight Sizzle and Stir*
1994	Child Road Safety
1992	Childhood Diseases Immunization
2004	Children's Hearings (Scottish Executive)*
2005	Children's Hearings System*
1990	Children's World
2001	Chiltern Railways (Clubman Service)
1984	Chip Pan Fires Prevention*
1990	Choosy Catfood*
1998	Christian Aid*
1992	Christian Aid
1994	CICA (Trainers)*
1992	Citroën Diesel Range
1988	Clairol Nice 'n Easy
1988	Clarks Desert Boots*
1996	Classic Combination Catalogue
1994	Clerical Medical

1992   Clorets
1988   Clover
1984   Clover
1980   Cointreau
1998   Colgate Toothpaste*
1990   Colman's Wholegrain Mustard
2000   Confetti.co.uk*
2005   Consensia/Police Service of Northern Ireland
2000   Co-op*
2004   Co-op Food Retail
1996   Cooperative Bank
1994   Cooperative Bank*
1990   Copperhead Cider
1982   Country Manor (Alcoholic Drink)
1986   Country Manor (Cakes)
1984   Cow & Gate Babymeals*
1982   Cracottes*
2004   Cravendale (Milk)*
2000   Crime Prevention
2003   Crimestoppers Northern Ireland
1990   Croft Original*
1982   Croft Original
1980   Croft Original
2003   Crown Paint
2002   Crown Paint
1999   Crown Paint
2004   Crown Paints
2000   Crown Paints*
1990   Crown Solo*
1999   Crown Trade
1999   Crown Wallcoverings
1984   Cuprinol*
1999   Cussons 1001 Mousse
1986   Cyclamon*

D

1996   Daewoo*
1982   Daily Mail*
2002   Dairy Council (Milk)*
2000   Dairylea*

1992	Danish Bacon & Meat Council
1980	Danum Taps
2003	Data Protection Act
1990	Data Protection Registrar
1980	Day Nurse
1994	Daz
1996	De Beers Diamonds*
2002	Debenhams
1980	Deep Clean*
2005	Deep River Rock – Win Big
2000	Degree
2003	Demand Broadband
1980	Dettol*
2002	DfES Higher Education
1984	DHL Worldwide Carrier
1998	Direct Debit
2004	Direct Line*
1992	Direct Line Insurance*
2003	District Policing Partnerships (Northern Ireland)
1990	Dog Registration
2000	Domestic Abuse*
2002	Domino's Pizza*
2002	Dr Beckmann Rescue*
2001	Dr Beckmann Rescue Oven Cleaner
1980	Dream Topping
1988	Drinking & Driving
1998	Drugs Education*
1994	Dunfermline Building Society
1980	Dunlop Floor Tiles
1990	Duracell Batteries
1980	Dynatron Music Suite

E

1988	E & P Loans*
2004	East of England Development Agency (Broadband)*
2000	easyJet*
2002	*Economist, The**
1992	*Economist, The**
1994	Edinburgh Club*
1990	Edinburgh Zoo

1980   Eggs Authority
2004   Electoral Commission (Northern Ireland)
2003   Electoral Commission/COI (DoE Northern Ireland)
1992   Electricity Privatization
1980   Ellerman Travel & Leisure
1996   Emergency Contraception
1986   EMI Virgin (records)*
1980   English Butter Marketing Company
1986   English Country Cottages
1992   Enterprise Initiative
2003   Equality Commission of Northern Ireland
1992   Equity & Law
1990   Eurax (Anti-Itch Cream)
1999   EuroSites (Continental camping holidays)
2004   Eurostar*
1994   Evening Standard Classified Recruitment
2004   Evergood Coffee (Norway)
1984   Exbury Gardens

F

1990   Family Credit
1998   Famous Grouse, The
1982   Farmer's Table Chicken
2000   Felix*
1996   Felix*
1980   Ferranti CETEC
1990   Fertilizer Manufacturers' Association
1982   Fiat Auto UK
1980   Findus Crispy Pancakes
1988   Findus French Bread Pizza & Crispy Pancakes
1992   Findus Lasagne
1984   Fine Fare
1982   Fine Fare*
2005   Fire Authority for Northern Ireland*
2005   First Choice*
1996   First Choice Holidays
2004   First Direct
1992   First Direct
1998   First Direct*
2005   First Great Western and First Great Western Link

2003   Fisherman's Friend
2002   Flowers & Plants Association
1992   Flowers & Plants Association
2003   Flymo Turbo Compact
1994   Fona Dansk Elektrik
1980   Ford Fiesta
1998   Ford Galaxy*
1986   Ford Granada*
1982   Ford Model Range
1980   Foster Grant
1984   Foster's
1995   Fox's Biscuits
2005   Fox's Rocky*
1998   French Connection
2000   Freschetta*
1999   Freschetta Pizzas
1982   Frish*
1996   Frizzell Insurance*
2002   Fruitopia
1994   Fruit-tella
2000   ft.com*
2005   Fybogel

G

1999   Gala Bingo Clubs
1997   Gala Bingo Clubs
2004   Garnier
1986   General Accident
2003   George Foreman Grills
1992   Gini (Schweppes)*
1986   Glasgow's Lord Provost
1986   GLC's Anti 'Paving Bill' Campaign*
2000   Glenmorangie*
1995   Glow-worm Boilers (Hepworth Heating)
1996   Glow-worm Central Heating
2001   GoByCoach.com (National Express)
1996   Gold Blend*
1988   Gold Spot
1984   Golden Wonder Instant Pot Snacks*
1980   Goodyear Grandprix

1984   Grant's Whisky
1992   Green Giant
1988   Green Science
1988   Greene King IPA Bitter
1990   Greenpeace
2004   Guardian, the*
1982   Guardian, the
1996   Guinness Book of Records
1990   Guinness (Draught) in Cans

H

1990   H. Samuel
1992   Häagen-Dazs*
2002   Halifax Building Society*
1994   Halifax Building Society
1992   Halifax Building Society
1982   Halifax Building Society
1980   Halifax Building Society Convertible Term Shares
1994   Halls Soothers*
1982   Hansa Lager
1999   Hartley's Jam
2002   Hastings Hotels (Golfing Breaks)*
2001   Hastings Hotels (Golfing Breaks in Northern Ireland)
2000   Health Education Board for Scotland
1994   Heineken Export
1980   Heinz Coleslaw
1980   Heinz Curried Beans
1984   Hellmann's Mayonnaise*
1982   Henri Winterman's Special Mild
1996   Hep30 (Building Products)
1992   Herta Frankfurters
1990   Herta Frankfurters
2005   Hidden Treasures of Cumbria*
2005   Highlands and Islands Broadband Registration Campaign
1980   Hoechst
1992   Hofels Garlic Pearles
1984   Hofmeister*
1984   Home Protection (Products)
1982   Home Protection (Products)
2004   Honda*
1990   Honda

1994 Horlicks
1986 Horlicks
1986 Hoverspeed
2002 Hovis*
1996 Hovis
1992 Hovis
1984 Hudson Payne & Iddiols
1996 Huggies Nappies
1994 Hush Puppies

I

1996 I Can't Believe It's Not Butter!*
1992 Iceland Frozen Foods
1980 ICI Chemicals
1984 ICI Dulux Natural Whites*
1992 IFAW*
1998 Imodium
2004 Imperial Leather*
2003 Imperial Leather
2002 Imperial Leather
2001 Imperial Leather
1990 Imperial War Museum
1998 Impulse
1988 Independent, the
1998 Inland Revenue Self Assessment
2005 Inland Revenue Self Assessment*
1988 Insignia
1982 International Business Show 1981
1990 International Wool Secretariat
1992 IPA Society
2005 Irish News, the
1992 Irn Bru
2003 Ironbridge Gorge Museums
1994 Israel Tourist Board

J

1998 Jammie Dodgers
1994 Jeep Cherokee

2002	Jeyes Bloo
2001	Jeyes Bloo
1992	Jif
1999	JJB Super League
1988	Job Clubs
2002	John Smith's Ale
1994	John Smith's Bitter*
1982	John Smith's Bitter*
1998	Johnson's Clean & Clear*

K

1992	K Shoes*
1995	K Shoes (Springers)
1996	Kaliber
1992	Kaliber
1990	Karvol
1980	Kays Catalogue
1992	Kellogg's All Bran*
1984	Kellogg's Bran Flakes*
2000	Kellogg's Coco Pops*
1994	Kellogg's Coco Pops
1984	Kellogg's Coco Pops*
1982	Kellogg's Cornflakes
1980	Kellogg's Frozen Waffles
2000	Kellogg's Nutri-Grain*
2002	Kellogg's Real Fruit Winders*
1980	Kellogg's Rice Krispies*
1982	Kellogg's Super Noodles*
2005	Kelso Racecourse
1998	Kenco
1986	Kensington Palace*
1998	KFC
1984	KFC
2000	KFC USA
1988	Kia Ora*
2004	Kiwi (SA)
1984	Kleenex Velvet
1990	Knorr Stock Cubes*
1988	Kodak Colour Print Film
1994	Kraft Dairylea

1984   Kraft Dairylea*
1980   Krona Margarine*
1986   Kronenbourg 1664

L

1990   Lada
1992   Ladybird
2004   Lamb (Meat & Livestock Australia)*
2005   Lancashire Short Breaks*
1990   Lanson Champagne*
2005   Lay Magistrates
1992   Le Creuset
1982   Le Crunch
1990   Le Piat d'Or
1986   Le Piat d'Or
1996   Le Shuttle
1990   Lea & Perrin's Worcestershire Sauce*
1980   Lea & Perrin's Worcestershire Sauce
1988   Leeds Permanent Building Society
1988   Lego
2004   Lego Bionicle
1984   Leicester Building Society
1996   Lenor
2002   Levi Strauss Engineered Jeans (Japan)
1992   Levi Strauss UK*
1980   Levi Strauss UK
1988   Levi's 501s*
2005   Lift Off
1996   Lil-lets
1990   Lil-lets*
1996   Lilt
1992   Limelite*
1980   Limmits
1999   Lincoln Financial Group
2000   Lincoln Insurance
2000   Lincoln USA
1980   Lion Bar
1992   Liquorice Allsorts
1988   Liquorice Allsorts
2004   Listerine

1988   Listerine*
1980   Listerine
1998   Littlewoods Pools
1992   Lloyds Bank
1984   Lloyds Bank*
1999   Local Enterprise Development Unit (NI)
1990   London Buses Driver Recruitment
1984   London Docklands*
1982   London Docklands
1990   London Philharmonic
1992   London Transport Fare Evasion
1986   London Weekend Television
1980   Lucas Aerospace*
1996   Lucky Lottery
1992   Lucozade
1980   Lucozade*
2000   Lurpak*
1988   Lurpak
2002   Lynx*
2004   Lynx Pulse*
1994   Lyon's Maid Fab
1988   Lyon's Maid Favourite Centres

M

2004   M&G
1988   Maclaren Prams
2003   Magna Science Adventure Centre
1999   Magnet Kitchens
2004   Magnum
1990   Malibu
2001   Manchester City Centre
1999   Manchester City Centre
2003   Manchester Evening News Jobs Section
2002   Manchester Evening News (Job Section)*
2003   Manchester IMAX
1982   Manger's Sugar Soap*
1988   Manpower Services Commission
1994   Marks & Spencer
2004   Marks & Spencer Lingerie*
2002   Marmite*

1998   Marmite*
1998   Marmoleum
1988   Marshall Cavendish Discovery
1994   Marston Pedigree*
2001   Maryland Cookies
1986   Mazda*
1986   Mazola*
1998   McDonald's
1996   McDonald's
1980   McDougall's Saucy Sponge
1990   Mcpherson's Paints
1988   Mcpherson's Paints
2004   McVitie's Jaffa Cakes
2000   McVitie's Jaffa Cakes
1992   Mercury Communications
2005   Metrication
1988   Metropolitan Police Recruitment*
2003   Microbake
1990   Midland Bank
1988   Midland Bank
1992   Miele
1988   Miller Lite*
2000   Moneyextra*
1999   Morrisons
1988   Mortgage Corporation*
2002   Mr Kipling*
1984   Mr Muscle
1995   Müller Fruit Corner
1994   Multiple Sclerosis Society
1996   Murphy's Irish Stout*
2000   Myk Menthol Norway*

N

2005   Nambarrie Tea
2000   National Code and Number Change
1996   National Dairy Council – Milk*
1992   National Dairy Council – Milk
1980   National Dairy Council – Milk
1992   National Dairy Council – Milkman*
1996   National Lottery (Camelot)

1999   National Railway Museum
1996   National Savings
1984   National Savings: Income Bonds
1982   National Savings: Save by Post*
1986   National Westminster Bank Loans
1982   Nationwide Building Society
1990   Nationwide Flex Account
1988   Nationwide Flex Account
1990   Navy Recruitment
1988   Nefax
1982   Negas Cookers
1982   Nescafé
2000   Network Q
1992   Neutrogena
2003   Newcastle Gateshead Initiative
1982   New Man Clothes
1994   New Zealand Lamb
1980   New Zealand Meat Producers Board
2001   NHS Missed Appointments
1996   Nike
1994   Nike
1994   Nissan Micra*
2000   No More Nails*
1986   No.7
2005   Noise Awareness*
1988   Norsk Data
1998   North West Water
1998   North West Water (drought)
1997   North West Water (drought)
2005   Northern Ireland Office Community Safety Unit*
2003   Northern Ireland Social Care Council
2003   Northern Ireland Tourist Board
1998   Norwich Union
2002   Norwich Union Pensions
2004   Northern Ireland Tourist Board
1990   Nouvelle Toilet Paper
2000   NSPCC*
1990   Nurofen
1986   Nursing Recruitment
1994   Nytol

O

2004	O₂*
1980	Observer, the – French Cookery School Campaign
2002	Ocean Spray*
1988	Oddbins*
1998	Olivio*
2002	Olivio/Bertolli*
1998	Olympus
1982	Omega Chewing Gum
1998	One2One*
2005	onlineni.net
1992	Optrex*
2005	Oral Cancer*
1998	Orange*
1996	Orange*
2000	Orange International
2000	Orange Just Talk*
1984	Oranjeboom
1990	Otrivine
2001	Our Dynamic Earth Visitor Attraction
1992	Oxo*
1990	Oxo
1988	Oxo
1998	Oxo Lamb Cubes
1988	Oxy 10

P

1986	Paignton Zoo
2000	Pampers South Africa*
1988	Paracodol*
1984	Paul Masson California Carafes
2005	Payment Modernization Programme
1982	Pedal Cycle Casualties*
1998	Penguin
1994	Peperami*
1994	Pepsi Max
1990	Perrier
1986	Perrier
2000	Persil*

2000	PG Tips*
1990	PG Tips*
1996	Philadelphia*
1994	Philadelphia
1994	Phileas Fogg
1988	Phileas Fogg
1980	Philips Cooktronic
1980	Philips Video
2003	Phoenix Natural Gas
2003	Phones 4u
1998	Physical Activity Campaign (HEB Scotland)
1990	Pilkington Glass
1992	Pilsner
1986	Pink Lady
1998	Pizza Hut*
1996	Pizza Hut
1994	Pizza Hut
1996	Pirelli
1990	Pirelli
1986	Pirelli
1984	Pirelli
1990	Plax
1980	Plessey Communications & Data Systems
1998	Polaroid*
1994	Police Federation of England and Wales
2004	Police Officer Recruitment (Hertfordshire Constabulary)*
2002	Police Recruitment*
2002	Police Recruitment (Could You?)
2002	Police Recruitment Northern Ireland
2001	Police Service of Northern Ireland
1996	Polo Mints
1984	Polyfoam
1986	Portsmouth News
2002	Post Office*
1980	Post Office Mis-sorts
1986	Post Office Special Issue Stamps
2004	Postbank (Post Office SA)
1998	Pot Noodle
1996	Potato Marketing Board
1984	Presto
1980	Pretty Polly*
1990	Price Waterhouse

2005   Progressive Building Society – Financial Services
1992   Prudential

Q

1984   QE2
2003   Qjump.co.uk
1988   Quaker Harvest Chewy Bars*
1982   Qualcast Concorde Lawn Mower*
1984   Qualcast Mow-n-trim and Rotasafe
1986   Quatro
1986   Quickstart
1996   Quorn Burgers

R

1982   Racal Redec Cadet
1994   Radio Rentals
1990   Radio Rentals
1990   Radion Automatic*
1996   RAF Recruitment
1980   RAF Recruitment*
2004   Rainbow (evaporated milk)*
1994   Range Rover
2000   Reading and Literacy*
1992   Real McCoys
2000   Rear Seatbelts*
1984   Red Meat Consumption
1998   Red Meat Market*
1988   Red Mountain*
1996   Reebok*
1992   Reebok
1990   Reliant Metrocabs
1994   Remegel
1998   Renault
1986   Renault 5
1990   Renault 19*
1996   Renault Clio*
1992   Renault Clio*
1984   Renault Trafic & Master

2005   ResponsibleTravel.Com
1996   Ribena
1982   Ribena*
2001   right to read (literacy charity)
2001   rightmove.co.uk
2002   Rimmel*
1986   Rimmel Cosmetics
2004   Road Safety (DoE Northern Ireland)*
2003   Road Safety (DoE Northern Ireland)
1999   Road Safety (DoE Northern Ireland)
1996   Rocky (Fox's Biscuits)
1988   Rolls-Royce Privatization*
1996   Ross Harper*
2004   Roundup
2005   Roundup Weedkiller*
1988   Rover 200
1982   Rowenta
1990   Rowntree's Fruit Gums
1992   Royal Bank of Scotland
1986   Royal College of Nursing
2002   Royal Mail
1986   Royal Mail Business Economy
1997   Royal Mint
1990   Royal National Institute for the Deaf
1996   RSPCA
1988   Rumbelows

S

2004   s1jobs
1994   S4C
1988   Saab*
1996   Safeway
2004   Safer Travel at Night (GLA)*
2002   Sainsbury's* (Jamie Oliver)
2002   Sainsbury's* (Promotion)
2001   Salford University
2003   Salvation Army, the
1996   Samaritans
1986   Sanatogen
1980   Sanatogen

1988	Sandplate*
1986	Sapur (Carpet Cleaner)
1992	Save the Children*
1988	Schering Greene Science
2001	Scholl Flight Socks
2000	scoot.com*
1980	Scotcade
2005	Scotch Beef
1984	Scotch Video Cassettes
1998	Scotland on Sunday
1992	Scotrail
1992	Scottish Amicable*
2005	Scottish Power*
1998	Scottish Prison Service
2005	Scruffs Hard Wear
2002	Seafish Industry Authority
2002	Seatbelts*
1980	Seiko
1992	Sellafield Visitors Centre
2002	Senokot
2001	Senokot
2005	Senokot
1999	Seven Seas Cod Liver Oil
1980	Shake 'n' Vac
1984	Shakers Cocktails*
2002	Shell Corporate
2002	Shell Optimax
1999	Shippam's Spread
1980	Shloer*
1986	Shredded Wheat
1990	Silent Night Beds*
2005	Silent Night My First Bed*
2002	Skoda*
1992	Skol
1982	Skol
1999	Slazenger (cricket bats)
1980	Slumberdown Quilts
1990	Smarties
1980	Smirnoff Vodka
1980	Smith's Monster Munch
1982	Smith's Square Crisps
1992	Smith's Tudor Specials

1994   Smoke Alarms*
1992   Smoke Alarms
1996   So ...? (Fragrance)
1986   Soft & Gentle
1996   Soldier Recruitment
1995   Solpadol
1994   Solvent Abuse
2000   Solvite*
1999   Solvite
1996   Solvite
1992   Sony
1988   Sony
1992   Sony Camcorders
2004   Sony Ericsson T610*
1996   Springers by K (Shoes)
1984   St Ivel Gold*
2004   Standard Bank (SA)
2005   Standard Life
2000   Standard Life
2000   Star Alliance
2002   Stella Artois*
2000   Stella Artois*
1998   Stella Artois
1996   Stella Artois*
1992   Stella Artois*
2002   Strathclyde Police
1994   Strepsils*
1990   Strongbow
1982   Summers the Plumbers
1980   Sunblest Sunbran
1990   Supasnaps
2000   Surf*
1980   Swan Vestas*
1984   SWEB Security Systems
1992   Swinton Insurance
1998   Switch
1996   Switch
2003   Syndol (painkillers)

T

1992	Tandon Computers
1990	Tango
1986	TCP*
2003	Teacher Training Agency
2001	Teacher Training Agency
1986	Teletext
1986	Territorial Army Recruitment
2000	Terry's Chocolate Orange*
2002	Tesco*
2000	Tesco*
1980	Tesco
1990	Tetley Tea Bags
2004	The Number 118 118*
1984	Thomas Cook
1992	Tia Maria
1990	Tia Maria
1990	Times, The
2005	Tizer*
1994	Tizer
1980	Tjaereborg Rejser*
2004	Tobacco Control (DH)*
1980	Tolly's Original
2002	Tommy's: The Baby Charity*
1984	Torbay Tourist Board*
1986	Toshiba*
1986	Touche Remnant Unit Trusts
1992	Tower of London
2004	Toyota Corolla
1996	Toyota RAV4
1982	Trans World Airlines
2003	Translink CityBus
2003	Translink Smartlink
2005	Travelocity.co.uk*
1984	Tri-ac (Skincare)
2004	Tritace
1980	Triumph Dolomite
1994	TSB
1988	TSB*
1986	TSB*
2004	TUI (Germany)

1982   Turkish Delight*
1986   TV Licence Evasion*
2000   Twix Denmark

U

1984   UK Canned Salmon
1986   Umbongo Tropical Juice Drink
2003   UniBond
1999   UniBond No More Nails
2005   UniBond Sealant Range*
2005   University of Dundee*
1998   UPS
2003   UTV Internet
2001   UTV Peak Soaps
1990   Uvistat*

V

1988   Varilux lenses
1994   Vauxhall Astra
1996   Vauxhall Cavalier
1990   Vauxhall Cavalier
1999   Vauxhall Network Q
1996   Vegetarian Society
2004   Vehicle Crime Reduction (Home Office)
2001   Vimto
1986   Virgin Atlantic
2004   Virgin Mobile*
2004   Virgin Mobile Australia*
2004   Virgin Trains*
1994   Visa
1986   Vodafone
1998   Volkswagen*
2002   Volkswagen (Brand)*
2004   Volkswagen Diesel*
2002   Volkswagen Passat*
1992   VW Golf*

W

1980	Waistline
2002	Waitrose*
2003	Wake Up To Waste (Northern Ireland)
1992	Wales Tourist Board
2002	Walkers Crisps*
1996	Walkers Crisps*
1998	Wallis
1980	Wall's Cornetto
1996	Wall's Viennetta
1984	Wall's Viennetta*
1984	Walnut Whips
2003	Warburtons
1990	Warburtons Bread*
2005	Waste Awareness
1984	Websters Yorkshire Bitter
2004	Weetabix*
1988	Weight Watchers Slimming Clubs
2002	West End Quay
2005	West Midlands Hub of Museums*
1990	Westwood Tractors
1992	Whipsnade Wild Animal Park*
1980	Whitegate's Estate Agents*
1990	Wilson's Ultra Golf Balls
1988	Winalot Prime*
1994	Wonderbra*

Y

2000	Yellow Pages Norway
1980	Yeoman Pie Fillings
1980	Yorkie
1982	Yorkshire Bank
2002	Yorkshire Forward/Yorkshire Tourist Board

Z

1984	Zanussi*
1994	Zovirax

Bibliography

Articles

Ansoff, I (1957) Strategies for diversification, *Harvard Business Review*, September

Ambler, T (2000) Persuasion, pride and prejudice: how ads work, *International Journal of Advertising*, **19** (3)

Ambler, T (2004) ROI is dead: now bury it, *Admap*, September

Ambler, T (2005) Customer capital: a good idea but still not the answer, *Market Leader*, Issue 28, Spring

Ambler, T (2006) Does the UK promotion of food and drink to children contribute to their obesity? *International Journal of Advertising*, **25** (2)

Ambler, T and Broadbent, S (2000) A dialogue on advertising effectiveness and efficiency, *Admap*, July

Armstrong, J S and Green, K C (2007) Competitor-oriented objectives: the myth of market share, *International Journal of Business*, **12** (1) winter

Barnard, N, Ehrenberg, A and Scriven, J (1997) Differentiation or salience, *Journal of Advertising Research*, **37** (6) November/December.

Benady, D (2006) Giving them the best start, *Marketing Week*, 15 June, pp 24–25

Bonney, D (2006) Sad-vertising, *Admap*, Issue 478, December

Deboo, M (2006) The dawn of the marketing venture capitalist, *Market Leader*, Issue 32, Summer

Dev, C and Schultz, D (2005) Time to kill off the four P's?, *Market Leader*, Issue 29, Summer

Conahan, T (2005) Being orange in a sea of blue, *The Advertiser*, October

Ehrenberg, A (2004) What brand loyalty can tell us, *Admap*, Issue 454, October

Ehrenberg, A, Barnard, N and Sharp, B (2000) Problems with marketing's 'decision' models, ANZMAC

Ehrenberg, A (1997) How do consumers come to buy a new brand? *Admap*, March

Fisk, P and Pringle, H (2004) Customer capital, *Market Leader*, Issue 27, Winter

Fitzgerald, N (2001) Life and death in the world of brands, *Market Leader*, Issue 14

Hastorf, A and Cantril, H (1954) They saw the game: A case study, *Journal of Abnormal and Social Psychology*, **49**, pp 129–34

Heath, R (1999) Can tracking studies tell lies? *International Journal of Advertising*, **18** (2)

Heath, R (1999) The low-involvement processing theory, *Admap*, March

Heath, R (2000) Low involvement processing 2, *Admap*, April

Heath, R (2000) Low involvement processing 1, *Admap*, March

Heath, R (2002) Low-involvement processing: does the LINK test measure it? *Admap*, Issue 431, September

Heath, R (2002) How the best ads work, *Admap*, Issue 427, April

Heath, R (2004) Emotional advertising works, *Market Leader*, Issue 26, Autumn

Heath, R and Howard-Spink, J (2000) And now for something completely different, *Marketing Research Society Conferences*

Heath, R and Hyder, P (2005) Measuring the hidden power of emotive advertising, *International Journal of Market Research*, **47** (5)

Heath, R and Nairn, A (2005) Measuring affective advertising: implications of low attention processing on recall, *Journal of Advertising Research*, **45** (2), June

Hofmeyr, J and Rice, J (1999) The impact of consumers' commitment to existing brands on new product launch strategies, *ESOMAR*, September

Kotler, P (2006) Alphabet soup, *Marketing Management*, March/April

Lauterborn, R (1990) New marketing litany: 4Ps passé; C words take over, *Advertising Age*, 1 October

Levitt, T (1960) Marketing myopia, *Harvard Business Review*, **38**, July/August

Madell, J (2004) Strategies for growth, *ESOMAR*, September

Marsden, P (2006) Customer advisory panels, *Market Leader*, Summer

Mercer, D (1993) Death of the product life cycle, *Admap*, September

Morgan, A (1999) Eating the big fish, *Market Leader*, Issue 6

Munoz, T (2004) A stretch too far: the challenge of the master brand, *Market Leader*. Issue 25, Summer

Page, G and Farr, A (2000) Do you have an elastic brand?, *Advertising Research Foundation Workshop*

Pirrie, A (2005) Customising new brand development, *Admap*, Issue 466, November

Pirrie, A (2006) What value brands?, *Admap*, Issue 476, October, pp 40–42

Porter, M (1979) How competitive forces shape strategy, *Harvard Business Review*, **57**, March/April

Schneider, J (2002) The launch: why new products blast off or fizzle, http://www.pdma.org/visions/jan02/launch.html

Sheth, J and Sisodia, R S (1999) Iridium's 66 pies in the sky, *Wall Street Journal*, June

Tam, M (2006) Tesco expands in Polish market, *Guardian*, 17 July

Wood, S and Moreau, P (2006) From fear to loathing? How emotion influences the evaluation and early use of innovations, *Journal of Marketing*, **70**, July, pp 44–57

Lectures

Jeremy Bullmore's Brands Lecture 'Posh Spice & Persil' to the British Brands Group 2001

Magazines

Brand Strategy, November 2005
Market Leader, Issue 32, Spring 2006

Reports

Ambler, T (2004) Does the UK promotion of food and drink to children contribute to their obesity? *Centre for Marketing Working Paper* No. 04-901, March

Binet, L and Field, P (2007) Marketing in the era of accountability, *IPA dataMINE*, WARC

Brand finance invisible business, *Brand Finance* (2005)

Digital music report 2007, *IFPI (2007)*

Buck, S (2001) Advertising and the long term success of a premium brand, *AA Economics Committee*, WARC

DMA preference service report, DMA (2006)

Dreaming with BRICs: The path to 2050, Goldman Sachs Global Economics Paper No. 99 (2003)

Hastings, G (2003) Does food promotion influence children? A systematic review of the evidence, *Food Standards Agency, September*

Institute of Practitioners in Advertising (2005) How analysts view marketing, *IPA*

Institute of Practitioners in Advertising (2006) The intangible revolution, *IPA*

Institute of Practitioners in Advertising (2007) The future of advertising and agencies, *IPA*

Ledbury Research (2007) Counterfeiting luxury report, *Davenport Lyons*

Livingstone, S (2004) A commentary on the research evidence regarding the effects of food promotion on children, *Research Department of the Office of Communications (OFCOM)*, February

Millward Brown (2006) *Perspectives*, Issue 32, February

Twose, D (2005) Driving top-line growth, *IPA dataMINE*, WARC

Books

Aaker, D and Joachimsthaler, E (2002) *Brand Leadership*, Free Press

Advertising Works Series (World Advertising Research Center)

Ambler, T (2003) *Marketing and the Bottom Line*, 2nd edn, Pearson Education

Barwise, P (1999) *Advertising in a Recession: The benefits of investing for the long term*, World Advertising Research Centre

Bedbury, S (2003) *A New Brand World*, Penguin

Briggs, R and Stuart, G (2006) *What Sticks: Why most advertising fails and how to guarantee yours succeeds, Kaplan Publishing*

Buchholtz, A and Wordemann, W (2000) *What Makes Winning Brands Different,* John Wiley & Sons

Bullmore, J (2003) *More Bullmore,* 3rd edn, World Advertising Research Center

Burkitt, H and Zealley, J (2006) *Marketing Excellence,* John Wiley & Sons

Butterfield, L (1999) *Excellence in Advertising*, Butterworth-Heinemann

Butterfield, L (2003) *AdValue: Twenty ways advertising works for brands*, Butterworth-Heinemann

Collins, J and Porras, J (1998) *Built to Last*, Random House Business Books

Damasio, A R (1994) *Descartes' Error: Emotion, reason and the human brain*, Putnam

Dennis, F (2007) *How to Get Rich*, Ebury Press

Doyle, P (2000) *Value-based Marketing*, John Wiley & Sons

Earls, M (2002) *Welcome to the Creative Age*, John Wiley & Sons

Earls, M (2007) *How to Change Mass Behaviour by Harnessing our True Nature*, John Wiley & Sons

Feldwick, P (2002) *What is Brand Equity, Anyway?* World Advertising Research Center

Fisk, P (2006) *Marketing Genius*, Capstone

Grant, J (1999) *The New Marketing Manifesto*, Texere

Green, L ed (2005) *Advertising Works and How*, World Advertising Research Center

Grove, A (1996) *Only the Paranoid Survive*, Currency

Haig, M (2003) *Brand Failures*, Kogan Page

Haig, M (2004) *Brand Royalty*, Kogan Page

Harford, T (2007) *The Undercover Economist*, Abacus

Hofmeyr, J and Rice, B (2004) *Commitment-Led Marketing*, Wiley

Jones, J P (1995) *When Ads Work*, Lexington Books

Kim, W C and Mauborgne, R (2005) *Blue Ocean Strategy*, Harvard Business School Press

Kotler, P (1967) *Marketing Management: Analysis, Planning and Control*, Prentice Hall

Kotler, P, Rein, I and Stoller, M (1997) *High Visibility*, NTC Business Books

Levitt, S and Dubner, S (2005) *Freakonomics*, Penguin Books

McCarthy, J (1960) *Basic Marketing*, Richard D Irwin

Miller, J and Muir, D (2004) *The Business of Brands*, John Wiley & Sons

Mitchell, A (2001) *Right Side Up*, Harper Collins Business

Morgan, A (1999) *Eating the Big Fish*, John Wiley & Sons

Morgan, A (2004) *The Pirate Inside*, John Wiley & Sons

Ormerod, P (2005) *Why Most Things Fail*, Faber & Faber

Porter, M (1980) *Competitive Strategy*, Free Press

Pringle, H (2004) *Celebrity Sells*, John Wiley & Sons

Pringle, H and Gordon, W (2001) *Brand Manners*, John Wiley & Sons

Pringle, H and Thompson, M (1999) *Brand Spirit*, John Wiley & Sons

Reichheld, F (1996) *The Loyalty Effect*, Bain & Company

Roberts, K (2004) *Lovemarks*, Powerhouse Books

Rutherford, D ed (2003) *Excellence in Brand Communication*, Institute of Communications and Advertising

Shaw, R (2005) *Marketing Payback: Is Your Marketing Profitable?* Financial Times/Prentice Hall

Stewart, T (1998) *Intellectual Capital: The New Wealth of Nations*, Nicholas Brealey

Surowiecki, J (2005) *The Wisdom of Crowds*, Abacus

Sveiby, K-E (1990) *The Invisible Balance Sheet*, Affarsvarlden Forlag

Trout, J (2001) *Big Brands Big Trouble*, John Wiley & Sons

Vamos, M and Lidsky, D ed (2006) *Ten Years of the Most Innovative Ideas in Business*, Penguin

Webography

http://www.ddblondon.com

http://www.grain.org

http://home.myspace.com/index.cfm?fuseaction=user

http://wearewhatwedo.org

http://web.ukonline.co.uk/k.frost/czech/skoda_jokes.html

http://www.118.com/

http://www.acupoll.com/
http://www.agbnielsen.net/
http://www.amazon.co.uk/Herd-Change-Behaviour-Harnessing-Nature/dp/0470060360/ref=sr_1_1?ie=UTF8&s=books&qid=120377401 5&sr=1-1
http://www.amazon.co.uk/Wisdom-Crowds-Many-Smarter-Than/dp/0349116059/ref=dp_return_1?ie=UTF8&n=266239&s=books &qid=1203773534&sr=1-1
http://www.birdseye.com/
http://www.bp.com
http://www.brandfinance.com/
http://www.cpsc.gov/
http://www.facebook.com/profile.php?id=667720076
http://www.fallon.co.uk
http://www.focalyst.com/
http://www.greenlabelart.com
http://www.guardian.co.uk
http://www.hall-and-partners.com/
http://www.hatads.org.uk
http://www.infores.com/
http://www.ipa.co.uk
http://www.ipa.co.uk/Marketing/CustomerCapital.cfm?fromsearch=1&search Txt=customer%20capital
http://www.ipsos-asi.com/
http://www.itv.com
http://www.lambie-nairn.com/
http://www.ledburyresearch.com/
http://www.marketingpower.com
http://www.marksandspencer.com/
http://www.masterbyte.co.uk/forensics/index.html
http://www.millwardbrown.com/
http://www.motorola.com/uk/
http://www.mruk.co.uk/
http://www.nielsenmedia.com/
http://www.ofcom.com
http://www.pernod-ricard.com/
http://www.rkcryr.com/
http://www.sveiby.com/
http://www.sveiby.com/Portals/0/articles/IntangAss/denosynl.htm
http://www.talkingretail.com/news/2118/Premium-gin-has-global-ambitio.ehtml
http://www.tesco.com/

http://www.thinkbox.tv
http://www.tnsglobal.com/
http://www.tns-mi.com/
http://www.vccp.com
http://www.virgin.com/
http://www.warc.com
http://www.wikipedia.org
http://www.youtube.com
http://www.youtube.com/user/hamishpringle

Index

NB: page numbers in *italic* indicate drawings, figures, photographs or tables